Other Books and Series by Jeff Bowen

Applications for Enrollment of Chickasaw Newborn Act of 1905
Volumes I thru VII

Cherokee Intermarried White 1906 Volume I thru X

Applications for Enrollment of Creek Newborn Act of 1905
Volumes I, II, III, IV & V

Visit our website at **www.nativestudy.com** to learn more about these and other books and series by Jeff Bowen

APPLICATIONS FOR ENROLLMENT OF CREEK NEWBORN ACT OF 1905

VOLUME VI

TRANSCRIBED BY
JEFF BOWEN

NATIVE STUDY
Gallipolis, Ohio
USA

Other Books and Series by Jeff Bowen

1901-1907 Native American Census Seneca, Eastern Shawnee, Miami, Modoc, Ottawa, Peoria, Quapaw, and Wyandotte Indians (Under Seneca School, Indian Territory)

1932 Census of The Standing Rock Sioux Reservation with Births And Deaths 1924-1932

Census of The Blackfeet, Montana, 1897- 1901 Expanded Edition

Eastern Cherokee by Blood, 1906-1910, Volumes I thru XIII

Choctaw of Mississippi Indian Census 1929-1932 with Births and Deaths 1924-1931   Volume I
Choctaw of Mississippi Indian Census 1933, 1934 & 1937, Supplemental Rolls to 1934 & 1935 with Births and Deaths 1932-1938, and Marriages 1936-1938 Volume II

Eastern Cherokee Census Cherokee, North Carolina 1930-1939 Census 1930-1931 with Births And Deaths 1924-1931 Taken By Agent L. W. Page Volume I
Eastern Cherokee Census Cherokee, North Carolina 1930-1939 Census 1932-1933 with Births And Deaths 1930-1932 Taken By Agent R. L. Spalsbury   Volume II
Eastern Cherokee Census Cherokee, North Carolina 1930-1939 Census 1934-1937 with Births and Deaths 1925-1938 and Marriages 1936 & 1938 Taken by Agents R. L. Spalsbury And Harold W. Foght Volume III

Seminole of Florida Indian Census, 1930-1940 with Birth and Death Records, 1930-1938

Texas Cherokees 1820-1839 A Document For Litigation 1921

Choctaw By Blood Enrollment Cards 1898-1914 Volumes I thru XVII

Starr Roll 1894 (Cherokee Payment Rolls) Districts: Canadian, Cooweescoowee, and Delaware Volume One
Starr Roll 1894 (Cherokee Payment Rolls) Districts: Flint, Going Snake, and Illinois   Volume Two
Starr Roll 1894 (Cherokee Payment Rolls) Districts: Saline, Sequoyah, and Tahlequah; Including Orphan Roll   Volume Three

Cherokee Intruder Cases Dockets of Hearings 1901-1909 Volumes I & II

Indian Wills, 1911-1921 Records of the Bureau of Indian Affairs Books One thru Seven;
Native American Wills & Probate Records 1911-1921

Other Books and Series by Jeff Bowen

Turtle Mountain Reservation Chippewa Indians 1932 Census with Births & Deaths, 1924-1932

Chickasaw By Blood Enrollment Cards 1898-1914 Volume I thru V

Cherokee Descendants East An Index to the Guion Miller Applications Volume I
Cherokee Descendants West An Index to the Guion Miller Applications Volume II (A-M)
Cherokee Descendants West An Index to the Guion Miller Applications Volume III (N-Z)

Applications for Enrollment of Seminole Newborn Freedmen, Act of 1905

Eastern Cherokee Census, Cherokee, North Carolina, 1915-1922, Taken by Agent James E. Henderson   *Volume I (1915-1916)*
Volume II (1917-1918)
Volume III (1919-1920)
Volume IV (1921-1922)

Complete Delaware Roll of 1898

Eastern Cherokee Census, Cherokee, North Carolina, 1923-1929, Taken by Agent James E. Henderson   *Volume I (1923-1924)*
Volume II (1925-1926)
Volume III (1927-1929)

Applications for Enrollment of Seminole Newborn Act of 1905 Volumes I & II

North Carolina Eastern Cherokee Indian Census 1898-1899, 1904, 1906, 1909-1912, 1914 Revised and Expanded Edition

1932 Hopi and Navajo Native American Census with Birth & Death Rolls (1925-1931) Volume 1 - Hopi
1932 Hopi and Navajo Native American Census with Birth & Death Rolls (1930-1932) Volume 2 - Navajo

Western Navajo Reservation Navajo, Hopi and Paiute 1933 Census with Birth & Death Rolls 1925-1933

Cherokee Citizenship Commission Dockets 1880-1884 and 1887-1889 Volumes I thru V

Copyright © 2011
by Jeff Bowen

ALL RIGHTS RESERVED
No part of this publication may be reproduced
or used in any form or manner whatsoever
without previous written permission from the
copyright holder or publisher.

Originally published:
Baltimore, Maryland
2011

Reprinted by:

Native Study LLC
Gallipolis, OH
www.nativestudy.com
2020

Library of Congress Control Number: 2020917992

ISBN: 978-1-64968-085-3

Made in the United States of America.

This series is dedicated to the descendants of the Creek newborn listed in these applications.

DEPARTMENT OF THE INTERIOR.
Commissioner to the Five Civilized Tribes.

NOTICE.

Opening of Land Office at Wewoka,
IN THE SEMINOLE NATION, INDIAN TERRITORY.

Notice is hereby given that on Monday, September 4, 1905, the Commissioner to the Five Civilized Tribes will establish a land office at Wewoka, in the Seminole Nation, Indian Territory, for the purpose of allowing citizens and freedmen of the Seminole Nation to select allotments of land for their minor children enrolled under the Act of Congress approved March 3, 1905 (33 Stat. L 1060), and for the further purpose of allowing citizens and freedmen of the Seminole Nation, whose allotments are incomplete, to select additional land in order to bring the value of their allotments up to the standard of $309.09, as nearly as may be practicable.

Each child whose enrollment in accordance with the Act of March 3, 1905, has been duly approved by the Secretary of the Interior, is entitled to receive an allotment of forty acres without regard to the character or value of the land selected.

Selection of allotments for minor children must be made by their citizen or freedmen parents or by a duly appointed guardian, or curator, or by a duly appointed administrator.

TAMS BIXBY,
Commissioner.

Muskogee, Indian Territory,
July 29, 1905.

This particular notice makes mention of the Act of 1905. The Creek and Seminole were closely related tribes. Both tribes' notices were like similar in nature.

DEPARTMENT OF THE INTERIOR,

Commission to the Five Civilized Tribes.

Closing of Citizenship Rolls

OF THE MUSKOGEE OR CREEK NATION.

WHEREAS, on June 13, 1904, the Secretary of the Interior, under the authority in him vested by the provisions of the act of Congress approved March 3, 1901, (31 Stat., 1058) ordered that September 1, 1904, be and the same is hereby fixed as the time when the rolls of the Muskogee or Creek Nation shall be closed:

Notice is hereby given that the Commission to the Five Civilized Tribes will, at its office in Muskogee, Indian Territory, up to and inclusive of September 1, 1904, receive applications for the enrollment of citizens and freedmen of the Muskogee or Creek Nation, and that after that date the application of no person whomsoever for enrollment as a citizen or freedman of said nation will be received by the Commission.

Commission to the Five Civilized Tribes,
TAMS BIXBY, Chairman,
T. B. NEEDLES,
C. R. BRECKINRIDGE,
Commissioners.

Muskogee, Indian Territory,
June 25, 1904.

A notice like this was printed in newspapers and posted throughout Indian Territory.

INTRODUCTION

This series concerns Applications for Enrollment of Creek Newborn, National Archive film M-1301 (Act of 1905), as described in the National Archives publication *American Indians*. It falls under the heading Applications for Enrollment of the Commission to the Five Civilized Tribes, 1898-1914, M-1301 and is transcribed from microfilm rolls 414-419. This shows the application forms filled out by individuals applying for enrollment in the Five Civilized Tribes under the Dawes Commission. These applications contain additional information that wasn't abstracted to the census cards that you find in series M-1186. This particular roll (Creek by Birth) contains its own series of numbers separate from M-1186. To find each party's roll number you would have to reference M-1186. On July 25, 1898, there was an Indian Territory Division created in the Office of the Department of Interior. This division was created because of the increased work caused by what was called the Curtis Act, named after Senator Charles Curtis. Basically, this law stated that the tribal rolls needed to be descriptive and pointed out that each tribal roll was without description and had to be redone. At this point there was such a struggle among the Creeks to accept that the Government was going to change their way of life, again, that their leaders were refusing to cooperate in handing over their census information. The Commission had found that enrolling the Creeks was a difficult task not only because the Creek feared what was coming but also because their tribal structure was consistent with being a confederacy with forty-four different bands whose tribesmen lived in different towns of which each had a king that was supposed to keep track of their citizenry. The Commission reported that there was very little evidence of any census that existed and what there was had been kept carelessly. There were attempts and tribal conflicts along the way, but the Curtis Act would make it so they had to do it again no matter what effort from the past. In 1899, Agent Wesley Smith educated Washington to the fact that it was difficult to verify Creek eligibility. The acts passed by the Creeks themselves concerning enrollment since 1893 had been strewn amongst the archives of the Creek Council in Muskogee, I.T., and there was no provision ever approved for the printing of the those enrollments. There was confusion and difficulty let alone the fact that surnames were practically unknown among the Creek. But there was no confusion on March 9, 1905, when the Commission stated they would come to seven towns in the Creek Nation and accept applications that had to be made on a standardized blank form and contain a notarized affidavit from the mother and the attending doctor or midwife. A few by mail, but most of them were offered to a field party led by Commissioner Needles. The Commission took in applications for 2,410 children by the deadline of midnight, May 2, 1905.

This series contains applications and correspondence from 1,171 of those claimants. Realizing there were over 2,400 applicants originally, it is understood that not all were accepted. Also included are names of doctors, lawyers, mid-wives, and others who attended to the Creek Nation before and during this time in history.

Jeff Bowen
Gallipolis, Ohio
NativeStudy.com

Applications for Enrollment of Creek Newborn
Act of 1905 Volume VI

BIRTH AFFIDAVIT.

DEPARTMENT OF THE INTERIOR
COMMISSION TO THE FIVE CIVILIZED TRIBES.

In Re Application for Enrollment as a citizen of the Creek Nation of Willie Byno McKim born on the 8th day of July 1902

Name of Father:	Robert A McKim	a citizen of the	Creek	Nation.
Name of Mother:	Minnie G. McKim	a citizen of the	not	Nation.

Postoffice Sapulpa I.T.

Affidavit of Mother

UNITED STATES OF AMERICA INDIAN TERRITORY }
Western DISTRICT.

I Minnie G. McKim on oath state that I am 25 years of age and a citizen by not of the not Nation; that I am the lawful wife of Robert McKim who is a citizen by blood of the Creek Nation; that a male child was born to me on 8th day of July 1902 that said child has been named Willie Byno and was living March 4 1905.

WITNESSES TO MARK:

Minnie G McKim

{

Subscribed and sworn to before me this 25 day of March 1905.

My Commission expires 10/20-1906

Joseph Bruner
Notary Public.

Affidavit of Attending Physician or Mid-Wife

UNITED STATES OF AMERICA INDIAN TERRITORY }
Western DISTRICT.

I Mrs. Dora Wilbanks a *(blank)* on oath state that I attended on Mrs. Minnie McKim wife of Robert A McKim on the 8th day of July 1902 ; that there was born to her on said date a boy child; that said child was living March 4 1905 and is said to have been named Willie Byno McKim

Dora Wilbanks

WITNESSES TO MARK:

{

1

Applications for Enrollment of Creek Newborn
Act of 1905   Volume VI

Subscribed and sworn to before me this 27 day of March 1905.

LMB
Notary Public.

My Com Ex Jan 2-1906

BIRTH AFFIDAVIT.

DEPARTMENT OF THE INTERIOR.
COMMISSION TO THE FIVE CIVILIZED TRIBES.

IN RE APPLICATION FOR ENROLLMENT as a citizen of the CREEK Nation of Willie Byno McKim born on the 8" day of July 1902

Name of Father:	Robert A. McKim	a citizen of the	Creek	Nation.
Name of Mother:	Minnie G. "	a citizen of the	U.S.	Nation.

Postoffice   Sapulpa

Child present

AFFIDAVIT OF ~~MOTHER~~. Father

UNITED STATES OF AMERICA Indian Territory
WESTERN   DISTRICT.

I Robert A. McKim on oath state that I am 29 years of age and a citizen by blood of the Creek Nation; that I am the lawful ~~wife~~ husband of Minnie G. McKim who is a citizen by ----- of the U.S. Nation; that a male child was born to me on 8" day of July 1902 that said child has been named Willie Byno McKim and is now living.

Robert A. McKim

Witnesses To Mark:
{

Subscribed and sworn to before me this 28" day of March 1905.

Edw C Griesel
Notary Public.

United States of America Indian Territory :
ss.
Western District.   :

Before me a Notary Public within and for the aforesaid District and Territory this day personally ap;eared[sic]   Ida Childers   to me well known who on oath

Applications for Enrollment of Creek Newborn
Act of 1905 Volume VI

declared that she was a citizen by blood of the Creek Nation and about 30 years of age; that she is the mother of Emmet Childers the son of Garfield Childers: that her maiden name was Ida Beaver and her father's name Tiller Beaver and her mother Nancy Fisher and that she then married Edmund Burgess and filed under the name of Ida Burgess all of which is truly of her own personal knowledge and belief.

Witnesses to Mark
(none given)

her
Ida x Childers
mark

Subscribed and sworn to before me this 5th day of Aug. 1905.

BJ Beaver
Notary Public.

My commission expires December 19 1905.

United States of America Indian Territory :
                                                       ss.
Western District.   :

Before me a Notary Public within and for the aforesaid District and Territory personally appeared James Childers to me well known who on oath declared that he was a citizen by blood of the Creek Nation and 66 years of age and a member of Cheyaha Town: that he is the grandfather of Emmet Childers an infant Creek and has known his mother Ida Childers and his daughter-in-law all her life; that Emmet Childers is the son of Ida Childers and Garfield Childers; that Ida Childers is the daughter of Tiller Beaver and Nancy Fisher; that she married Edmund Burgess and was enrolled as Ida Burgess; that she then married lawfully Garfield Childers and to this marriage Emmet was born; that Ida Childers is the identical person who was Ida Burgess and Ida Beaver and of Brown Arrown[sic] Town all of which is of my own personal knowledge.

Witnesses to Mark
  T W Tiger

his
James x Childers
mark

Hattie Childers
Subscribed and sworn to before me this 5th day of Aug. 1905.

B.J. Beavers
Notary Public.

My commission expires December 19 1905[sic].

Birth Affidavit.
        Department of the Interior
                Commission to the Five Civilized Tribes.

--------------O--------------

Applications for Enrollment of Creek Newborn
Act of 1905 Volume VI

In re application for enrollment as a citizen of the Creek Nation of Emmet Childers born on the 7th day of May 1902 Name of Father Garfield Childers a citizen of the ~~Cherokee~~ Creek Nation Name of Mother Ida Childers a citizen of the Creek Nation. Post office Coweta Ind. Ter.

Affidavit of Mother.

United States of America[sic] Indian Territory :
    Western District.   : ss.

I Ida Childers on my oath state that I am nineteen years of age and a citizen by blood of the Creek Nation; that I am the lawful wife of Garfield Childers who is a citizen by blood of the Creek Nation; that a male child was born to me on 7th day of May 1902; that said child was named Emmet Childers and is now living.

                        her
                      Ida x Childers
Witnesses to Mark.   mark
N E Charles
Shirly Wofford

Subscribed and sworn to before me this 23rd day of March 1905.

                      BJ Beavers
                        Notary Public.
My commission expires Dec. 19th. 1908.

Affidavit of attending Physician or Midwife.

United States of America Indian Territory :
    Western District.   : ss.

I Eliza Childers a midwife on my oath state that I attended on Mrs. Ida Childers wife of Garfield Childers on the 7 day of May 1902 that there was born to her on said date a male child; that said child is now living and is said to have been named Emmet Childers

                    Eliza Childers

Witnesses to mark
N E Charles
Shirly Wofford
                    BJ Beavers
                      Notary Public.
My commission expires Dec. 19th. 1908.

Applications for Enrollment of Creek Newborn
Act of 1905   Volume VI

NC-422.

Muskogee Indian Territory August 3 1905.

Agnes Simpson
Eufaula Indian Territory.

Dear Madam:

  In the matter of the application for the enrollment of your minor daughter Mary Elizabeth Simpson as a citizen by blood of the Creek Nation it will be necessary for you to file with this office evidence of your marriage to Robert L. Simpson the father of said child.

  Such evidence may consist of either the original or a certified copy of your marriage license and certificate.

  It is also advisable that you furnish this office with the affidavit of said Robert L. Simpson relative to the birth of said child and a blank for that purpose partially filled out is inclosed herewith. You are requested to have the same properly executed and return to this office in the inclosed envelope.

        Respectfully

              Commissioner.

CTD-21
Env.

CERTIFICATE OF RECORD.

United States of America
 INDIAN TERRITORY } ss.
 Northern District.

  I CHARLES A. DAVIDSON Clerk of the United States Court in the Northern District Indian Territory do hereby certify that the instrument hereto attached was filed for record in my office the   31   day of   May   1902 at   ? A-   M. and duly recorded in Book   M   Marriage Record Page   453

  WITNESS my hand and seal of said Court at Muscogee in said Territory this   31   day of   May   A. D. 1902

      Chas A Davidson   *Clerk.*
     By   *(blank)*   *Deputy.*

Applications for Enrollment of Creek Newborn
Act of 1905   Volume VI

MARRIAGE LICENSE

✿ ✿ ✿

United States of America
  INDIAN TERRITORY } ss.   *No.* **872**
  Northern District.

To Any Person Authorized by Law to Solemnize Marriage---Greeting:

You are Hereby Commanded to Solemnize the Rite and publish the Banns of Matrimony between Mr.   R. L. Simpson   of   Eufaula   in the Indian Territory aged   27   years and Miss   Agnes Whatley   of   Eufaula   in the Indian Territory aged   20   years according to law and do you officially sign and return this License to the parties therein named.

WITNESS my hand and official seal at Muscogee Indian Territory this   12"   day of   May   A.D. 190 2

                            Chas. A. Davidson
                                 Clerk of the U.S. Court

By   (blank)   Deputy

CERTIFICATE OF MARRIAGE.

✿ ✿

United States of America
  Indian Territory } ss.
  Northern District.

I   A Lee Boyd   a Minister of the Gospel DO HEREBY CERTIFY that on the   14   day of   May   A. D. 1902 I did duly and according to law as commanded in the foregoing License solemnize the Rite and publish the Banns of Matrimony between the parties therein named.

WITNESS my hand   15   day of   May   A. D. 1902

My credentials are recorded in the office of the Clerk of the United States Court Indian Territory Northern District Book   (blank)   Page   (blank)   .

                            A. Lee Boyd
                            A Minister of the Gospel

Note—This License and Certificate of Marriage must be returned to the Office of the Clerk of the United States Court in the Northern District Indian Territory from whence it was issued within sixty days from the date thereof or the party to whom the license was issued will be liable in the amount of the One Hundred Dollars ($100.00)

Applications for Enrollment of Creek Newborn
Act of 1905   Volume VI

Commission to the Five Civilized Tribes

In Re Application for enrollment of Mary Elizabeth Simpson born on 4th day of January 1905. Name of father Robert L. Simpson a citizen by blood of the Creek Nation. Name of mother Agnes Simpson. Post Office Eufaula Indian Territory.

Affidavit of mother.   Non Citizen

Indian Territory
Western District

      Agnes Simpson being duly sworn on oath states that I am 24 years of age; that I am the lawful wife of Robert L. Simpson a citizen by blood of the Creek Nation; that on the 4th day of January 1905 there was born unto me a female child; that said child is now living and has been named Mary Elizabeth Simpson.

Agnes Simpson

Sworn and subscribed to before me this 5th day of March 1905.

M Washington
Notary Public

My Commission Expires July 8th 1906.

Indian Territory
Western District

      W. A. Tolleson a physician being duly sworn on oath states that he attended on Mrs Agnes Simpson wife of Robert L. Simpson on the 4th day of January 1905; that there was born unto her on said date a female child that said child is now living and has been named Mary Elizabeth Simpson.

W. A. Tolleson

Sworn and subscribed to before me this 5th day of March 1905.

F. L. Moss
Notary Public

My Commission expires Jan. 20th 1908.

Applications for Enrollment of Creek Newborn
Act of 1905 Volume VI

BIRTH AFFIDAVIT.

DEPARTMENT OF THE INTERIOR.
COMMISSION TO THE FIVE CIVILIZED TRIBES.

IN RE APPLICATION FOR ENROLLMENT as a citizen of the Creek Nation of Mary Elizabeth Simpson born on the 4 day of Jan 1905

Name of Father:	Robert L. Simpson	a citizen of the	Creek	Nation.
Name of Mother:	Agnes Simpson	a citizen of the	U S	Nation.

Postoffice Eufaula Ind. Ter.

AFFIDAVIT OF ~~MOTHER~~. Father

UNITED STATES OF AMERICA Indian Territory
Western DISTRICT.

I Robert L. Simpson on oath state that I am 31 years of age and a citizen by blood of the Creek Nation; that I am the lawful ~~wife~~ husband of Agnes Simpson who is a citizen by *(blank)* of the U.S. Nation; that a female child was born to ~~me~~ her on 4 day of January 1905 that said child has been named Mary Elizabeth Simpson and was living March 4 1905.

Robert L. Simpson

Witnesses To Mark:

Subscribed and sworn to before me this 14 day of Aug 1905.

Edw C Griesel
Notary Public.

BIRTH AFFIDAVIT.

DEPARTMENT OF THE INTERIOR.
COMMISSION TO THE FIVE CIVILIZED TRIBES.

IN RE APPLICATION FOR ENROLLMENT as a citizen of the Creek Nation of Robert Fixico born on the 5 day of November 1903

Name of Father:	Tul mo chus Fixico	a citizen of the	Creek	Nation.
Name of Mother:	Salley Fixico	a citizen of the	Creek	Nation.

Postoffice Castle Ind Ter.

Applications for Enrollment of Creek Newborn
Act of 1905 Volume VI

AFFIDAVIT OF MOTHER.

UNITED STATES OF AMERICA Indian Territory }
Western DISTRICT.

I Salley Fixico on oath state that I am 35 years of age and a citizen by blood of the Creek Nation; that I am the lawful wife of Tul mo chus Fixico who is a citizen by blood of the Creek Nation; that a male child was born to me on 5 day of November 1903 that said child has been named Robert Fixico and was living March 4 1905.

                                        her
                               Salley x Fixico

Witnesses To Mark: mark
{ HG Malot
  Tupper Dunn

Subscribed and sworn to before me this 17 day of March 1905.

My com exp Aug 19-1908   Tupper Dunn
                                                Notary Public.

AFFIDAVIT OF ATTENDING PHYSICIAN OR MID-WIFE.

UNITED STATES OF AMERICA Indian Territory }
Western DISTRICT.

I Dela Fixico a midwife on oath state that I attended on Mrs. Salley Fixico wife of Tul mo chus Fixico on the 5 day of November 1903 ; that there was born to her on said date a *(blank)* child; that said child was living March 4 1905 and is said to have been named Robert Fixico
                                        her
                               Dela x Fixico

Witnesses To Mark: mark
{ HG Malot
  Tupper Dunn

Subscribed and sworn to before me this 17 day of March 1905.

My com exp Aug 19-1908   Tupper Dunn
                                                Notary Public.

Applications for Enrollment of Creek Newborn
Act of 1905   Volume VI

BIRTH AFFIDAVIT.
DEPARTMENT OF THE INTERIOR
COMMISSION TO THE FIVE CIVILIZED TRIBES.

IN RE Application for Enrollment as a citizen of the Creek Nation of Edith Woodward born on the 30 day of July 1904

Name of Father:	Herbert E. Woodward	a citizen of the	U.S.	Nation.
Name of Mother:	Nellie W. Woodward	a citizen of the	Creek	Nation.

Post-office: Tulsa I.T.

AFFIDAVIT OF MOTHER.

UNITED STATES OF AMERICA
   INDIAN TERRITORY.
   Western   District.

I Nellie E. Woodward on oath state that I am 29 years of age and a citizen by Blood of the Creek Nation; that I am the lawful wife of   Herbert E. Woodward who is a citizen by Blood of the United States Nation; that a Female child was born to me on 30" day of July 1904 that said child has been named Edith Woodward and is now living.

Nellie E. Woodward

WITNESSES TO MARK:
{

Subscribed and sworn to before me this 18 *day of* March *1905.*

Com Ex July 3" 1906

Robert E. Lynch
Notary Public.

AFFIDAVIT OF ATTENDING PHYSICIAN OR MID-WIFE.

UNITED STATES OF AMERICA
   INDIAN TERRITORY.
   Western   District.

I J. E. Webb a physician on oath state that I attended on Mrs. Nellie E. Woodward wife of Herbert E. Woodward on the 30 day of July 1904 ; that there was born to her on said date a Female child; that said child is now living and is said to have been named Edith Woodward

J.E. Webb

Applications for Enrollment of Creek Newborn
Act of 1905   Volume VI

WITNESSES TO MARK:

{

Subscribed and sworn to before me 18 day of Mch 1905.

My Commission Expires July 7th 1907.

D. C. *(Illegible)*
Notary Public.

B. V. Leonard
Lawyer.

Wagoner Ind. Ter.

United States of America
Western Judicial District   S.S.
Indian Territory.

Amanda E. Skeen being first duly sworn states on oath that she attended Mrs. Laura Cunningham a citizen of the Creek Nation by blood wife of C.N. Cunningham on the 2nd. day of August 1903 when a male child was born to her said to be named William Leo Cunningham and that said child is living at this date the 31st. day of March 1905

Witness   Amanda E. Skeen
B.V. Lenard
H O Skeen

Subscribed and sworn to before me this 31st. day of March 1905 by the above named Amanda E. Skeen; and I further certify that the above affidavit was first read over to her in her hearing before she subscribed to same

B V Leonard
Notary Public.

BIRTH AFFIDAVIT.

DEPARTMENT OF THE INTERIOR.
COMMISSION TO THE FIVE CIVILIZED TRIBES.

IN RE APPLICATION FOR ENROLLMENT as a citizen of the CREEK Nation of Wm Leo Cunningham born on the 2 day of Aug 1903

Name of Father:	C.N. Cunningham		a citizen of the	U. S.	Nation.
Name of Mother:	Laura "		a citizen of the	Creek	Nation.

Postoffice   Wagoner

Applications for Enrollment of Creek Newborn
Act of 1905   Volume VI

BIRTH AFFIDAVIT.

DEPARTMENT OF THE INTERIOR
COMMISSION TO THE FIVE CIVILIZED TRIBES.

IN RE Application for Enrollment as a citizen of the Creek Nation of Edith Woodward born on the 30 day of July 1904

Name of Father: Herbert E. Woodward   a citizen of the   U.S.   Nation.
Name of Mother: Nellie W. Woodward   a citizen of the   Creek   Nation.

Post-office: Tulsa I.T.

AFFIDAVIT OF MOTHER.

UNITED STATES OF AMERICA
INDIAN TERRITORY.
Western   District.

I Nellie E. Woodward on oath state that I am 29 years of age and a citizen by Blood of the Creek Nation; that I am the lawful wife of Herbert E. Woodward who is a citizen by Blood of the United States Nation; that a Female child was born to me on 30" day of July 1904 that said child has been named Edith Woodward and is now living.

Nellie E. Woodward

WITNESSES TO MARK:

Subscribed and sworn to before me this 18 *day of* March 1905.

Robert E. Lynch
Com Ex July 3" 1906   *Notary Public.*

AFFIDAVIT OF ATTENDING PHYSICIAN OR MID-WIFE.

UNITED STATES OF AMERICA
INDIAN TERRITORY.
Western   District.

I J. E. Webb a physician on oath state that I attended on Mrs. Nellie E. Woodward wife of Herbert E. Woodward on the 30 day of July 1904 ; that there was born to her on said date a Female child; that said child is now living and is said to have been named Edith Woodward

J.E. Webb

Applications for Enrollment of Creek Newborn
Act of 1905   Volume VI

WITNESSES TO MARK:
{

Subscribed and sworn to before me 18 day of Mch 1905.

D. C. *(Illegible)*
Notary Public.

My Commission Expires July 7th 1907.

B. V. Leonard
Lawyer.

Wagoner Ind. Ter.

United States of America
Western Judicial District   S.S.
Indian Territory.

  Amanda E. Skeen being first duly sworn states on oath that she attended Mrs. Laura Cunningham a citizen of the Creek Nation by blood wife of C.N. Cunningham on the 2nd. day of August 1903 when a male child was born to her said to be named William Leo Cunningham and that said child is living at this date the 31st. day of March 1905

Witness   Amanda E. Skeen
B.V. Lenard
H O Skeen

Subscribed and sworn to before me this 31st. day of March 1905 by the above named Amanda E. Skeen; and I further certify that the above affidavit was first read over to her in her hearing before she subscribed to same

              B V Leonard
                Notary Public.

BIRTH AFFIDAVIT.

DEPARTMENT OF THE INTERIOR.
COMMISSION TO THE FIVE CIVILIZED TRIBES.

  IN RE APPLICATION FOR ENROLLMENT as a citizen of the CREEK Nation of Wm Leo Cunningham born on the 2 day of Aug 1903

Name of Father:	C.N. Cunningham	a citizen of the	U. S.	Nation.
Name of Mother:	Laura "	a citizen of the	Creek	Nation.

         Postoffice   Wagoner

Applications for Enrollment of Creek Newborn
Act of 1905 Volume VI

(child present)

AFFIDAVIT OF MOTHER.

UNITED STATES OF AMERICA Indian Territory
WESTERN DISTRICT.

I Laura Cunningham on oath state that I am 21 years of age and a citizen by blood of the Creek Nation; that I am the lawful wife of C. N. Cunningham who is a citizen by ----- of the U. S. Nation; that a male child was born to me on 2 day of August 1903 that said child has been named William Lee Cunningham and is now living.

                  Her
               Laura x Cunningham
Witnesses To Mark: mark
 Irwin Donovan
 EC Griesel

Subscribed and sworn to before me this 24" day of March 1905.

             Edw C Griesel
               Notary Public.

NC-426.

           Muskogee Indian Territory August 3 1905.

Minnie Richard
  c/o Jasper Richard
    Checotah Indian Territory.

Dear Madam:

  On March 22 1905 your husband Jasper Richard appeared before the Commission to the Five Civilized Tribes and made application for the enrollment of your minor daughter Annie Richard as a citizen by blood of the Creek Nation and at that time submitted his affidavit as to the birth of said child it appearing therefrom that she was born on December 24 1902. Subsequently on April 23 1905 you filed with the said Commission your affidavit and the affidavit of Louisa Simmons midwife relative to the birth of said child from which it appears that she was born January 31 1904.

  You are requested to immediately inform this office as to which of the above dates if either of them is the correct date of the birth of said child.

           Respectfully
               Commissioner.

Applications for Enrollment of Creek Newborn
Act of 1905   Volume VI

N.C. 426.

DEPARTMENT OF THE INTERIOR
COMMISSIONER TO THE FIVE CIVILIZED TRIBES.
Muskogee Indian Territory August 10 1905.

In the matter of the application for the enrollment of Annie Richard as a citizen by blood of the Creek Nation.

Minnie Richard being duly sworn testified as follows:

By Commissioner:

Q What is your name? A Minnie Richard.
Q What is your age? A I cant[sic] tell (Witness appears to be about thirty years old.)
Q What is your post office address? A Checotah.
Q Have you a child named Annie Richard? A Yes sir
Q Where is she? A Right here.
Q When was Annie born? A The last day of January.
Q How old was she last January? A She is going on two years old.
Q She was one last January? A Yes sir.
Q Are you certain of that? A Yes sir

The child is present and appears to be about the age given.)

Q You made out an affidavit before Charles Buford notary public and gave the date as January 31 1904 the midwife also gave that date. Who is the father of this child? A Jasper Richard.
Q He made out an affidavit before the Commission and gave December 24 1902 which would make the child two years old and over A No that's not correct he never waited on me and never got a doctor to wait on me I waited on myself that is a mistake of his
Q The correct date is January 31 1904? A Yes sir.

I Anna Garrigues on oath state that the above and foregoing is a true and correct copy of my stenographic notes taken in said case on said date.

Anna Garrigues

Subscribed and sworn to before me
this 10th day of August 1905.

Henry G. Hains
Notary Public.

Applications for Enrollment of Creek Newborn
Act of 1905 Volume VI

BIRTH AFFIDAVIT.

DEPARTMENT OF THE INTERIOR.
COMMISSION TO THE FIVE CIVILIZED TRIBES.

IN RE APPLICATION FOR ENROLLMENT as a citizen of the CREEK Nation of Annie Richard born on the 24 day of Dec. 1902

Name of Father:	Jasper Richard	a citizen of the	Creek	Nation.
Name of Mother:	Minnie "	a citizen of the	Creek	Nation.

Postoffice   Checotah IT

AFFIDAVIT OF MOTHER.

UNITED STATES OF AMERICA Indian Territory
WESTERN DISTRICT.

I Jasper Richard on oath state that I am 31 years of age and a citizen by blood of the CREEK Nation; that I am the lawful ~~wife~~ husband of Minnie who is a citizen by blood of the CREEK Nation; that a *(blank)* child was born to me on 24 day of Dec 1902 that said child has been named Annie Richard and is now living.

                       his
                 Jasper x Richard

Witnesses To Mark: mark
  H.G. Hains
  Irwin Donovan

Subscribed and sworn to before me this 22" day of March 1905.

                J. McDermott
                    Notary Public.

BIRTH AFFIDAVIT.

DEPARTMENT OF THE INTERIOR.
COMMISSION TO THE FIVE CIVILIZED TRIBES.

IN RE APPLICATION FOR ENROLLMENT as a citizen of the Creek Nation of Annie Richard born on the 31st day of January 1904

Name of Father:	Jasper Richard	a citizen of the	Creek	Nation.
Name of Mother:	Minnie Richard	a citizen of the	Creek	Nation.

Postoffice   Checotah Ind. Terr.

Applications for Enrollment of Creek Newborn
Act of 1905 Volume VI

AFFIDAVIT OF MOTHER.

UNITED STATES OF AMERICA Indian Territory
Western DISTRICT.

    I Minnie Richard on oath state that I am 21 years of age and a citizen by blood of the Creek Nation; that I am the lawful wife of Jasper Richard who is a citizen by blood of the Creek Nation; that a female child was born to me on the 31st day of January 1904 that said child has been named Annie Richard and was living March 4 1905.

                                                      her
Witnesses To Mark: Minnie x Richard
    F.A. McIntosh   mark
    Daniel N. Bard

    Subscribed and sworn to before me this 20th day of March 1905.

My commission expires July 3rd 1906.   Charles Buford
                                                    Notary Public.

AFFIDAVIT OF ATTENDING PHYSICIAN OR MID-WIFE.

UNITED STATES OF AMERICA Indian Territory
Western DISTRICT.

    I Louisa Simmons a mid-wife on oath state that I attended on Mrs. Minnie Richard wife of Jasper Richard on the 31st day of January 1904 ; that there was born to her on said date a female child; that said child was living March 4 1905 and is said to have been named Annie Richard

                                                      her
Witnesses To Mark: Louisa x Simmons
    Daniel N. Bard   mark
    F.A. McIntosh

My commission expires July 3rd 1906.   Charles Buford
                                                    Notary Public.

Applications for Enrollment of Creek Newborn
Act of 1905 Volume VI

N. C. 427.   JWH

Muskogee Indian Territory January 29 1907.

Annie McNac
    c/o Fred McNac
        Rush Hill Indian Territory.

Dear Madam :--

    In the matter of the application for the enrollment of your minor child Lizzie McNac as a citizen of the Creek Nation you are advised that you should appear at this office at once to give testimony relative to the date of her birth bringing with you any records you may have pertaining thereto.

                Respectfully

                Commissioner.

DEPARTMENT OF THE INTERIOR

Commissioner to the five Civilized Tribes.

In re application for Enrollment as a citizen of the Creek Nation of Nellie E Self born on the 6 day of Feb 1905

Name of the father: James A Self	a citizen of Creek	Nation.
Name of the Mother: Mattie Self	a citizen of the U.S.	Nation.

        Post office   Kellyville I.T.

AFFIDAVIT OF MOTHER.

UNITED STATES OF AMERICA)
  Indian Territory   )
  Western   District   )

    I Mattie Self on oath state that I am 26 years of age and a citizen by Birth of the U S Nation that I am the lawful wife of James A Self who is a citizen by Blood of the Creek Nation; that a female child was born to me on 6 day of Feb 1905 that said child has been named Nellie E Self and is now living.

                Mattie Self

Applications for Enrollment of Creek Newborn
Act of 1905   Volume VI

Witness to Mark   :
  Must be   :
two witnesses   :

Subscribed and sworn to before me this 16 day of March 1905.

W W Holder
Notary Public.

Affidavit of attending Physician or Mid-wife.

UNITED STATES OF AMERICA   )
  Indian Territory   )
Western   District   )

    I J. P. Cox   a Physician   on oath state that I attended on Mrs.   Mattie Self wife of   James A Self   on the 6   day of   Feb   1905; that there was born to her on said date a female child; that said child is now living and is said to have been named   Nellie E Self.

J P Cox MD

Witness to Mark   :
  must be two   :
  witnesses   :

Subscribed and sworn to before me this 16 day of March 1905.

W W Holder
Notary Public.

BIRTH AFFIDAVIT.

Department of the Interior
COMMISSION TO THE FIVE CIVILIZED TRIBES.

    IN RE Application for Enrollment as a citizen of the Creek Nation of   Ivory Bell Self born on the 20 day of March   1903

Name of Father:	James A Self	a citizen of the	Creek	Nation.
Name of Mother:	Mattie Self	a citizen of the	Creek	Nation.

Post-office   Kellyville

Applications for Enrollment of Creek Newborn
Act of 1905 Volume VI

AFFIDAVIT OF MOTHER.

UNITED STATES OF AMERICA
    INDIAN TERRITORY
Western   District.

    I Mattie Self on oath state that I am 26 years of age and a citizen by U.S. of the *(blank)* Nation; that I am the lawful wife of James A Self who is a citizen by blood of the Creek Nation; that a Female child was born to me on 20 day of March 1903 that said child has been named Ivory Bell Self and is now living.

                                     Mattie Self

WITNESSES TO MARK:

{

    Subscribed and sworn to before me this 16 day of March 1905.

Com Expires 9/8/06   W W Holder
                                               Notary Public.

AFFIDAVIT OF ATTENDING PHYSICIAN OR MID-WIFE.

UNITED STATES OF AMERICA
    INDIAN TERRITORY
Western   District.

    I J.P. Cox a physician on oath state that I attended on Mrs. Mattie Self wife of James A Self on the 20 day of March 1903 ; that there was born to her on said date a female child; that said child is now living and is said to have been named Ivory Bell Self

                                     J.P. Cox M.D.

WITNESSES TO MARK:

{

    Subscribed and sworn to before me this 16 day of March 1905.

                                     W W Holder
                                     Notary Public.

Applications for Enrollment of Creek Newborn
Act of 1905 Volume VI

DEPARTMENT OF THE INTERIOR

Commissioner to the Five Civilized Tribes.

In re application for Enrollment as a citizen of the Creek Nation of William K Self born on the 25 day of Oct 1902

Name of the father: John H Self   a citizen of   Creek   Nation.
Name of the mother: Dollie Self   a citizen of the   U.S.   Nation.

Post Office   Kellyville I.T.

Affidavit of Mother.

UNITED STATES OF AMERICA)
Indian Territory)
Western   District   )

I Dollie Self on oath state that I am 24 years of age and a citizen by *(blank)* of the U.S. Nation that I am the lawful wife of John H Self who is a citizen by blood of the Creek Nation; that a male child was born to me on 25 day of Oct 1902 that said child has been named William K Self and is now living.

Dollie Self

Witness to Mark :
 Must be   :
two witnesses :

Subscribed and sworn to before me this 16 day of March 1905.

Com expires 9.8.06   W W Holder
                                       Notary Public.

Affidavit of attending Physician or Mid-wife.

UNITED STATES OF AMERICA)
Indian Territory)
Western   District   )

I M A Self a midwife on oath state that I attended on Mrs. Dollie Self wife of John H Self on the 25 day of Oct 1902; that there was born to her on said date a male child; that said child is now living and is said to have been named William K Self

M A Self

Witness to Mark :
 must be two   :
  witnesses   :

Applications for Enrollment of Creek Newborn
Act of 1905 Volume VI

Subscribed and sworn to before me this 16 day of March 1905.

Com expires 9.8.06   W W Holder
              Notary Public.

DEPARTMENT OF THE INTERIOR

Commissioner to the five civilized tribes.

In re application for Enrollment as a citizen of the Creek Nation of Edward N Self born on the 15 day of Sept 1904

Name of the father: John H Self   a citizen of   Creek   Nation.
Name of the Mother: Dollie Self   a citizen of the U.S.   Nation.

         Post office   Kellyville

AFFIDAVIT OF MOTHER.

UNITED STATES OF AMERICA)
  Indian Territory   )
Western   District   )

   I Dollie Self on oath state that I am 24 years of age and a citizen by *(blank)* of the U S Nation that I am the lawful wife of John H Self who is a citizen by Blood of the Creek Nation; that a male child was born to me on 15 day of Sept 1904 that said child has been named Edward N Self and is now living.

             Dollie Self

Witness to Mark :
  Must be   :
two witnesses   :

Subscribed and sworn to before me this 16 day of March 1905.

Com expires 9.8.06   W W Holder
              Notary Public.

Affidavit of attending Physician or Mid-wife.

UNITED STATES OF AMERICA)
  Indian Territory   )
Western   District   )

Applications for Enrollment of Creek Newborn
Act of 1905 Volume VI

  I J. P. Cox a Physician on oath state that I attended on Mrs. Dollie Self wife of John H Self on the 15 day of Sept 1904; that there was born to her on said date a male child; that said child is now living and is said to have been named Edward N Self.

                J P Cox MD

Witness to Mark :
 must be two :
 witnesses :

Subscribed and sworn to before me this 16 day of March 1905.

               W W Holder
                Notary Public.

Department of the Interior.

COMMISSION TO THE FIVE CIVILIZED TRIBES.

In Re Application for Enrollment as a citizen of the Creek Nation of Minnie Chisholm born on the 17" day of May 1903.

Name of Father: Anderson Chisholm a citizen of the Creek Nation.
Name of Mother: Rosa Chisholm a citizen of the Creek Nation.

          Postoffice: Fry I.T.

          Affidavit of Mother

United States of America
Indian Territory
Western District.

  I Rosa Chisholm on oath state that I am 24 years of age and a citizen by blood of the Creek Nation that I am the wife of Anderson Chisholm who is a citizen by blood of the Creek Nation that a female child was born to me on the 17" day of May *(remainder illegible).*
               her
            Rosa x Chisholm
Witnesses to Mark: mark
 Frank L. Haymes
 D. Harslman

Applications for Enrollment of Creek Newborn
Act of 1905 Volume VI

Subscribed and sworn to before me this *(remainder illegible).*

(Illegible)

        Z.I.J. Holt
         Notary Public.

Affidavit of Attending Midwife.

United States of America
Indian Territory
Western District.

(Entire Affidavit illegible)

          her
        Kizzie x Loler
         mark

Frank L. Haymes
D. Harslman

        Z.I.J. Holt

Department Of The Interior.

COMMISSION TO THE FIVE CIVILIZED TRIBES.

In Re Application For Enrollment as a citizen of the Creek Nation of Almarine Larney born on the 9" day of Aril 1904.

Name of Father Dave Larney a citizen of the Creek Nation.
Name of Mother Nancy (<u>Larney</u>) Alexander a citizen of the Creek Nation

      Post Office Fry I.T.

      Affidavit of Mother.

United States of America
Indian Territory.
Western District.
  I Nancy (Larney) Alexander on oath state that I am 20 years of and a citizen by blood of the Creek Nation; that I am the wife of Willie Alexander who is a citizen by

Applications for Enrollment of Creek Newborn
Act of 1905   Volume VI

blood of the Creek Nation; that my former husband Dave Larney the father of this child died March 4 1904; that he was a citizen by blood of the Creek Nation; that a male child was born to me on the 9" day of April 1904; that said child was living on March 4 1905 and has been named Almarine Larney.

                                        Nancy Larney Alexander (Signed)

Witness to mark

_____
_____

SEAL

    Subscribed and sworn to before me this 16" day of March A. D. 1905.

                                        S. I. J. Holt (Signed)
                                                Notary Public.

My commission expires May 9" 1907.

_____

Affidavit of Attending Mid-Wife.

United States of America
Indian Territory
Western District.

    I Kizzie Loler a mid-wife on oath state that I attended on Mrs. Nancy Larney (now Nancy Alexander) Wife of Willie Alexander (then wife of Dave Larney) on the 9" day of April 1904; that there was born to her on said date a male child; that said child was living on March 4 1905 and is said to have been named Almarine Larney.

                                                 her
                                      Kizzie X Loler
                                          mark

Witnesses to mark:

    Frank L. Haymes
    D. Harslman

SEAL
    Subscribed and sworn to before me this 16" day of March A. D. 1905.

                                        Z. I. J. Holt
                                               Notary Public.

My commission expires May 9" 1907.

_____

Applications for Enrollment of Creek Newborn
Act of 1905 Volume VI

(Page illegible except for signatures)

                Nancy Larney Alexander

                Z.I.J. Holt

(Page illegible except for signatures)

                her
             Kizzie x Loler
                mark

Frank L. Haymes
D. Harslman

                Z.I.J. Holt

BIRTH AFFIDAVIT.

DEPARTMENT OF THE INTERIOR.
COMMISSION TO THE FIVE CIVILIZED TRIBES.

IN RE APPLICATION FOR ENROLLMENT as a citizen of the CREEK Nation of Hattie Swingle born on the 10 day of Dec 1902

Name of Father: Willoughby Swingle   a citizen of the   U. S.   Nation.
Name of Mother: Corda   "   a citizen of the   Creek   Nation.

            Postoffice   Bixby

(child present)

AFFIDAVIT OF MOTHER.

UNITED STATES OF AMERICA Indian Territory }
    WESTERN   DISTRICT.

    I Corda Swingle on oath state that I am 21 years of age and a citizen by blood of the Creek   Nation; that I am the lawful wife of   Willoughby Swingle   who is a

Applications for Enrollment of Creek Newborn
Act of 1905 Volume VI

citizen by ----- of the U. S. Nation; that a female child was born to me on 10 day of Dec 1902 that said child has been named Hattie Swingle and is now living.

         Corda Swingle

Witnesses To Mark:
{

 Subscribed and sworn to before me this 22 day of March 1905.

         Edw C Griesel
         Notary Public.

AFFIDAVIT OF ATTENDING PHYSICIAN OR MID-WIFE.

UNITED STATES OF AMERICA Indian Territory }
  WESTERN DISTRICT.

 I Dollie Bowman a midwife on oath state that I attended on Mrs. Corda Swingle wife of Willoughby Swingle on the 10 day of Dec 1902 ; that there was born to her on said date a female child; that said child is now living and is said to have been named Hattie Swingle

         Dollie Bowman

Witnesses To Mark:
{

 Subscribed and sworn to before me this 22 day of March 1905.

         Edw C Griesel
         Notary Public.

NC 432.

    DEPARTMENT OF THE INTERIOR
  COMMISSIONER TO THE FIVE CIVILIZED TRIBES.
    MUSKOGEE INDIAN TERRITORY
      OCTOBER 27 1906.

 In the matter of the application for the enrollment of Chitto Harjo Bullett as a citizen by blood of the Creek Nation.

 JOHN BULLETT being duly sworn by H.G. Hains a Notary Public testified as follows through Official Interpreter Lona Merrick.

Applications for Enrollment of Creek Newborn
Act of 1905   Volume VI

Examination by the Commissioner.

Q What is your name? A John Bullette[sic].
Q What is your age? A 26.
Q What is your post office address? A Hanna.
Q What is the name of your father? A Bailey Bullett.
Q Is he living? A No sir he is dead.
Q What is the name of your mother? A Hullie Yarby.
Q What Creek Indian town do you belong to? A Hillabee Canadian

  Witness is identified as John Bullett opposite Creek Indian roll number 8776.

Q Are you married? A Yes sir.
Q What is the name of your wife? A Zoye.
Q Is she living? A Yes sir.
Q When were you married to her? A I don't know how long we have been married; we have two children.
Q Have you your marriage license with you? A No sir but I have it at home.

  Witness is advised that it would be well for him to furnish this office with a copy of said marriage license.

Q You say you had two children by Zoye? A Yes sir.
Q What is the name of the oldest? A Jemima Bullett.
Q Is that child living? A Yes sir.
Q How old is she? A About ten years old.
Q Is it enrolled? A Yes sir I have filed for her I enrolled before the field party.
Q Was she ever known by any other name? A No sir.
Q Did you have a child by the name of Chitto Harjo Bullett? A Yes sir.
Q Is it a boy or girl? A Boy.
Q Is he living? A Yes sir.
Q How old is he? A About three years old.
Q We have an affidavit here sign[sic] by Zoye Bullett which says the child was born August 8 1904 that is two years ago last August? A I was guessing at its age when I said it was three years old.
Q Don't you know---do you know whether it was born in the summer time or winter or when? A It was born in the summer time.
Q Was it two years old this last summer that has just passed? A Yes sir.
Q His mother is not an Indian she is a white man is she? A Yes sir.
Q Can you read or write? A No sir.
Q Your name appears on the roll and identified as John Bullett that is our correct name is it??[sic] A Yes sir.
Q Is this the correct name of Chitto Harjo Bullett---it is B-u-l-l-e-t-t-e instead of B-u-l-l-e-t the way the first affidavit is written? A Yes sir.
Q What was your wife's name before you married her Zoye what? A Zoye Lucas.
Q Who was the midwife when Chitto Harjo Bullette was born? A My wife's mother.

Applications for Enrollment of Creek Newborn
Act of 1905 Volume VI

Lona Merrick being duly sworn states that the above and foregoing is a true and correct transcript of her stenographic notes as taken in said cause on said date.

Lona Merrick

Subscribed and sworn to before me this 3rd day of November 1906.

H.G. Hains
Notary Public.

N.C. 432

DEPARTMENT OF THE INTERIOR
COMMISSIONER TO THE FIVE CIVILIZED TRIBES
Wetumka Indian Territory November 1906.

In the matter of the application for the enrollment of Chitto Harjo Bullet as a citizen by blood of the Creek Nation.

ZOYE TIGER Being duly sworn testified as follows:

BY COMMISSIONER:

Q What is your name? A Zoye Tiger was Bullet.
Q What is your age? A Twnety[sic] three will be twenty four the 16th.
Q What is your postoffice address? A Wetumka c/o John Lucas.
Q Are you a Creek citizen? A No sir.
Q Are you a citizen of any of the five tribes? A No claimed to be a Cherokee but not enroled[sic].
Q Have you a child for whom you made application for enrollment in the Creek Nation? A Yes sir.
Q What is the name of that child? A Chitto Harjo Bullet.
Q When was he born? A He was three years old last Augst[sic] the 8th.
Q Do you know what year? A I've forgot.
Q If he was three years old last 8th of August he must have been born in the year 1903 would he not? A Yes sir thats[sic] right.

There is an affidavit on file at the office of the Commissioner to the Five Civilized Tribes executed by you on March 22 1905 stating that Chitto Harjo Bullet was born August 8 1904.

Q Is that the correct date of his birth? A No it couldn't be. I know the child was three years old last August.
Q Are you positive that your child Chitto was three years ago last August? A Yes I am. When Posey made out those papers there was a big crowd there then and he might have misunderstood me and made out the papers wrong.
Q Who is the father of Chitto Harjo Bullet? A John Bullet.

Applications for Enrollment of Creek Newborn
Act of 1905   Volume VI

Q Is he a Creek citizen A Yes sir.
Q Were you lawfully married to John Bullet when this child was born? A Yes I was.
Q Can you procure the marriage license and certificate between yourself and John Bullet? A I haven't got them now cause I sent them to my lawyer at Wewoka. He said he would have to have it when [sic] tried the case.
Q What case? A I sued him for a divource[sic].
Q Was the divource[sic] granted? A I guess so; my lawyer said it was.
Q What is the lawyer's name? A Skinner he lives in Wetumka.
Q Can you furnish the Commissioner the decree of the Court in the divource[sic] suit between yourself and John Bullet? A I don't know but I have some papers here that my lawyer sent to me.

The witness presents a copy of the Master's Report dated April 18 1906 which is made a part of the record in the case. She requests that a copy of the report be made and filed in the case and the original returned to her.

Q Do you know where John Bullet lives now? A I think he's down at Hanna.
Q Are you married to another man now? A Yes.

I Jesse McDermott on oath state that the above and foregoing is a full and true transcript of my notes as taken in said cause on said date.

Jesse McDermott

Subscribed and sworn to before me this 5th day of November 1906.

MB Glesher
Notary Public.

My Com Expires Dec 12-1906

IN THE UNITED STATES COURT IN THE INDIAN TERRITORY

WESTERN DISTRICT AT WEWOKA.

NO. 694 EQUITY.

Zoie Bullet	Plaintiff	:		
		:		
vs		:		MASTER'S REPORT
		:		
John Bullet	Defendant.	:		
		:		

Applications for Enrollment of Creek Newborn
Act of 1905   Volume VI

To the Honorable Louis Sulzbacher Judge of said Court:

The undersigned Thomas A. Sanson Master in Chancery of this Court to whom the above entitled cause was referred to take the proof and report his findings of fact and conclusions of law begs leave to make the following report:

I.

The plaintiff filed her bill of complaint in this cause on December 15 1905 in which she prays a decree of divorce from the defendant her husband upon the following grounds: First that the defendant offered such indignities to the person of the plaintiff as to render her condition intolerable and Second on the ground of desertion.

Upon this bill of complaint the Clerk of this Court issued a writ of summons to the defendant returnable at the present April term of this court and the same was on February 2 1906 returned into the office of the clerk of this Court personally served upon the defendant at Hanna in this District on the 16th day of January 1906 and the defendant not having appeared nor answered herein was heretofore adjudged to be in default and this cause referred to the Master.

II.

This cause came on for hearing before me at the United States Court House at Wewoka in this District on the 16th day of April 1906 the plaintiff appearing in person and by her attorney the defendant making no appearance and the following witnesses were produced and sworn and their testimony reduced to writing is hereto attached and made a part of this report:

        Zoie Bullet plaintiff Wetumka I. T.
        Earnest Hill Wetumka I. T.
        S. L. Lucas Wetumka I. T.

From the testimony of said witnesses I find the facts hereinto be as follows:

III.

I find that the plaintiff has resided in the Creek Nation Indian Territory for about twenty-three years and that she resided in this District at the time this suit was brought; that she and the defendant were lawfully intermarried on the 30th day of January 1899 by Rev. G. A. Alexander a Minister of the Gospel under a marriage license issued out of this court and duly returned and recorded; that they lived together as husband and wife until the 3rd day of July 1904 when the defendant left the plaintiff and since that time they have not lived together as husband and wife nor has he contributed anything towards her support.

I find that two children were born of this marriage Gemima aged six years and Chitaggo aged two years; that these children are now in the custody and possession of the

Applications for Enrollment of Creek Newborn
Act of 1905 Volume VI

plaintiff their mother and since the said separation the defendant has furnished nothing towards their support.

I find that just prior to the separation that the defendant cursed and abused the plaintiff his wife and that he struck her in the head with his fist; that there are no property rights involved; that the equities are with the plaintiff and against the defendant.

IV.

CONCLUSIONS OF LAW.

From the testimony in this cause and the foregoing findings of fact I conclude first that the defendant offered such indignities to the person of the plaintiff as to make her condition intolerable and second that on the 3rd day of July A. D. 1904 the defendant willfully deserted the plaintiff his wife without just cause and that since that time has remained separate and apart from her with legal excuse.

RECOMMENDATIONS/[sic]

I therefore recommend that the bonds of matrimony which now exist between the plaintiff and defendant be dissolved set aside and held for naught; that the plaintiff be restored to all the rights of a single and unmarried person; that she be awarded the care and custody of their two minor children; that the defendant pay the cost of this proceeding and that a decree be made and entered herein accordingly

All of which is respectfully submitted.

Master in Chancery.

April 18 1906.

BIRTH AFFIDAVIT.

DEPARTMENT OF THE INTERIOR.
COMMISSION TO THE FIVE CIVILIZED TRIBES.

IN RE APPLICATION FOR ENROLLMENT as a citizen of the Creek Nation of Chitto Harjo Bullet born on the 3 day of August 1904

Name of Father: John Bullet   a citizen of the   Creek   Nation.
Name of Mother: Zoye Bullet   a citizen of the United States Nation.

Postoffice   Wetumka Ind. Ter.

Applications for Enrollment of Creek Newborn
Act of 1905   Volume VI

AFFIDAVIT OF MOTHER.

UNITED STATES OF AMERICA Indian Territory }
Western   DISTRICT.

I Zoye Bullet on oath state that I am 24 years of age and a citizen by *(blank)* of the United States ~~Nation~~; that I am the lawful wife of John Bullet who is a citizen by blood of the Creek Nation; that a male child was born to me on 8 day of August 1904 that said child has been named Chitto Harjo Bullet and was living March 4 1905.

                                          her
Witnesses To Mark: Zoye x Bullet
  { Alex Posey   mark
    DC Skaggs

Subscribed and sworn to before me this 22 day of March 1905.

                      Drennan C Skaggs
                      Notary Public.

AFFIDAVIT OF ATTENDING PHYSICIAN OR MID-WIFE.

UNITED STATES OF AMERICA Indian Territory }
Western   DISTRICT.

I Martha Lucus a midwife on oath state that I attended on Mrs. Zoye Bullet wife of John Bullet on the 8 day of August 1904 ; that there was born to her on said date a *(blank)* child; that said child was living March 4 1905 and is said to have been named Chitto Harjo Bullet

                                          her
Witnesses To Mark: Martha x Lucus
  { Alex Posey   mark
    DC Skaggs

Subscribed and sworn to before me this 22 day of March 1905.

                      Drennan C Skaggs
                      Notary Public.

BIRTH AFFIDAVIT.
DEPARTMENT OF THE INTERIOR
COMMISSIONER TO THE FIVE CIVILIZED TRIBES.

ENROLLMENT OF MINORS.   ACT OF CONGRESS APPROVED APRIL 26 1906.

IN RE APPLICATION FOR ENROLLMENT as a citizen of the Creek Nation of Chitto Harjo Bullett born on the ----- day of August 1904

Applications for Enrollment of Creek Newborn
Act of 1905   Volume VI

Name of Father: John Bullett   a citizen of the   Creek   Nation.
Name of Mother: Zoye   "   a citizen of the   U.S.   Nation.

Tribal enrollment of father   (blank)   Tribal enrollment of mother   (blank)

Postoffice   Hanna I.T. for father

AFFIDAVIT OF ~~MOTHER~~.
Father

UNITED STATES OF AMERICA Indian Territory }
Western   District.

I John Bullett on oath state that I am 26 years of age and a citizen by blood of the Creek Nation; that I am the lawful ~~wife~~ husband of Zoye Bullett who is a citizen by ----- of the U. S. Nation; that a male child was born to me on ----- day of August 1904 that said child has been named Chitto Harjo Bullett and was living March 4 1906.

                                          his
                                 John x Bullett
WITNESSES TO MARK: mark
{ H.G. Hairn
{ Lona Merrick

Subscribed and sworn to before me this   27" day of October   1906.

H.G. Hains
Notary Public

(The first Birth Affidavit was given again)

BIRTH AFFIDAVIT.
DEPARTMENT OF THE INTERIOR.
COMMISSION TO THE FIVE CIVILIZED TRIBES.

IN RE APPLICATION FOR ENROLLMENT as a citizen of the Creek Nation of Chitto Harjo Bullet born on the 8 day of Aug 1903

Name of Father: John Bullet   a citizen of the   Creek   Nation.
Name of Mother: Zoye Bullet   a citizen of the   US   Nation.

Postoffice   Wetumka ITy

Applications for Enrollment of Creek Newborn
Act of 1905 Volume VI

AFFIDAVIT OF MOTHER.

UNITED STATES OF AMERICA Indian Territory }
Western   DISTRICT.

I Zoye Bullet (now Tiger) on oath state that I am 24 years of age and a citizen by *(blank)* of the U.S. ~~Nation~~; that I ~~am~~ was the lawful wife of John Bullet who is a citizen by blood of the Creek Nation; that a male child was born to me on 8 day of August 1903 that said child has been named Chitto Harjo Bullet and was living March 4 1905.

                                      her
                                Zoye x Bullet Tiger
Witnesses To Mark: mark
{ J McDermott

Subscribed and sworn to before me this 2" day of Nov 1906.

My Commission   J McDermott
Expires July 25" 1907   Notary Public.

AFFIDAVIT OF ATTENDING PHYSICIAN OR MID-WIFE.

UNITED STATES OF AMERICA Indian Territory }
Western   DISTRICT.

I Martha Lucas a midwife on oath state that I attended on Mrs. Zoye Bullet who was the wife of John Bullet on the 8th day of Aug 1903 ; that there was born to her on said date a male child; that said child was living March 4 1905 and is said to have been named Chitto Harjo Bullet

                                Martha Lucas
Witnesses To Mark:
{

Subscribed and sworn to before me this 2" day of Nov 1906.

My Com   J McDermott
Exp. July 25" 1907   Notary Public.

REFER IN REPLY TO THE FOLLOWING:
NC-432.

DEPARTMENT OF THE INTERIOR
COMMISSIONER TO THE FIVE CIVILIZED TRIBES.

Muskogee Indian Territory August 3 1905.

John Bullett
    Wetumka Indian Territory.

Applications for Enrollment of Creek Newborn
Act of 1905 Volume VI

Dear Sir:

    In the matter of the application for the enrollment of your minor son Chitto Harjo Bullett as a citizen by blood of the Creek Nation it will be necessary for you to file with this office either the original or a certified copy of the marriage license and certificate between you and Zoye Bullett the noncitizen mother of said child.

    You are also requested to supply this office with your affidavit as to the birth of said child and a blank for proof of birth which has been partially filled out is inclosed herewith and you are requested to appear before a notary public swear to the same and return it to this office in the inclosed envelope together with the evidence of marriage above requested.

                            Respectfully
                                       Tams Bixby

                                                Commissioner.

CTD-21.
Env.

                                                           HGH

REFER IN REPLY TO THE FOLLOWING:
NC-432.

DEPARTMENT OF THE INTERIOR
COMMISSIONER TO THE FIVE CIVILIZED TRIBES.

                        Muskogee Indian Territory August 30 1905.

Zoye Bullett
    Care of John Bullett
        Wetumka Indian Territory.

Dear Madam:

    In the matter of the application for the enrollment of your minor son Chitto Harjo Bullett as a citizen by blood of the Creek Nation it will be necessary for you to file with this office either the original or a certified copy of the marriage license and certificate between you and John Bullett.

    You are also requested to supply this office with an affidavit of John Bullett as to the birth of said child and a blank for proof of birth which has been partially filled out is inclosed herewith and you are requested to appear before a notary public swear to the same and return it to this office in the inclosed envelope together with the evidence of marriage above requested.

                            Respectfully
                            Tams Bixby   Commissioner.

CTD-21.
Env.

Applications for Enrollment of Creek Newborn
Act of 1905   Volume VI

HGH

REFER IN REPLY TO THE FOLLOWING:

NC-432.

DEPARTMENT OF THE INTERIOR
COMMISSIONER TO THE FIVE CIVILIZED TRIBES.

Muskogee Indian Territory December 12 1905.

Zoye Bullett
    Care of John Bullett
        Wetumka Indian Territory.

Dear Madam:

    In the matter of the application for the enrollment of your minor child Chitto Harjo Bullett born August 8 1904 as a citizen by blood of the Creek Nation it will be necessary for you to file with this office either the original or a certified copy of the marriage license and certificate between you and John Bullett the father of said child. In the event that no license was issued for your marriage to said John Bullett it will be necessary for you to furnish this Office with the affidavit of John Bullett stating that he is your lawful husband and the father of said child giving the date of the child's birth and whether or not he was living March 4 1905 March 4 1905. A blank for that purpose is herewith enclosed.

    This matter should receive your prompt attention.

                Respectfully
                Wm. O. Beall
1 B A   Acting Commissioner.

NC 432   EK

Muskogee Indian Territory March 1 1907.

John Bullet
    Wetumka Indian Territory.

Dear Sir:

    You are hereby advised that on February 15 1907 the Secretary of the Interior approved the enrollment of your minor child Chitto Harjo Bullet as a citizen by blood of the Creek Nation and that the name of said child appears upon the roll of New Born citizens by blood of the Creek Nation enrolled under the Act of Congress approved March 3rd 1905 as number 1140.

    The child is now entitled to allotment and application therefor should be made without delay at the Creek Land Office Muskogee Indian Territory.

Applications for Enrollment of Creek Newborn
Act of 1905 Volume VI

Dear Sir:

In the matter of the application for the enrollment of your minor son Chitto Harjo Bullett as a citizen by blood of the Creek Nation it will be necessary for you to file with this office either the original or a certified copy of the marriage license and certificate between you and Zoye Bullett the noncitizen mother of said child.

You are also requested to supply this office with your affidavit as to the birth of said child and a blank for proof of birth which has been partially filled out is inclosed herewith and you are requested to appear before a notary public swear to the same and return it to this office in the inclosed envelope together with the evidence of marriage above requested.

      Respectfully
          Tams Bixby

            Commissioner.

CTD-21.
Env.

            HGH

REFER IN REPLY TO THE FOLLOWING:
NC-432.

DEPARTMENT OF THE INTERIOR
COMMISSIONER TO THE FIVE CIVILIZED TRIBES.

    Muskogee Indian Territory August 30 1905.

Zoye Bullett
  Care of John Bullett
    Wetumka Indian Territory.

Dear Madam:

In the matter of the application for the enrollment of your minor son Chitto Harjo Bullett as a citizen by blood of the Creek Nation it will be necessary for you to file with this office either the original or a certified copy of the marriage license and certificate between you and John Bullett.

You are also requested to supply this office with an affidavit of John Bullett as to the birth of said child and a blank for proof of birth which has been partially filled out is inclosed herewith and you are requested to appear before a notary public swear to the same and return it to this office in the inclosed envelope together with the evidence of marriage above requested.

      Respectfully
        Tams Bixby Commissioner.

CTD-21.
Env.

Applications for Enrollment of Creek Newborn
Act of 1905   Volume VI

REFER IN REPLY TO THE FOLLOWING:
NC-432.

DEPARTMENT OF THE INTERIOR
COMMISSIONER TO THE FIVE CIVILIZED TRIBES.

HGH

Muskogee Indian Territory December 12 1905.

Zoye Bullett
    Care of John Bullett
        Wetumka Indian Territory.

Dear Madam:

    In the matter of the application for the enrollment of your minor child Chitto Harjo Bullett born August 8 1904 as a citizen by blood of the Creek Nation it will be necessary for you to file with this office either the original or a certified copy of the marriage license and certificate between you and John Bullett the father of said child. In the event that no license was issued for your marriage to said John Bullett it will be necessary for you to furnish this Office with the affidavit of John Bullett stating that he is your lawful husband and the father of said child giving the date of the child's birth and whether or not he was living March 4 1905 March 4 1905. A blank for that purpose is herewith enclosed.

    This matter should receive your prompt attention.

                Respectfully
                Wm. O. Beall
1 B A   Acting Commissioner.

NC 432   EK

Muskogee Indian Territory March 1 1907.

John Bullet
    Wetumka Indian Territory.

Dear Sir:

    You are hereby advised that on February 15 1907 the Secretary of the Interior approved the enrollment of your minor child Chitto Harjo Bullet as a citizen by blood of the Creek Nation and that the name of said child appears upon the roll of New Born citizens by blood of the Creek Nation enrolled under the Act of Congress approved March 3rd 1905 as number 1140.

    The child is now entitled to allotment and application therefor should be made without delay at the Creek Land Office Muskogee Indian Territory.

Applications for Enrollment of Creek Newborn
Act of 1905 Volume VI

Respectfully

Commissioner.

BIRTH AFFIDAVIT.

DEPARTMENT OF THE INTERIOR.
COMMISSION TO THE FIVE CIVILIZED TRIBES.

IN RE APPLICATION FOR ENROLLMENT as a citizen of the Creek Nation of Sealy Deer born on the 9th day of March 1904

Name of Father: Joe Deer	a citizen of the	Creek Nation.
Name of Mother: Yarner Deer	a citizen of the	Creek Nation.

Postoffice   Morse I.T.

AFFIDAVIT OF MOTHER.

UNITED STATES OF AMERICA Indian Territory
Western Judicial   DISTRICT.

I Yarner Deer on oath state that I am 25 years of age and a citizen by Blood of the Muskokee[sic] or Creek Nation; that I am the lawful wife of Joe Deer who is a citizen by Blood of the Muskokee[sic] or Creek Nation; that a Female child was born to me on 9th day of March 1904 that said child has been named Sealy Deer and was living March 4 1905.

                                                          her
Witnesses To Mark: Yarner x Deer
   James E. Porter   mark
   John H. Phillips

Subscribed and sworn to before me this 20th day of March 1905.

John H. Phillips
Notary Public.

My Commission Expires Sept. 6th 1906.

Applications for Enrollment of Creek Newborn
Act of 1905   Volume VI

AFFIDAVIT OF ATTENDING PHYSICIAN OR MID-WIFE.

UNITED STATES OF AMERICA Indian Territory }
Western Judicial   DISTRICT.

I Amanda Deer a Mid-Wife on oath state that I attended on Mrs. Yarner Deer wife of Joe Deer on the 9th day of March 1904 ; that there was born to her on said date a Female child; that said child was living March 4 1905 and is said to have been named Sealy Deer

                                    Amanda Deer

Witnesses To Mark:
{

Subscribed and sworn to before me this 20th day of March 1905.

                                John H. Phillips
                                Notary Public.

My Commission Expires Sept. 6th 1906.

BIRTH AFFIDAVIT.
DEPARTMENT OF THE INTERIOR.
COMMISSION TO THE FIVE CIVILIZED TRIBES.

IN RE APPLICATION FOR ENROLLMENT as a citizen of the CREEK Nation of William Albert Eubanks born on the 26 day of Feb. 1905

Name of Father: William Eubanks   a citizen of the Creek Na[sic] Nation.
                              Evans
Name of Mother: Minnie Eubanks   a citizen of the Creek   Nation.

                    Postoffice   Oktaha I.T.

AFFIDAVIT OF MOTHER.

UNITED STATES OF AMERICA Indian Territory }
WESTERN   DISTRICT.

I Minnie Eubanks on oath state that I am 16 years of age and a citizen by blood of the Creek Nation; that I am the lawful wife of William Eubanks who is a citizen by Mariage[sic] of the Creek Nation; that a male child was born to me on 26 day of Feb. 1905 that said child has been named William Albert Eubanks and is now living.

                                Minnie Eubanks

Applications for Enrollment of Creek Newborn
Act of 1905   Volume VI

Witnesses To Mark:
{ R.L. Burt
{ Ruth Cain

Subscribed and sworn to before me this 21 day of March 1905.

W. A. Cain
Notary Public.

AFFIDAVIT OF ATTENDING PHYSICIAN OR MID-WIFE.

UNITED STATES OF AMERICA Indian Territory }
Western Dist.   DISTRICT. }

I Dr. William L. Lett a M.D. on oath state that I attended on Mrs. Minnie Eubanks wife of William Eubanks on the 26 day of Feb. 1905 ; that there was born to her on said date a Male child; that said child is now living and is said to have been named William Albert Eubanks

Wm L. Lett M.D.

Witnesses To Mark:
{ R.L. Burt
{ Ruth Cain

Subscribed and sworn to before me this 21 day of March 1905.

W. A. Cain
Notary Public.

NC-436

DEPARTMENT OF THE INTERIOR
COMMISSIONER TO THE FIVE CIVILIZED TRIBES.

Muskogee Indian Territory July 21 1905.

In the matter of the application for the enrollment of Christie Richard Chisholm James and Amos Robison Jr. as citizens by blood of the Creek Nation.

Amos R. Robison being duly sworn testified as follows:

EXAMINATION BY THE COMMISSION:
Q What is your name? A Amos R. Robison.
W How old are you? A 34 past.
Q What is your postoffice address? A Weleetka.

Applications for Enrollment of Creek Newborn
Act of 1905   Volume VI

Q Are you a citizen of the Creek Nation? A Yes sir.

    The witness is identified as Amos R. Robison on Creek Indian card 1466 opposite Roll No. 4665.

Q Have you some children enrolled here already? A Yes sir.
                                                        Eddie
Q Name them. A Ben Holmes Josephus and Annie A. Robison.
Q What is the name of the mother of those children? A Louise.

    On card 1451 appear the names of Louisa Robison and the four children mentioned opposite numbers 4612 to 4616. The father of said children is there mentioned as Amos Robison.

Q Have you any new-born children by this woman? A No sir.
Q You have since separated from her? A Yes sir.
Q Did you get a divorce? A Did not have to; we were married by the Creek law.
Q You have married since have you? A Yes sir.
Q What is the name of your wife now? A Lizzie.
Q What was her name before that? A Lizzie Chisholm.
Q Have you had some children by her? A Yes sir.
Q Name them. A James Amos Richard Chisholm Robison.
Q Those three? A Yes sir.
Q When was Richard Chisholm Robison born? A 1890 I think; I am not sure.
Q You have it a little mixed ain't you? have you a new-born child by that name?
A Yes sir; he was born the 7th of last February.
Q The 7th of this February--of this year? A Yes sir.
Q Is he living? A Yes sir.
Q The other two children are dead aren't they? A Yes sir
Q How long has James been dead about? A About three years.
Q How long has Amos been dead? A About two years.
Q Aren't you a little mistaken it is about four years? A Yes sir; about four years.
Q Amos about three years? A Yes sir.
Q The mother is said children made affidavit that James died July 10 1901 and that Amos died October 15 1902; that is about right is it? A Yes sir.
Q Who is the father of Christie Robison do you know? A No sir.
Q Weren't you the father? A No sir.
Q You had quit living with her when that child was born? A Yes sir.
Q How long before the birth of that child was it that you quit living with her? A I think it is about seven or eight years ago since we separted[sic].
Q Did not have anything to do with her since that time? A No sir.
Q You are certain are you that from the time you parted with her until about a year ago when this child Christie was born you had never had any dealings with her as man and wife--no sexual intercourse? A No sir.
Q So it would be absolutely impossible for it to be your child? A Yes sir.

Applications for Enrollment of Creek Newborn
Act of 1905 Volume VI

Q She stated in an affidavit that you are the father of that child. A I don't know. She is the mother of four of my children; they are named Robison and they just wanted to keep their name.
Q That would not be any reason for stating in an affidavit that this child was yours when you did not have anything to do with her in the last seven years? (No answer)
Q Do you know the name of the father? A No sir.
Q You absolutely know the fact that you are not the father? A No sir.
Q Is Richard Chisholm Robison living with you? A Yes sir.
Q Where is this Louisa Robison living now? A Five miles east of Weleetka with her father.
Q What is his name? A Lumber (or Lambert) Scott.
Q Their postoffice would be Weleetka? A Yes sir.

INDIAN TERRITORY Western District.

I J. Y. Miller a stenographer to the Commission to the Five Civilized Tribes do hereby certify that the above and foregoing is a true and complete translation of my notes as same appear in my stenographic report of this case.

JY Miller

Sworn to and subscribed before me
this the 22 day of July 1905.

J. McDermott

Notary Public.

BIRTH AFFIDAVIT.

DEPARTMENT OF THE INTERIOR.
COMMISSION TO THE FIVE CIVILIZED TRIBES.

IN RE APPLICATION FOR ENROLLMENT as a citizen of the Creek Nation of Richard Chisholm Robison born on the 7 day of February 1905

Name of Father: Amos R. Robison   a citizen of the   Creek   Nation. Thlopthlocco Town
Name of Mother: Lizzie Robison (nee Chisholm) a citizen of the   Creek   Nation. Tuskegee Town
                        Postoffice   Weleetka Ind. Ter.

AFFIDAVIT OF MOTHER.

UNITED STATES OF AMERICA Indian Territory
Western   DISTRICT.

Child is present

I Lizzie Robison on oath state that I am 21 years of age and a citizen by blood of the Creek Nation; that I am the lawful wife of Amos R. Robison who is a citizen

Applications for Enrollment of Creek Newborn
Act of 1905   Volume VI

by   blood of the   Creek   Nation; that a   male   child was born to me on   7   day of February   1905   that said child has been named   Richard Chisholm Robison   and was living March 4 1905.

Lizzie Robison

Witnesses To Mark:
{

Subscribed and sworn to before me this 21   day of March   1905.

Drennan C Skaggs
Notary Public.

AFFIDAVIT OF ATTENDING PHYSICIAN OR MID-WIFE.

UNITED STATES OF AMERICA Indian Territory }
Western   DISTRICT.

I   Mary Chisholm   a   midwife   on oath state that I attended on Mrs.   Lizzie Robison wife of   Amos R. Robison   on the   7 day of   February   1905 ; that there was born to her on said date a   male   child; that said child was living March 4 1905 and is said to have been named   Richard Chisholm Robison

her
Mary x Chisholm
mark

Witnesses To Mark:
{ Alex Posey
  DC Skaggs

Subscribed and sworn to before me this 27 day of March 1905.

Drennan C Skaggs
Notary Public.

BIRTH AFFIDAVIT.

DEPARTMENT OF THE INTERIOR.
COMMISSION TO THE FIVE CIVILIZED TRIBES.

IN RE APPLICATION FOR ENROLLMENT as a citizen of the Creek Nation of   James Robinson[sic] born on the 27th day of June 1901

Name of Father:	Amos Robinson[sic]	a citizen of the Creek	Nation.
Name of Mother:	Lizzie Robinson[sic]	a citizen of the Creek	Nation.

Postoffice   Weleetka I.T.

Applications for Enrollment of Creek Newborn
Act of 1905   Volume VI

AFFIDAVIT OF MOTHER.

UNITED STATES OF AMERICA Indian Territory }
Western   DISTRICT.

I Lizzie Robinson on oath state that I am 21 years of age and a citizen by Blood of the Creek Nation; that I am the lawful wife of Amos Robinson who is a citizen by blood of the Creek Nation; that a male child was born to me on 27th day of June 1901 that said child has been named James Robinson and ~~was living March 4 1905~~. died the 10th day of July 1901

Lizzie Robison

Witnesses To Mark:
{

Subscribed and sworn to before me this 28th day of March 1905.

G.F. Clark
Notary Public.

My Com ex. 7/8-06

AFFIDAVIT OF ATTENDING PHYSICIAN OR MID-WIFE.

UNITED STATES OF AMERICA Indian Territory }
Western   DISTRICT.

I Mary Chisholm a midwife on oath state that I attended on Mrs. Lizzie Robinson wife of Amos Robinson on the 27th day of June 1901 ; that there was born to her on said date a male child; that said child ~~was living March 4 1905~~ died July 10 1901 and is said to have been named James Robinson

her
Mary x Chisholm
mark

Witnesses To Mark:
{ G.F. Clark
  Ida Chisholm

Subscribed and sworn to before me this 28th day of March 1905.

G.F. Clark
Notary Public.

My Com ex. 7/8-06

Applications for Enrollment of Creek Newborn
Act of 1905   Volume VI

BIRTH AFFIDAVIT.

DEPARTMENT OF THE INTERIOR.
COMMISSION TO THE FIVE CIVILIZED TRIBES.

IN RE APPLICATION FOR ENROLLMENT as a citizen of the Creek Nation of Amos Robinson[sic] Jr born on the 18th day of May 1902

Name of Father: Amos Robinson[sic]   a citizen of the   Creek   Nation.
Name of Mother: Lizzie Robinson[sic]   a citizen of the   Creek   Nation.

Postoffice   Weleetka I.T.

AFFIDAVIT OF MOTHER.

UNITED STATES OF AMERICA Indian Territory }
Western   DISTRICT.

I Lizzie Robinson on oath state that I am 21 years of age and a citizen by blood of the Creek Nation; that I am the lawful wife of Amos Robinson who is a citizen by blood of the Creek Nation; that a male child was born to me on 18th day of May 1902 that said child has been named Amos Robinson Jr and ~~was living March 4 1905~~. died Oct 15th 1902

Lizzie Robison

Witnesses To Mark:
{

Subscribed and sworn to before me this 28th day of March 1905.

G.F. Clark
My Com ex. 7/8-06.   Notary Public.

AFFIDAVIT OF ATTENDING PHYSICIAN OR MID-WIFE.

UNITED STATES OF AMERICA Indian Territory }
Western   DISTRICT.

I Mary Chisholm a Midwife on oath state that I attended on Mrs. Lizzie Robinson wife of Amos Robinson on the 18th day of May 1902 ; that there was born to her on said date a male child; that said child ~~was living March 4 1905~~ died Oct 15th 1902 and is said to have been named Amos Robinson Jr

Mary x Chisholm

Witnesses To Mark:
{ G.F. Clark
  Ida Chisholm

Applications for Enrollment of Creek Newborn
Act of 1905 Volume VI

Subscribed and sworn to before me this 28th day of March 1905.

G.F. Clark
Notary Public.

My Com ex. 7/8-06

Commission to the Five Civilized Tribes.

-----oOo-----

IN RE APPLICATION FOR ENROLLMENT as a citizen of the Creek Nation of Christie Robison born on the 4th day of March 1904. Name of Father Amos Robison a citizen of the Creek Nation. Name of Mother Louisa Robison a citizen of the Creek Nation.

Post office Weleetka Ind. Ter.

Affidavit of Mother.

United States of America,)
Western District of the Indian Territory.) SS.

I Louisa Robison on my oath state that I am 35 (?) years of age and a citizen by birth of the Muskogee or Creek Nation; that I am the lawful wife of Amos Robison who is a citizen by Birth of the Muskogee or Creek Nation; that a Female child was born to me on the 4th day of March 1904; that said child was named Christie Robison and was living on the 4" day of March, 1905.

her
Louisa x Robison
mark

Witness to Mark:
AM Harral
C.H. Harral

Subscribed and sworn to before me this 22nd day of March 1905.

MY COMMISSION EXPIRES FEBY. 29 1906.

John B Patterson
Notary Public.

Affidavit of attending Physician or Midwife.

United States of America,)
Western District of the Indian Territory.) SS.

I Lucy Scott a Midwife on oath state that I attended on Mrs. Louisa Robison wife of Amos Robison on the 4th day of March 1904 that there was

Applications for Enrollment of Creek Newborn
Act of 1905 Volume VI

born to her on said date a Female child; that said child was living on the 4" day of March, 1905 and is said to have been named Christie Robison

Witness to Mark :

Lucy Scott

_____

_____

Subscribed and sworn to before me this 22nd day of March 1905.

MY COMMISSION EXPIRES FEBY. 29 1906.

John B Patterson
Notary Public.

_____

NC 436.

JLDe.

DEPARTMENT OF THE INTERIOR,
COMMISSIONER TO THE FIVE CIVILIZED TRIBES.

In the matter of the application for the enrollment of James Robinson, deceased, and Amos Robinson, Jr., deceased, as citizens by blood of the Creek Nation.

STATEMENT AND ORDER.

The record in this case shows that on March 31, 1905, application was made, in affidavit form, supplemented by sworn testimony taken July 21, 1905, for the enrollment of James Robinson, deceased, and Amos Robinson, Jr., deceased, as citizens by blood of the Creek Nation, under the provisions of the Act of Congress approved March 3, 1905.

It appears that the evidence filed in this matter that said James Robinson and Amos Robinson, Jr. were born June 27, 1901, and May 18, 1902, respectively, and died July 10, 1901, and October 15, 1902, respectively, and were the children of Amos R. Robison and Lizzie Robison, whose names appear on the approved roll of citizens by blood of the Creek Nation, opposite Nos., 4665 and 6025, respectively.

The Act of Congress approved March 3, 1905, (33 Stat., 1048), in part provides:

> "That the Commission to the Five Civilized Tribes is authorized for sixty days after the date of the approval of this act to receive and consider applications for enrollment, of children, born subsequent to May twenty-fifth, nineteen hundred and one, and prior to March fourth, nineteen hundred and five, and living on said latter date, to citizens of the Creek tribe of Indians whose enrollment has been approved by the Secretary of the Interior prior to the approval of this act; and to enroll and make allotments to such children."

It is, therefore, ordered that the applications for the enrollment of James Robinson, deceased, and Amos Robinson, Jr. deceased, as citizens by blood of the Creek Nation, be and the same are hereby dismissed.

Applications for Enrollment of Creek Newborn
Act of 1905   Volume VI

Muskogee, Indian Territory.
JAN 18 1907

Tams Bixby Commissioner.

Cr NC-436

Muskogee, Indian Territory, June 9, 1905.

Amos Robison,
    Weleetka, Indian Territory.

Dear Sir:

    In the matter of the application for the enrollment of your minor children, Christie and Richard Chisholm Robison, you are advised that the Commission cannot identify Louisa Lizzie Robison, the mother of said children, on its rolls.

    You are requested to furnish the Commission with the maiden name of said mother, the names of her parents, the Creek Indian Town to which she claims to belong, and any other information that may help identify her as a citizen of the Creek Nation.

Respectfully,

Chairman.

NBC 436.

Muskogee, Indian Territory, January 19, 1907.

Lizzie Robinson,
    c/o Amos Robinson,
        Weleetka, Indian Territory.

Dear Madam:

    There is herewith enclosed one copy of the statement and order of the Commissioner to the Five Civilized Tribes, dated January 18, 1907, dismissing the application made by you for the enrollment of your minor children, James and Amos Robinson, Jr., as citizens by blood of the Creek Nation.

Respectfully,

Commissioner.

Register.
LM-27.

Applications for Enrollment of Creek Newborn
Act of 1905   Volume VI

NC-437.

Muskogee, Indian Territory, August 3, 1905.

Jack Lewis,
　　Wealaka, Indian Territory.

Dear Sir:

　　In the matter of the application for the enrollment of your minor daughter Ella Lewis, born July 15, 1903, as a citizen by blood of the Creek Nation, it appearing from the evidence now on file that there was no physician or midwife in attendance on your wife when said child was born, it will be necessary for you to furnish this office with the affidavits of two disinterested persons who are acquainted with said child, know when she was born, the names of her parents and whether or not she was living on March 4, 1905. All of said facts should be set forth in their affidavits and the source of the knowledge of the affiants should also be set forth.

　　You should give this matter your immediate attention.

　　　　　　　　　　　Respectfully,

　　　　　　　　　　　　　　　　　　Commissioner.

BIRTH AFFIDAVIT.

DEPARTMENT OF THE INTERIOR.
COMMISSION TO THE FIVE CIVILIZED TRIBES.

　　IN RE APPLICATION FOR ENROLLMENT, as a citizen of the Creek Nation, of Ella Lewis, born on the 15 day of July, 1903

| Name of Father: | Jack Lewis | a citizen of the | Creek | Nation. |
| Name of Mother: | Delila " | a citizen of the | Creek | Nation. |

　　　　　　　　　　Postoffice　　Wealaka, I.T.

　　　　　　　　　　　Acquaintance
AFFIDAVIT OF ~~MOTHER~~.

UNITED STATES OF AMERICA, Indian Territory,　⎫
　　Western　　　　　DISTRICT.　　　　　⎭

　　　　We　　　　　　　　　　　　　　are
　　~~I~~, the undersigned　, on oath state that ~~I am~~　we ~~years of age and~~ a citizen by blood, of the Creek Nation; we are personally acquainted with Delila Lewis that ~~I am~~

Applications for Enrollment of Creek Newborn
Act of 1905 Volume VI

she is the lawful wife of Jack Lewis , who is a citizen, by blood of the Creek Nation; that a female child was born to ~~me~~ her ~~on~~ about the 15" day of July , 1903 , that said child has been named Ella Lewis , and was living March 4, 1905.

              her
           (Illegible) x Colbert
             her mark
Witnesses To Mark: Ella x Isaac
 { Anna Garrigues   mark
   Jesse McDermott

Subscribed and sworn to before me this 15" day of Aug , 1905.

          J McDermott
           Notary Public.

BIRTH AFFIDAVIT.

DEPARTMENT OF THE INTERIOR.
COMMISSION TO THE FIVE CIVILIZED TRIBES.

  IN RE APPLICATION FOR ENROLLMENT, as a citizen of the CREEK Nation, of Ella Lewis, born on the 15 day of July , 1903

Name of Father: Jack Lewis   a citizen of the Creek Nation.
Name of Mother: Delila "   a citizen of the   "   Nation.

         Postoffice Wealaka

(child present)
        AFFIDAVIT OF MOTHER.

UNITED STATES OF AMERICA, Indian Territory, ⎫
  WESTERN   DISTRICT. ⎭

  I, Delila Lewis , on oath state that I am 31 years of age and a citizen by blood , of the Creek Nation; that I am the lawful wife of Jack Lewis , who is a citizen, by blood of the Creek Nation; that a female child was born to me on 15" day of July , 1903 , that said child has been named Ella Lewis , and is now living.

           Her
         Delila x Lewis
Witnesses To Mark: mark
 { J McDermott
   EC Griesel

Subscribed and sworn to before me this 28" day of March , 1905.

Applications for Enrollment of Creek Newborn
Act of 1905   Volume VI

Edw C Griesel
Notary Public.

No Mid Wife
AFFIDAVIT OF ATTENDING ~~PHYSICIAN OR MID-WIFE~~. or
Doctor.

UNITED STATES OF AMERICA, Indian Territory, }
WESTERN   DISTRICT. }

I, Jack Lewis , a Father , on oath state that I attended on Mrs. Delila Lewis , wife of myself on the 15 day of July , 1903 ; that there was born to her on said date a female child; that said child is now living and is said to have been named Ella Lewis

His
Jack x Lewis
mark

Witnesses To Mark:
{ J McDermott
{ EC Griesel

Subscribed and sworn to before me this 28 day of March, 1905.

Edw C Griesel
Notary Public.

L.C.
~~En.438~~

Muskogee, Indian Territory, September 27, 1905.

Sam Beaver,
  Sapulpa, Indian Territory.

Dear Sir:

Receipt is acknowledged of your letter of September 25, 1905, in which you ask when you will be allowed to file for your minor child, Mary Capitola Beaver.

In reply you are advised that the matter of the application for the enrollment of said Mary Capitola Beaver as a citizen by blood of the Creek Nation, is now pending before the Secretary of the Interior the Interior and when final action is had in the matter, you will be duly notified.

Respectfully,

Commissioner.

Applications for Enrollment of Creek Newborn
Act of 1905 Volume VI

BIRTH AFFIDAVIT.

DEPARTMENT OF THE INTERIOR.
COMMISSION TO THE FIVE CIVILIZED TRIBES.

IN RE APPLICATION FOR ENROLLMENT, as a citizen of the Creek Nation, of Mary Capitola, born on the 21st day of Nov, 1903

Name of Father: Samuel Beaver   a citizen of the   Creek   Nation.
Name of Mother: Ollie Beaver   not a citizen of the Creek Nation.

Postoffice   Sapulpa, I.T.

AFFIDAVIT OF MOTHER.

UNITED STATES OF AMERICA, Indian Territory, ⎱
    Western   DISTRICT.   ⎰

I, Ollie Beaver, on oath state that I am 25 years of age and a citizen by non, of the non Nation; that I am the lawful wife of Samuel Beaver, who is a citizen, by blood of the Creek Nation; that a Female child was born to me on 21st day of Nov, 1903, that said child has been named Mary Capitola, and was living March 4, 1905.

                                   Ollie Beaver
Witnesses To Mark:
{

Subscribed and sworn to before me this 20th day of March, 1905.

                                   Joseph Bruner
My Commission   Notary Public.
expires 10/20.1906

AFFIDAVIT OF ATTENDING PHYSICIAN OR MID-WIFE.

UNITED STATES OF AMERICA, Indian Territory, ⎱
    Western   DISTRICT.   ⎰

I, Mrs. B E Bradley, a Mid-Wife, on oath state that I attended on Mrs. Ollie Beaver, wife of Samuel Beaver on the 21st day of Nov, 1903; that there was born to her on said date a Female child; that said child was living March 4, 1905, and is said to have been named Mary Capitola

                                   B E Bradley
Witnesses To Mark:
{

Applications for Enrollment of Creek Newborn
Act of 1905   Volume VI

Subscribed and sworn to before me this 20th day of March, 1905.

My Commission expires
10/20.1906

Joseph Bruner
Notary Public.

NC-439.

Muskogee, Indian Territory, August 3, 1905.

Emma West,
    Henryetta, Indian Territory.

Dear Madam:

    On March 23, 1905 you appeared before the Commission to the Five Civilized Tribes and made application for the enrollment of your minor children William West born in October 1901, and Robert West, born in October 1904, and at that time submitted your affidavit only as to the birth of said children, stating that no one attended you when said children were born.

    You are advised that in lieu of the affidavit of the attending physician or midwife at the birth of said children it will be necessary for you to furnish this office with the affidavits, relative to the birth of said children, of two disinterested persons. Said affidavits to set forth the names of said children, the dates of their birth, the names of their parents and whether or not they were living on March 5, 1905.

    It is noted that you stated at the time you made application for these children that you were a citizen by blood of the Creek Nation. This office has been unable to identify you upon the final roll of citizens by blood of said nation and you are therefore requested to inform this office of the name under which you were finally enrolled, the names of your parents and other members of your family, the Creek town to which you belong and if you have received your allotment certificate and deed your final roll number as the same appears thereon.

                            Respectfully,

                                         Commissioner.

Applications for Enrollment of Creek Newborn
Act of 1905   Volume VI

NC-439

Muskogee, Indian Territory, December 12, 1905.

Emma West,
    Care of Lumsey West,
        Henryetta, Indian Territory.

Dear Madam:

    In the matter of the application for the enrollment of your minor child, Robert West, born during the month of October, 1904, and in the matter of the application for the enrollment of your minor child, William West, born in the month of October, 1901, as citizens by blood of the Creek Nation, it will be necessary for you to furnish this Office, in lieu of the affidavits of the midwives or attending physicians at the birth of said children, with the affidavits of two disinterested persons as to the birth of each of said children. Said affidavits should set forth the names of the children, the names of their parents, the dates of the children's births, and whether or not they were living March 4, 1905.

    Your affidavit relative to the birth of said William West is defective, inasmuch as a certain erasure made on the form of said affidavit causes same to fail to show whether or not said William West is in fact your child. There is herewith enclosed a blank form of birth affidavit which you are requested to execute relative to the birth of said William West, being careful to give the correct information desired. The notary public before whom the affidavits are sworn should date, sign and seal each affidavit.

                Respectfully,

                            Acting Commissioner.

1 B A
2 Dis

NC 439.

Muskogee, Indian Territory, March 1, 1907.

Emma West,
    C/o Lumsey West,
        Henryetta, Indian Territory.

Dear Madam:

    You are hereby advised that on February 15, 1907, the Secretary of the Interior approved the enrollment of your minor children, Robert West and William West, as citizens by blood of the Creek Nation, and that the names of said children appear upon the roll of New Born citizens by blood of the Creek Nation, enrolled under the Act of Congress approved March 3rd, 1905, as numbers 1141 and 1142, respectively.

Applications for Enrollment of Creek Newborn
Act of 1905   Volume VI

These children are now entitled to allotment and application should be made without delay at the Creek Land Office, Muskogee, Indian Territory.

Respectfully,

Commissioner.

Indian Territory)
) SS
Western District)

We, the undersigned, on oath state that we are personally acquainted with Emma West   wife of   Lumsey West   ; that ~~on or about the~~ sometime ~~day of~~ in October, 1904, a   male   child was born to them and has been named   Robert West   ; that said child was living March 4, 1905.

We further state that we have no interest in the above case.

M J Miller

George Tiger

Witnesses to mark:

_____

_____

Subscribed and sworn to before me this 16 day of March 1904.

Alex Posey
Notary Public.

BIRTH AFFIDAVIT.

DEPARTMENT OF THE INTERIOR.
COMMISSION TO THE FIVE CIVILIZED TRIBES.

IN RE APPLICATION FOR ENROLLMENT, as a citizen of the Creek Nation, of Robert West , born ~~on the~~ *(blank)* ~~day of~~ October, 1904

Name of Father:	Lumsey West	a citizen of the	Creek	Nation.
Name of Mother:	Emma West	a citizen of the	Creek	Nation.

Postoffice   Henryetta, Ind. Ter.

Applications for Enrollment of Creek Newborn
Act of 1905   Volume VI

AFFIDAVIT OF MOTHER.

UNITED STATES OF AMERICA, Indian Territory, }
    Western   DISTRICT.

      I, Emma West , on oath state that I am about 30 years of age and a citizen by blood , of the Creek Nation; that I am the lawful wife of Lumsey West , who is a citizen, by blood of the Creek Nation; that a male child was born to me ~~on~~ *(blank)* ~~day of~~ October , 1904 , that said child has been named Robert West , and was living March 4, 1905. That no one attended on me as midwife or physician at the birth of the child.

                                                  her
                                    Emma x West
Witnesses To Mark: mark
  { Alex Posey
    DC Skaggs

      Subscribed and sworn to before me this 23 day of March , 1905.

                                  Drennan C Skaggs
                                  Notary Public

Indian Territory I
             I SS
Western District I

      We, the undersigned, on oath state that we are personally acquainted with Emma West   wife of   Lumsey West ; that ~~on or about the~~ sometime ~~day of~~ in October, 1901, a male child was born to them and has been named William West , that said child was living March 4, 1905.

      We further state that we have no interest in the above case.

                                    M J Miller

                                  George Tiger

Witnesses to mark:

_____

_____

      Subscribed and sworn to before me this 17 day of March 1904.

                                  Alex Posey
                                  Notary Public.

Applications for Enrollment of Creek Newborn
Act of 1905 Volume VI

BIRTH AFFIDAVIT.

DEPARTMENT OF THE INTERIOR.
COMMISSION TO THE FIVE CIVILIZED TRIBES.

IN RE APPLICATION FOR ENROLLMENT, as a citizen of the Creek Nation, of William West, born ~~on the~~ *(blank)* ~~day of~~ October, 1901

Name of Father: Lumsey West   a citizen of the   Creek   Nation.
(Illegible) Town
Name of Mother: Emma West   a citizen of the   Creek   Nation.
Thlewathle[sic] Town

                        Postoffice   Henryetta, Ind. Ter.

AFFIDAVIT OF MOTHER.

UNITED STATES OF AMERICA, Indian Territory,
    Western   DISTRICT.

    I, Emma West , on oath state that I am about 28 years of age and a citizen by blood , of the Creek Nation; that I am the lawful wife of Lumsey West , who is a citizen, by blood of the Creek Nation; that a male child was born to me ~~on~~ in ~~day of~~ October , 1901 , that said child has been named William West , and was living March 4, 1905.

                                         her
                                Emma x West
Witnesses To Mark: mark
   { Alex Posey
   { DC Skaggs

    Subscribed and sworn to before me this 16 day of March , 1905.

                                         Alex Posey
                                              Notary Public

BIRTH AFFIDAVIT.

DEPARTMENT OF THE INTERIOR.
COMMISSION TO THE FIVE CIVILIZED TRIBES.

IN RE APPLICATION FOR ENROLLMENT, as a citizen of the Creek Nation, of William West, born ~~on the~~ *(blank)* ~~day of~~ October, 1901

Name of Father: Lumsey West   a citizen of the   Creek   Nation.
Name of Mother: Emma West   a citizen of the   Creek   Nation.

                        Postoffice   Henryetta, Ind. Ter.

Applications for Enrollment of Creek Newborn
Act of 1905   Volume VI

AFFIDAVIT OF MOTHER.

UNITED STATES OF AMERICA, Indian Territory,
Western DISTRICT.

I, Emma West, on oath state that I am about 30 years of age and a citizen by blood, of the Creek Nation; that I am the lawful wife of Lumsey West, who is a citizen, by blood of the Creek Nation; that a male child was born to me ~~on~~ *(blank)* ~~day of~~ October, 1901, that said child has been named William West, and was living March 4, 1905. That no one attended on me as midwife or physician in the birth of the child.

                her
Emma x West
     mark

Witnesses To Mark:
  { Alex Posey
   DC Skaggs

Subscribed and sworn to before me this 23 day of March, 1905.

Drennan C Skaggs
Notary Public

NC-440.

Muskogee, Indian Territory, August 3, 1905.

Martha Haynes,
   c/o James Haynes,
      Dustin, Indian Territory.

Dear Madam:

On March 23, 1905 you appeared before the Commission to the Five Civilized Tribes and made application for the enrollment of your minor son Roley Haynes, born May 16, 1902, as a citizen by blood of the Creek Nation, and at that time submitted your affidavit only as to the birth of said child stating that no one attended you when he was born.

You are advised that it will be necessary for you to furnish this office, in lieu of the affidavit of the attending physician or midwife at the birth of said child, with the affidavits, relative to the birth of said child, of two disinterested persons. Said affidavits to set forth the name of said child, when he was born, the names of his parents and whether or not he was living on March 4, 1905.

Applications for Enrollment of Creek Newborn
Act of 1905 Volume VI

Respectfully,

Commissioner.

BIRTH AFFIDAVIT.

DEPARTMENT OF THE INTERIOR.
COMMISSION TO THE FIVE CIVILIZED TRIBES.

IN RE APPLICATION FOR ENROLLMENT, as a citizen of the Creek Nation, of Roley Haynes, born on the *(blank)* day of *(blank)*, 1*(blank)*

Name of Father:	James Haynes	a citizen of the	Creek	Nation.
Name of Mother:	Martha Haynes	a citizen of the	Creek	Nation.

Postoffice   Dustin, I.T.

two disinterested persons
AFFIDAVIT OF ~~ATTENDING PHYSICIAN OR MID-WIFE~~.

UNITED STATES OF AMERICA, Indian Territory,
Western   DISTRICT.

we are personally acquainted with We, the undersigned , a *(blank)* , on oath state that ^ ~~I attended on~~ Mrs. Martha Haynes , wife of James Haynes on the *(blank)* day of *(blank)* , 1*(blank)* ; that there was born to her ~~on said date~~ a male child; that said child was living March 4, 1905, and is said to have been named Roley Raynes

Willie Hope

her
Melinda x Hope
mark

Witnesses To Mark:
- Alex Posey
- Jesse McDermott

Subscribed and sworn to before me this 25" day of Nov., 1905.

J. McDermott
Notary Public.

Applications for Enrollment of Creek Newborn
Act of 1905 Volume VI

BIRTH AFFIDAVIT.

DEPARTMENT OF THE INTERIOR,
COMMISSIONER TO THE FIVE CIVILIZED TRIBES.

ENROLLMENT OF MINORS. ACT OF CONGRESS, APPROVED APRIL 26, 1906.

IN RE APPLICATION FOR ENROLLMENT, as a citizen of the Creek Nation, of Alva Arizona Evans, born on the 14" day of August, 1905

Name of Father:	Charley Evans	a citizen of the	Creek	Nation.
Name of Mother:	Mary J.E. Evans	a citizen of the	U.S.	Nation.

Tribal enrollment of father   Creek   Tribal enrollment of mother   U.S.

Postoffice   Oktaha, Ind. Ter.

AFFIDAVIT OF MOTHER.

UNITED STATES OF AMERICA, Indian Territory, } Western District.

I, Mary J.E. Evans, on oath state that I am Twenty one years of age and a citizen by *(blank)*, of the United States Nation; that I am the lawful wife of Charlie Evans, who is a citizen, by Blood of the Creek Nation; that a Female child was born to me on 14th day of August, 1905, that said child has been named Alva Arizona Evans, and was living March 4, 1906.

Mary J. E. Evans

WITNESSES TO MARK:
{

Subscribed and sworn to before me this Eleventh day of May, 1906.

My Com will expire Aug. 1, 1906   L. W. Mead
Notary Public.

AFFIDAVIT OF ATTENDING PHYSICIAN OR MID-WIFE.

UNITED STATES OF AMERICA, Indian Territory, } Western District.

I, Malissa C. Moore, a Midwife, on oath state that I attended on Mrs. Mary J.E. Evans, wife of Charlie Evans on the 14th day of August, 1905; that there was born to her on said date a Female child; that said child was living March 4, 1906, and is said to have been named Alva Arizona Evans

Malissa x C Moore
mark
(her)

Applications for Enrollment of Creek Newborn
Act of 1905   Volume VI

WITNESSES TO MARK:
{ W P Stone
{ Varie Stone

Subscribed and sworn to before me this Eleventh day of May , 1906.

My Com will expire Aug. 1, 1906   L. W. Mead
                                              Notary Public.

NC-441.

Muskogee, Indian Territory, August 3, 1905.

Emma Sewel,
    c/o Ben Sewel,
        Holdenville, Indian Territory.

Dear Madam:

    On March 28, 1905 you appeared before the Commission to the Five Civilized Tribes and made application for the enrollment of your minor children Ellen Sewel and Elliott Sewel as citizens by blood of the Creek Nation, at that time submitting your affidavit and the affidavit of Sophia Sewel relative to the birth of said children.

    The midwife's affidavit, relative to the birth of Elliott Sewel, fails to set forth the date of the birth of said child and there also appears a discrepancy in both affidavits as to your surname, it appearing from said affidavits that your name is Sewell while your husband is identified upon the final roll of Creek citizens by blood as Ben Sewel.

    It will therefore be necessary for you to furnish this office with new and proper affidavits as to the birth of said children and for that purpose two blanks for proof of birth, which have been filled out, are inclosed herewith and you are requested to have the same executed, taking care to see that the notary public, before whom the affidavits are sworn to, attaches his name and seal to each affidavit, and return to this office in the inclosed envelope. In case any signature is by mark the same must be attested by two disinterested witnesses.

                        Respectfully,

                                          Commissioner.

CTD-23.
Env.

Applications for Enrollment of Creek Newborn
Act of 1905 Volume VI

BIRTH AFFIDAVIT.

DEPARTMENT OF THE INTERIOR.
COMMISSION TO THE FIVE CIVILIZED TRIBES.

IN RE APPLICATION FOR ENROLLMENT, as a citizen of the Creek Nation, of Ellen Sewel, born on the 12th day of February, 1903

Name of Father:	Ben Sewel	a citizen of the	Creek	Nation.
Name of Mother:	Emma Sewel	a citizen of the	Creek	Nation.

Postoffice Holdenville, I.T.

AFFIDAVIT OF MOTHER.

UNITED STATES OF AMERICA, Indian Territory,
Western DISTRICT.

I, Emma Sewel, on oath state that I am 25 years of age and a citizen by blood, of the Creek Nation; that I am the lawful wife of Ben Sewel, who is a citizen, by blood of the Creek Nation; that a female child was born to me on 12th day of February, 1903, that said child has been named Ellen Sewel, and was living March 4, 1905.

Emma Sewel

Witnesses To Mark:

Subscribed and sworn to before me this 30th day of August, 1905.

Chas Rider
Notary Public.

AFFIDAVIT OF ATTENDING PHYSICIAN OR MID-WIFE.

UNITED STATES OF AMERICA, Indian Territory,
Western DISTRICT.

I, Sophia Sewel, a mid-wife, on oath state that I attended on Mrs. Emma Sewel, wife of Ben Sewel on the 12th day of February, 1903; that there was born to her on said date a female child; that said child was living March 4, 1905, and is said to have been named Ellen Sewel

her
Sophia Sewel x
mark

Witnesses To Mark:
 J. T. Regan
 Chas Rider

Applications for Enrollment of Creek Newborn
Act of 1905   Volume VI

Subscribed and sworn to before me this 30th day of August, 1905.

                                                  Chas Rider
                                                  Notary Public.

BIRTH AFFIDAVIT.

DEPARTMENT OF THE INTERIOR.
COMMISSION TO THE FIVE CIVILIZED TRIBES.

IN RE APPLICATION FOR ENROLLMENT, as a citizen of the Creek Nation, of Ellen Sewell, born on the 12 day of February, 1903

Name of Father:	Ben Sewell	a citizen of the	Creek	Nation.
Tulsa L.R. Town				
Name of Mother:	Emma Sewell	a citizen of the	Creek	Nation.
Tulsa L.R. Town				

                                Postoffice   Holdenville, Ind. Ter.

AFFIDAVIT OF MOTHER.

UNITED STATES OF AMERICA, Indian Territory,
    Western   **DISTRICT.**   <u>Child is present</u>

    I, Emma Sewell, on oath state that I am 25 years of age and a citizen by blood, of the Creek Nation; that I am the lawful wife of Ben Sewell, who is a citizen, by blood of the Creek Nation; that a female child was born to me on 12 day of February, 1903, that said child has been named Ellen Sewell, and was living March 4, 1905.

                                                    her
Witnesses To Mark: Emma x Sewell
   { Alex Posey   mark
   { DC Skaggs

Subscribed and sworn to before me this 28 day of March, 1905.

                                            Drennan C Skaggs
                                            Notary Public.

Applications for Enrollment of Creek Newborn
Act of 1905 Volume VI

AFFIDAVIT OF ATTENDING PHYSICIAN OR MID-WIFE.

UNITED STATES OF AMERICA, Indian Territory,
Western DISTRICT.

I, Sophia Sewell , a midwife , on oath state that I attended on Mrs. Emma Sewell , wife of Ben Sewell on the 12 day of February , 1903 ; that there was born to her on said date a female child; that said child was living March 4, 1905, and is said to have been named Ellen Sewell

          her
        Sophia x Sewell
         mark

Witnesses To Mark:
{ Alex Posey
{ DC Skaggs

Subscribed and sworn to before me this 28 day of March , 1905.

      Drennan C Skaggs
      Notary Public.

BIRTH AFFIDAVIT.

DEPARTMENT OF THE INTERIOR.
COMMISSION TO THE FIVE CIVILIZED TRIBES.

IN RE APPLICATION FOR ENROLLMENT, as a citizen of the Creek Nation, of Elliott Sewell, born on the 2 day of July , 1904

Name of Father: Ben Sewell a citizen of the Creek Nation.
Tulsa Little River Town
Name of Mother: Emma Sewell a citizen of the Creek Nation.
Tulsa Little River Town
       Postoffice Holdenville, Ind. Ter.

AFFIDAVIT OF MOTHER.

UNITED STATES OF AMERICA, Indian Territory, Child is present
Western DISTRICT.

I, Emma Sewell , on oath state that I am 25 years of age and a citizen by blood, of the Creek Nation; that I am the lawful wife of Ben Sewell , who is a citizen, by blood of the Creek Nation; that a male child was born to me on 2 day of July , 1904 , that said child has been named Elliott Sewell , and was living March 4, 1905.

        her
      Emma x Sewell
        mark

Applications for Enrollment of Creek Newborn
Act of 1905 Volume VI

Witnesses To Mark:
{ Alex Posey
{ DC Skaggs

Subscribed and sworn to before me this 28 day of March, 1905.

Drennan C Skaggs
Notary Public.

AFFIDAVIT OF ATTENDING PHYSICIAN OR MID-WIFE.

UNITED STATES OF AMERICA, Indian Territory,
Western DISTRICT.

I, Sophia Sewell, a midwife, on oath state that I attended on Mrs. Emma Sewell, wife of Ben Sewell ~~on the (blank) day of (blank), 1~~ *(blank)*; that there was born to her on said date a male child; that said child was living March 4, 1905, and is said to have been named Elliott Sewell

her
Sophia x Sewell
mark

Witnesses To Mark:
{ Alex Posey
{ DC Skaggs

Subscribed and sworn to before me this 28 day of March, 1905.

Drennan C Skaggs
Notary Public.

BIRTH AFFIDAVIT.

DEPARTMENT OF THE INTERIOR.
COMMISSION TO THE FIVE CIVILIZED TRIBES.

IN RE APPLICATION FOR ENROLLMENT, as a citizen of the Creek Nation, of Elliott Sewel, born on the 2nd day of July, 1904

Name of Father:	Ben Sewel	a citizen of the	Creek	Nation.
Name of Mother:	Emma Sewel	a citizen of the	Creek	Nation.

Postoffice   Holdenville, I.T.

Applications for Enrollment of Creek Newborn
Act of 1905 Volume VI

AFFIDAVIT OF MOTHER.

UNITED STATES OF AMERICA, Indian Territory,
Western DISTRICT.

I, Emma Sewel, on oath state that I am 25 years of age and a citizen by blood, of the Creek Nation; that I am the lawful wife of Ben Sewel, who is a citizen, by blood of the Creek Nation; that a male child was born to me on 2nd day of July, 1904, that said child has been named Elliott Sewel, and was living March 4, 1905.

Emma Sewel

Witnesses To Mark:

Subscribed and sworn to before me this 30th day of August, 1905.

Chas Rider
Notary Public.

AFFIDAVIT OF ATTENDING PHYSICIAN OR MID-WIFE.

UNITED STATES OF AMERICA, Indian Territory,
Western DISTRICT.

I, Sophia Sewel, a mid-wife, on oath state that I attended on Mrs. Emma Sewel, wife of Ben Sewel on the 2nd day of July, 1904; that there was born to her on said date a male child; that said child was living March 4, 1905, and is said to have been named Elliott Sewel

Sophia Sewel x her mark

Witnesses To Mark:
    J. T. Regan
    Chas Rider

Subscribed and sworn to before me this 30th day of August, 1905.

Chas Rider
Notary Public.

Applications for Enrollment of Creek Newborn
Act of 1905 Volume VI

BIRTH AFFIDAVIT.

DEPARTMENT OF THE INTERIOR.
COMMISSION TO THE FIVE CIVILIZED TRIBES.

IN RE APPLICATION FOR ENROLLMENT, as a citizen of the Creek Nation, of Iva M. Bruner, born on the 28th day of July, 1904

Name of Father:	Freeland Bruner	a citizen of the	Creek	Nation.
Name of Mother:	Rhoda Bruner	a citizen of the	Creek	Nation.

Postoffice   Edna, Ind. Terr.

AFFIDAVIT OF MOTHER.

UNITED STATES OF AMERICA, Indian Territory,
Western   DISTRICT.

I, Rhoda Bruner, on oath state that I am 26 years of age and a citizen by blood, of the Creek Nation; that I am the lawful wife of Freeland Bruner, who is a citizen, by blood of the Creek Nation; that a female child was born to me on 28th day of July, 1904, that said child has been named Iva M. Bruner, and was living March 4, 1905.

Rhoda Bruner

Witnesses To Mark:
{ L. L. Longfellow
{ Frank Zimmermann

Subscribed and sworn to before me this 22nd day of March, 1905.

T.W. Flynn
Notary Public.

AFFIDAVIT OF ATTENDING PHYSICIAN OR MID-WIFE.

UNITED STATES OF AMERICA, Indian Territory,
Western   DISTRICT.

I, Sina Kay, a Midwife, on oath state that I attended on Mrs. Rhoda Bruner, wife of Freeland Bruner on the 28th day of July, 1904; that there was born to her on said date a female child; that said child was living March 4, 1905, and is said to have been named Iva M. Bruner

her
Sina Kay x
mark

Witnesses To Mark:
{ Hendrson[sic] Gooden
{ Bessie Kay

Applications for Enrollment of Creek Newborn
Act of 1905   Volume VI

Subscribed and sworn to before me this 22nd day of March, 1905.

                T.W. Flynn
                Notary Public.

DEPARTMENT OF THE INTERIOR,
COMMISSIONER TO THE FIVE CIVILIZED TRIBES.
WETUMKA, INDIAN TERRITORY.
JULY 18, 1906.

In the matter of the application for the enrollment; as citizens of the Creek Nation, of minor children born to duly enrolled citizens, members of the so called Snake faction.

        D.W. Field[sic], being duly sworn, testified as follows: Through Official Interpreter, Alex Posey.

Q What is your name? A D.W. Fields.
Q What is your age? A Twenty-seven.
Q What is your post office address? A Henryetta.
Q Are you a citizen of the Creek Nation? A Yes sir.
Q To what Creek Indian town do you belong? A Hutchechuppa.
Q Do you know of any minor children in your town or neighborhood for whose enrollment application has not been made? A Sandy Wildcat and Losanna Wildcat, both of Thlewarthle town have a child between two and three years old. If is a boy. I don't know its name. The post office address of the parents is Bryant.

        Sandy and Losanna Wildcat are identified opposite Creek Indian Roll Nos. 5072 and 5073.

        Lona Merrick, being duly sworn, states that the above and foregoing is a true and correct of the original.

                Lona Merrick

Subscribed and sworn to before me this 21st day of August, 1906.

                (No name given)
                Notary Public.

Applications for Enrollment of Creek Newborn
Act of 1905   Volume VI

DEPARTMENT OF THE INTERIOR,
COMMISSIONER TO THE FIVE CIVILIZED TRIBES.
Wetumka, Indian Territory.
July 18, 1906.

In the matter of the application for the enrollment; as citizens of the Creek Nation, of minor children born to duly enrolled citizens, members of the so called Snake faction.

D.W. Fields, being duly sworn, testified as follows:
Through Official Interpreter, Alex Posey.

Q What is your name? A DW. Fields.
Q What is your age? A Twenty-seven.
Q What is your post office address? A Henryetta.
Q Are you a citizen of the Creek Nation? A Yes sir.
Q To what Creek Indian town do you belong? A Hutchechuppa.
Q Do you know of any minor children in your town or neighborhood for whose enrollment application has not been made? A Billy West and Louisa his wife, have a child, a girl but I don't know its name.
Q Is the child living? A Yes sir.
Q To what Creek Indian town do the parents belong? A Billy West belongs to Kialigee and Louisa to Thlopthlocco.
Q What is the post office address of the parents? A Weleetka.
(Note: Notation on the page indicates the number 434 for this party)

Sun Thloppa an old ~~man~~ woman living at Hutchechuppa has an illegitimate child of Joe Brown and Betsey Barnett; the child is two years old and is a girl. I don't know its name.
Q What is the post office address of the parents? A Dustin.
Q To what Creek Indian towns do they belong? A Joe Brown belongs to Okchiye and Betsey Barnett belongs to Hutchechuppa.

Little Tommy Johnson of Nuyaka and his wife Arlie Johnson, also of Nuyaka, have a girl about two years old but I don't know its name.
Q What is the post office address of the parents? A Henryetta.
Q Is little Tommy Johnson known by any other name? A That is the only name by which I know him.
Little Tommy Johnson is identified opposite Creek Indian Roll No. 5372 as Little Tom Johnson and Arlie Johnson is identified opposite No. 5373 as Ellie Johnson.
Q Is the child living? A Yes sir.
(Note: Notation on the page indicates the number 435 for this party)

Nannie Scott of Artussee has a child, a boy, about a year and a half old; I don't know its name. The father is said to be Sandy Watson of Okchiye. The child is living.
Q What is the post office address of the parents? A Weleetka.
(Note: Notation for this party is NB (Mar. 3.05) Card #393)

Applications for Enrollment of Creek Newborn
Act of 1905 Volume VI

McDaniels Watson of Hutchechuppa and Louisa Watson his wife have a boy child about a year and a half old. I don't know the child's name or the town of its mother. The post office address of the parents is Dustin. The mother's maiden name was Louisa Bird.
Q Is the child living? A Yes sir.

Sandy Wildcat and Losanna Wildcat, both of Thlewarthle town, have a child between two and three years old. It is a boy. I don't know its name. The post office address of the parents is Bryant.

Sandy and Losanna Wildcat are identified opposite Creek Indian roll Nos. 5072 and 5073.
(Notation for this entry: Thinks this is Peter Wildcat on N.B. (Mar.3.05) Card No. 443)

Cotchoche and his wife Lucinda have four children. I don't think any of them are enrolled as the father is a strong snake sympathizer and much opposed to the work of the Dawes Commission among the Indians. I don't know the names of any of the children or what their ages are. I three[sic] three[sic] girls and one a boy. Cotchoche belongs to Thlewathle town but I don't know to what town his wife belongs. Lucinda is probably enrolled as Lucinda Mitchell as that was her maiden name. The post office of the parents is Henryetta.
Q Are all these children living? A Yes sir.

Lumsey West of Kialigee town and Emma West of the same town have three children; one boy and two girls that are probably not enrolled but I don't know the children's names or ages. The post office address of the parents is Bryant. The children are all living.
Lumsey West is identified opposite Creek Indian roll No, 4944.

Sam Lowe of Cussehta has one child. I think it is a boy. I don't know the name of the mother nor to what town she belongs.
Q What is the post office address of the parents? A Schulter.
Q What is the post office address of the parents? A Schulter.[sic]
Q Is the child living? A Yes sir.
Sam Lowe is identified opposite No. 8343 as Samuel Lowe.
Q You don't think that application has been made for the enrollment of any of the above children about whom you have given information? A No sir, because their parents all belong to the Snake faction.

I, Alex Posey, on oath state that the above and foregoing is a true and correct transcript of my notes as taken in said cause on said date.

SEAL   (Signed) Alex Posey
Subscribed and sworn to before me this 1 day of August, 1906.

                         (Signed) Edward Merrick,
                                   Notary Public.

Applications for Enrollment of Creek Newborn
Act of 1905 Volume VI

Lona Merrick, being duly sworn, states that she copied the above and foregoing and that the same is a correct copy of the original testimony.

Lona Merrick

Subscribed and sworn to before me this 6th day of August, 1906.

Edward Merrick
Notary Public.

DEPARTMENT OF THE INTERIOR.
COMMISSION TO THE FIVE CIVILIZED TRIBES.

IN RE APPLICATION FOR ENROLLMENT, as a citizen of the Creek Nation, of Peter Wildcat, born on the 22 day of May, 1902

Name of Father:	Sandy Wildcat	a citizen of the Creek	Nation.
Name of Mother:	Losanna Wildcat	a citizen of the Creek	Nation.

Postoffice   Weleetka, Ind. Ter.

AFFIDAVIT OF MOTHER.

UNITED STATES OF AMERICA, Indian Territory,
Western   DISTRICT.

I, Losanna Wildcat, on oath state that I am about 40 years of age and a citizen by blood, of the Creek Nation; that I am the lawful wife of Sandy Wildcat, who is a citizen, by blood of the Creek Nation; that a male child was born to me on 22 day of May, 1902, that said child has been named Peter Wildcat, and was living March 4, 1905. That no one attended on me as midwife or physician at the birth of child.

                                                       her
                                         Losanna x Wildcat

Witnesses To Mark: mark
  { Alex Posey
    DC Skaggs

Subscribed and sworn to before me this 23 day of March, 1905.

Drennan C Skaggs
Notary Public.

Applications for Enrollment of Creek Newborn
Act of 1905   Volume VI

(The above Birth Affidavit given again)

Western District
Indian Territory   SS

We, the undersigned, on oath state that we are personally acquainted with Losanna Wildcat wife of Sandy Wildcat that on or about the 22 day of May, 1902, a male child was born to them and has been named Peter Wildcat; and that said child was living March 4, 1905 and is now living

We further state that we have no interest in the above case.

                                            his
                                  (Illegible) x King
                                        her mark
                                   Nellie x Jacob

Witness to mark: mark
  Alex Posey
  JB *(Illegible)*
  Alex Posey
  JB *(Illegible)*

Subscribed and sworn to before
me this 15 day of Nov 1906   Alex Posey
                                              Notary Public.

N.B. 443   COPY
N.C. 443

Commissioner to the Five Civilized Tribes,
       Muskogee, Indian Territory.
Sir:

      In the matter of the application for the enrollment of an unnamed minor child of Sandy and Losanna Wildcat as a citizen by blood of the Creek Nation, I have the honor to report that, upon investigation, I find that application has already been made for the enrollment of said minor child as Peter Wildcat, and it does not appear that further evidence is desired in said cause.
                                Respectfully,

                                (Signed) Alex Posey
                                              In Charge
JBM   Creek Field Party.

Applications for Enrollment of Creek Newborn
Act of 1905   Volume VI

HGH

REFER IN REPLY TO THE FOLLOWING:

NC-443.

**DEPARTMENT OF THE INTERIOR,
COMMISSIONER TO THE FIVE CIVILIZED TRIBES.**

Muskogee, Indian Territory, August 3, 1905.

Losanna Wildcat,
   c/o Sandy Wildcat,
      Weleetka, Indian Territory.

Dear Madam:

    On March 23, 1905 you appeared before the Commission to the Five Civilized Tribes and made application for the enrollment of your son Peter Wildcat, born May 22, 1902, as a citizen by blood of the Creek Nation, and at that time submitted your affidavit only as to the birth of said child stating that there was no physician or midwife in attendance when he was born.

    You are advised that it will be necessary, before the rights of said child as a citizen by blood of the Creek Nation can be finally determined, for you to file with this office the affidavits, relative to the birth of said child, of two disinterested persons. Said affidavits to set forth the name of said child, the date of his birth, the names of his parents and whether or not he was living on March 4, 1905.

Respectfully,

Tams Bixby
    Commissioner.

NC 443.

Muskogee, Indian Territory, December 12, 1905.

Losanna Wildcat,
   Care of Sandy Wildcat,
      Weleetka, Indian Territory.

Dear Madam:

    In the matter of the application for the enrollment of your minor child, Peter Wildcat, born May 22, 1902, as a citizen by bloof[sic] of the Creek Nation, it will be necessary for you to furnish this office with the affidavit of two disinterested persons as to the birth of said child. Said affidavit must set forth said child's name, the names of his parents, the date of his birth, and whether or not he was living March 4, 1905. A blank for that purpose is herewith enclosed.

Applications for Enrollment of Creek Newborn
Act of 1905   Volume VI

Respectfully,

Dis.   Acting Commissioner.

NC 443

JWH

Muskogee, Indian Territory, March 1, 1907.

Losanna Wildcat,
    c/o Sandy Wildcat,
        Bryant, Indian Territory.

Dear Madam:--

You are hereby advised that on February 15, 1907, the Secretary of the Interior approved the enrollment of your minor child, Peter Wildcat, as a citizen by blood of the Creek Nation, and that the name of said child appears upon the roll of New Born citizens by blood of the Creek Nation, enrolled Act of Congress approved March 3, 1905, as number 1143.

This child is now entitled to allotment, and application therefor should be made without delay at the Creek Land Office, Muskogee, Indian Territory.

Respectfully,

Commissioner.

DEPARTMENT OF THE INTERIOR,
COMMISSION TO THE FIVE CIVILIZED TRIBES.
April 24, 1905.

In the matter of the application for the enrollment of certain new borns as citizens of the Creek Nation.

Alex Posey, being duly sworn, testified as follows:

By Commission:
Q What is your name, age and post office address? A Alex Posey, 31, Muskogee.
Q Are you a citizen of the Creek Nation? A Yes sir.
Q Got your land, have you? A Yes sir.
Q You have been engaged recently in the field for the Dawes Commission securing evidence about Creek citizens or new borns? A Yes sir.
Q Have you a list of children for whom application could not be made and about whom you have succeeded in obtaining some information? A Yes sir.

Applications for Enrollment of Creek Newborn
Act of 1905   Volume VI

Q You may state the conditions and the names of these children? You desire to make application for them? A Yes sir.

Q Name them. [sic] Jaly Proctor, Weogufky Town, Sukey Proctor, Weogufky Town, have two children --one about three years old and one about six months old. Post office, Hanna, Indian Territory.

Jacob Bullet, about three years old. Parents: Maxey Bullet, Seminole, and Hannah Bullet, Hillabbee[sic]. Post Office, Hanna, Indian Territory.

Connie Hawkins, Hillabee Town, Sabella Hawkins, Okchiye, have two children-- one about three years old and a younger child. Post Office, Hanna, Indian Territory.

Willie Fisher, Hickory Ground Town, Lussee Fisher, Okfusky[sic] Canadian Town, have two children--one about three years old and a baby. Post Office, Slumpker, Indian Territory.

Lizzie Lasley, about three years old, Sam Lasley, born in either August or September, 1904. Parents: Sam Lasley, Okchiye, Wisey Lasley, Weogufky. Post Office, Hanna, Indian Territory.

Jim Haynes (or Sangee), Okchiye Town, Folotkokee, Weogufky Town have a male child about three years old named Joe. Post Office, Hanna, Indian Territory.

Taylor Foley, Weogufky, Melinda Foley, Okchiye, have a child about two years old. Post Office Slumpka[sic], Indian Territory.

Phillip Lindsey, Tuckabatchee[sic], Cilla Lindsey, Hillabee, have a child about three years old. Post Office, Hanna, Indian Territory.

Big William (or William Thlocco), Okchiye Town, Cinda Williams, Weogufky Town, have two children -- one about three years old-- one born in February 1905. Post Office, Hanna, Indian Territory.

Freeland Lindsey, Tuckabctehee[sic] or Hillabee, Nancy Proctor, Tullahassoche[sic], have a child about two years old. Post Officer, Hanna, Indian Territory.

Timonthluppy George, Weogufky Town, Nellie George, Pukon Tullahassee[sic], have a child about three years old. Post Office, Slumpker, Indian Territory.

Walter Simmons, Weogufky, Chippie Simmons, Pukon Tulahassee[sic], have a child about one years old. Post Office, Hanna, Indian Territory.

Jacob Larney (or Green), Arbeka Tulledega Town, Bettie Larney, (or Green), Hillabee, Town, have a child. Post Office, Hanna, Indian Territory.

John Hill, Okchiye, Millie Hill, Weogufky, have a child about three months old. Post Office, Hanna, Indian Territory.

Jim Pigeon, Okchiye Town, Jennie Pigeon, Okchiye Town, gave a child about five months old. Post Office, Hanna, Indian Territory.

Thomas Deo, Okchiye Town, Nancy Deo, Fish Pond Town, have a child about three months old. Post Office, Hanna, Indian Territory.

Jack Buckner, born December 17, 1904. Parents: Wiley Buckner, Okchiye, Susie Buckner, Cussehta. Post Office, Hanna, Indian Territory.

Q This is the information you received from relatives right around there on April 24, 1905? A Yes sir.

Applications for Enrollment of Creek Newborn
Act of 1905 Volume VI

Q Were you informed that the parents of these children were unwilling to make application for their enrollment? A Yes sir.
Q This was the only way that the rights of these children would be saved? A Yes sir. I made every effort to obtain direct information from the parents but in every instance they refused to give their testimony.

Lona Merrick being duly sworn, states that the above and foregoing is a true and correct transcript of her stenographic notes as taken in said cause on said date.

Lona Merrick

Subscribed and sworn to before me this 9th day of May, 1905.

Edw C Griesel
Notary Public.

N.C. 444.

DEPARTMENT OF THE INTERIOR,
COMMISSIONER TO THE FIVE CIVILIZED TRIBES.
Hanna, I. T., October 7, 1905.

In the matter of the application for the enrollment of Ceboly and Nahsa Deo as citizens by blood of the Creek Nation.

THOMAS DEO, being duly sworn, testified as follows:

Through Alex Posey Official Interpreter:

BY THE COMMISSIONER:
Q What is your name? A Thomas Deo.
Q How old are you? A About twenty-nine.
Q What is your post office address? A Hanna.
Q Are you a citizen of the Creek Nation? A Yes, sir.
Q To what town do you belong? A Okchiye.
Q Have you two children named Ceboly and Nahsa Deo? A Yes, sir.
Q Who is the mother of those children? A Nancy Deo.
Q Are these children known by any other names? A Yes, sir. The proper name of Ceboly is Amos and the proper name of Nahsa is Susie. Ceboly and Nahsa are nicknames.
Q When were these two children born? A Amos was born June 17, 1902, and Susie was born January 4, 1905.
Q Cumsey Green appeared before the Commission and executed an affidavit stating that Nahsa was born January 15, 1905, is that a mistake? A Yes, sir. He told me after making application for the children that he had made a mistake.

---oooOOOooo---

Applications for Enrollment of Creek Newborn
Act of 1905   Volume VI

I, D. C. Skaggs, on oath state that the above and foregoing is a full and true transcript of my stenographic notes as taken in said cause on said date.

D.C. Skaggs

Subscribed and sworn to before me this 16 day of Oct, 1905.

Edw C Griesel

BIRTH AFFIDAVIT.

DEPARTMENT OF THE INTERIOR.
COMMISSION TO THE FIVE CIVILIZED TRIBES.

IN RE APPLICATION FOR ENROLLMENT, as a citizen of the Creek Nation, of Ceboly Deo, born on the 17 day of June, 1902

Name of Father:	Thomas Deo	a citizen of the	Creek	Nation.
Name of Mother:	Nancy Deo	a citizen of the	Creek	Nation.

Postoffice   Hanna, I.T.

AFFIDAVIT OF ATTENDING PHYSICIAN OR MID-WIFE.

UNITED STATES OF AMERICA, Indian Territory,
   Western   **DISTRICT.**

personally acquainted with ~~I,~~ We the undersigned , ~~a~~ *(blank)* , on oath state that ~~I~~ we are ~~attended on~~ Mrs. Nancy Deo, wife of Thomas Deo ~~on the (blank) day of (blank) , 1~~ ; that there was born to her on June 17, 1902, ~~said date~~ a male child; that said child was living March 4, 1905, and is said to have been named Ceboly Deo

Tom Tiger

Witnesses To Mark: his
 { D C Skaggs   Wilson x Gibson
 { Alex Posey   mark

Subscribed and sworn to before me this 7 day of Oct, 1905.

Drennan C Skaggs
Notary Public.

Applications for Enrollment of Creek Newborn
Act of 1905   Volume VI

BIRTH AFFIDAVIT.

DEPARTMENT OF THE INTERIOR.
COMMISSION TO THE FIVE CIVILIZED TRIBES.

IN RE APPLICATION FOR ENROLLMENT, as a citizen of the Creek Nation, of Ceboly Deo, born ~~on the~~ *(blank)* ~~day of~~ June, 1903

Name of Father:	Thomas Deo	a citizen of the	Creek	Nation.
Name of Mother:	Nancy Deo	a citizen of the	Creek	Nation.

Postoffice   Hanna, Ind. Ter.

AFFIDAVIT OF MOTHER.

UNITED STATES OF AMERICA, Indian Territory,
Western   DISTRICT.

I, Cumsey Green, on oath state that I am about 45 years of age and a citizen by blood, of the Creek Nation; that I am the ~~lawful wife of~~ Uncle by marriage of Nancy Deo, who with her husband, refuses to make application for the enrollment of her children that a male child was born to ~~me on~~ her ~~day of~~ June, 1903, that said child has been named Ceboly Deo, and was living March 4, 1905.

his
Cumsey x Green
mark

Witnesses To Mark:
{ Alex Posey
{ DC Skaggs

Subscribed and sworn to before me this 23 day of March, 1905.

Drennan C Skaggs
Notary Public.

BIRTH AFFIDAVIT.

DEPARTMENT OF THE INTERIOR.
COMMISSION TO THE FIVE CIVILIZED TRIBES.

IN RE APPLICATION FOR ENROLLMENT, as a citizen of the Creek Nation, of Amos Deo, born on the 17 day of June, 1902

Name of Father:	Thomas Deo	a citizen of the	Creek	Nation.
Okchiye Town.				
Name of Mother:	Nancy Deo	a citizen of the	Creek	Nation.
Fish Pond Town				

Applications for Enrollment of Creek Newborn
Act of 1905 Volume VI

Postoffice   Hanna, I.T.

AFFIDAVIT OF MOTHER.

UNITED STATES OF AMERICA, Indian Territory, ⎫
Western   DISTRICT.   ⎭

I, Nancy Deo, on oath state that I am about 25 years of age and a citizen by blood, of the Creek Nation; that I am the lawful wife of Thomas Deo, who is a citizen, by blood of the Creek Nation; that a male child was born to me on 17 day of June, 1902, that said child has been named Amos Deo, and is now living. and was living March 4, 1905.

                            her
                        Nancy x Deo
                          mark

Witnesses To Mark:
{ D C Skaggs
  Alex Posey

Subscribed and sworn to before me this 1 day of June, 1905.

                        Drennan C Skaggs
                        Notary Public.

AFFIDAVIT OF ATTENDING PHYSICIAN OR MID-WIFE.

UNITED STATES OF AMERICA, Indian Territory, ⎫
Western   DISTRICT.   ⎭

                                                  my wife
I, Thomas Deo, a (blank), on oath state that I attended on ^ Mrs. Nancy Deo, wife of (blank) on the 17 day of June, 1902 ; that there was born to her on said date a male child; that said child is now living and was living March 4, 1905 and is said to have been named Amos Deo

                        Thomas Deo

Witnesses To Mark:
{

Subscribed and sworn to before me this 1 day of June, 1905.

                        Drennan C Skaggs
                        Notary Public.

Applications for Enrollment of Creek Newborn
Act of 1905 Volume VI

BIRTH AFFIDAVIT.

DEPARTMENT OF THE INTERIOR.
COMMISSION TO THE FIVE CIVILIZED TRIBES.

IN RE APPLICATION FOR ENROLLMENT, as a citizen of the Creek Nation, of Ceboley Deo, born ~~on the~~ *(blank)* ~~day of~~ June, 1903

Name of Father:	Thomas Deo	a citizen of the	Creek	Nation.
Name of Mother:	Nancy Deo	a citizen of the	Creek	Nation.

Postoffice   Hanna, Ind. Ter.

AFFIDAVIT OF MOTHER.

UNITED STATES OF AMERICA, Indian Territory, ⎫
Western   DISTRICT.   ⎭

I, Cumsey Green, on oath state that I am about 45 years of age and a citizen by blood, of the Creek Nation; that I am the ~~lawful wife of~~ Uncle by marriage of Nancy Deo, who with her husband, refuses to make application for the enrollment of her children that a male child was born to ~~me on~~ her ~~day of~~ June, 1903, that said child has been named Ceboly Deo, and was living March 4, 1905.

            his
          Cumsey x Green
Witnesses To Mark: mark
 { Alex Posey
   DC Skaggs

Subscribed and sworn to before me this 23 day of March, 1905.

          Drennan C Skaggs
           Notary Public.

BIRTH AFFIDAVIT.

DEPARTMENT OF THE INTERIOR.
COMMISSION TO THE FIVE CIVILIZED TRIBES.

IN RE APPLICATION FOR ENROLLMENT, as a citizen of the Creek Nation, of Nasha Deo, born on the 15 day of January, 1905

Name of Father:	Thomas Deo	a citizen of the	Creek	Nation.
Name of Mother:	Nancy Deo	a citizen of the	Creek	Nation.

Postoffice   Hanna, Ind. Ter.

Applications for Enrollment of Creek Newborn
Act of 1905   Volume VI

Uncle
AFFIDAVIT OF ~~MOTHER~~.

UNITED STATES OF AMERICA, Indian Territory,
Western   DISTRICT.

I, Cumsey Green , on oath state that I am about 45 years of age and a citizen by blood , of the Creek Nation; that I am ~~the lawful wife of~~ Uncle by marriage of Nancy Deo , who with her husband, refuses to make application for the enrollment her children that a female child was born to ~~me~~ her on 15 day of January , 1905 , that said child has been named Nasha Deo , and was living March 4, 1905.

his
Cumsey x Green
mark

Witnesses To Mark:
{ Alex Posey
{ DC Skaggs

Subscribed and sworn to before me this 23 day of March , 1905.

Drennan C Skaggs
Notary Public.

BIRTH AFFIDAVIT.

DEPARTMENT OF THE INTERIOR.
COMMISSION TO THE FIVE CIVILIZED TRIBES.

IN RE APPLICATION FOR ENROLLMENT, as a citizen of the Creek Nation, of Nasha Deo , born on the 4 day of Jan , 1904

Name of Father: Thomas Deo   a citizen of the   Creek   Nation.
Name of Mother: Nancy Deo   a citizen of the   Creek   Nation.

Postoffice   Hanna, I.T.

AFFIDAVIT OF ATTENDING PHYSICIAN OR MID-WIFE.

UNITED STATES OF AMERICA, Indian Territory,
Western   DISTRICT.

personally acquainted with ~~I,~~ We the undersigned , ~~a~~ (blank) , on oath state that ~~I~~ we are ^ ~~attended on~~ Mrs. Nancy Deo, wife of Thomas Deo ~~on the (blank) day of (blank) , 1~~ ; that there was born to her on, ~~said date~~ January 4, 1905 a female child; that said child was living March 4, 1905, and is said to have been named Nasha Deo

Tom Tiger

Applications for Enrollment of Creek Newborn
Act of 1905 Volume VI

Witnesses To Mark:
{ D C Skaggs
{ Alex Posey

his
Wilson x Gibson
mark

Subscribed and sworn to before me this 7 day of October, 1905.

Drennan C Skaggs
Notary Public.

BIRTH AFFIDAVIT.

DEPARTMENT OF THE INTERIOR.
COMMISSION TO THE FIVE CIVILIZED TRIBES.

IN RE APPLICATION FOR ENROLLMENT, as a citizen of the Creek Nation, of Susie Deo, born on the 4 day of January, 1905

Name of Father: Thomas Deo a citizen of the Creek Nation. Okchye[sic] Town.
Name of Mother: Nancy a citizen of the Creek Nation. Fish Pond Town

Postoffice Hanna, I.T.

AFFIDAVIT OF MOTHER.

UNITED STATES OF AMERICA, Indian Territory, }
Western DISTRICT. }

I, Nancy Deo, on oath state that I am about 25 years of age and a citizen by blood, of the Creek Nation; that I am the lawful wife of Thomas Deo, who is a citizen, by blood of the Creek Nation; that a female child was born to me on 4 day of January, 1905, that said child has been named Susie Deo, and is now living. and was living March 4, 1905.

her
Nancy x Deo
mark

Witnesses To Mark:
{ D C Skaggs
{ Alex Posey

Subscribed and sworn to before me this 1 day of June, 1905.

Drennan C Skaggs
Notary Public.

Applications for Enrollment of Creek Newborn
Act of 1905 Volume VI

AFFIDAVIT OF ATTENDING PHYSICIAN OR MID-WIFE.

UNITED STATES OF AMERICA, Indian Territory,
Western DISTRICT.

my wife
I, Thomas Deo , ~~a (blank)~~, on oath state that I attended on ^ Mrs. Nancy Deo, ~~wife of (blank)~~ on the 4 day of January , 1905 ; that there was born to her on said date a female child; that said child is now living and was living March 4, 1905 and is said to have been named Susie Deo

Thomas Deo

Witnesses To Mark:

Subscribed and sworn to before me this 1 day of June, 1905.

Drennan C Skaggs
Notary Public.

DEPARTMENT OF THE INTERIOR,
COMMISSION TO THE FIVE CIVILIZED TRIBES.
APRIL 24, 1905.

In the matter of the application for the enrollment of certain new borns as citizens of the Creek Nation.

Alex Posey, being duly sworn, testified as follows:

Statement: Thomas Deo, of Okchiye Town, Nancy Deo, Fish Pond Town, hva[sic] child about five months old. Post Office, Hanna, Indian Territory.

NC 444.

Muskogee, Indian Territory, August 3, 1905.

Cumsey Green,
Hanna, Indian Territory.

Dear Sir:

On March 23, 1905, you appeared before the Commission to the Five Civilized Tribes and made application for the enrollment of Ceboly Deo, born in June 1903, and Nahsa Deo, born January 15, 1905, as citizens by blood of the Creek Nation, at that time submitting your affidavits relative to the birth of said children and also stating that the parents of said children refused to make application for their enrollment.

Applications for Enrollment of Creek Newborn
Act of 1905   Volume VI

This office is unable to identify Nancy Deo, the mother of said children upon the final roll of Creek citizens by blood. You are, therefore, requested to state the name under which she is enrolled, the names of her parents and other members of her family, the Creek town to which she belongs and if she has in her possession her allotment certificate and deed her final roll number as the same appears thereon.

You are also advised that, before the rights of said children as citizens by blood of the Creek Nation can be finally determined, it will be necessary that this office be supplied with the affidavits of the mother of said children and the attending physician or midwife at their birth, and in order that the same may be supplied there are inclosed herewith two blanks for proof of birth. In having same executed be careful to see that the notary public, before whom the affidavits are sworn to attaches his name and seal to each affidavit. In case any signature is by mark it must be attested by two disinterested witnesses.

Respectfully,

Commissioner.

Dustin, Indian Territory, October 12, 1905.

Commissioner to the Five Civilized Tribes,
Muskogee, Indian Territory.

Sir:

There is enclosed herewith supplemental proof in the following Creek new born enrollment cases:

No
444   Ceboly & Nasha Deo

Alex P

Dustin, Indian Territory, October 12, 1905.

Commissioner to the Five Civilized Tribes,
Muskogee, Indian Territory.

Sir:

There is enclosed herewith supplemental proof in the following Creek new born enrollment cases:

No.	Name.
444	Ceboly and Nahsa Deo.

Applications for Enrollment of Creek Newborn
Act of 1905   Volume VI

994	Jacob Bullet.
995	Pink and Nellie Hawkins.
998	Hettie Fisher.
1009	Emma Simmons.
1012	Nache Pigeon.
1051	Lillie Sloan.
1130	Posey Fish.

Respectfully,

Alex Posey
Clerk in Charge Creek Field Party.

Dustin, Indian Territory, October 13, 1905.

Commissioner to the Five Civilized Tribes,
   Muskogee, Indian Territory.

Sir:

There is enclosed herewith supplemental proof in the following Creek new born enrollment cases:

	Name.
No. 444	Ceboly and Nahsa Deo.
998	Bettie Fisher.
1069	Sandy and Sarty Emarthla.

I find it impossible to obtain further evidence in the case of Sandy and Sarty Emarthla. The parents of these children belong to the so called Snake faction and refuse to give any information, whatever.

Respectfully,

Alex Posey
Clerk in Charge C. F. P.

NC 444.

Muskogee, Indian Territory, December 12, 1905.

Nandy Deo,
   Care Thomas Deo,
      Hannah, Indian Territory.

Applications for Enrollment of Creek Newborn
Act of 1905 Volume VI

Dear Madam:

In the matter of the application for the enrollment of your minor children, Amos Deo, born June 17, 1902, and Susie Deo, born January 4, 1905, as citizens by blood of the Creek Nation, you are advised that this office is unable to identify you on its final rolls of citizens of the Creek Nation.

You are requested to write this office at an early date giving your maiden name, the names of your parents and other members of your family, the Creek Indian Town to which you belong, and, if possible, your name and roll number as same appear on your allotment certificate or deeds to land in the Creek Nation.

This matter should receive your prompt attention receive your prompt attention.

> Respectfully,
>
> Acting Commissioner.

JWH

N C 444

Muskogee, Indian Territory, March 1, 1907.

Nancy Deo,
    c/o Thomas Deo,
        Hanna, Indian Territory.

Dear Madam:--

You are hereby advised that on February 15, 1907, the Secretary of the Interior approved the enrollment of your minor children, Amos and Susie Deo, as citizens by blood of the Creek Nation, and that the names of said children appear upon the roll of New Born citizens by blood of the Creek Nation, enrolled under the Act of Congress approved March 3, 1905, as numbers 1144 and 1145, respectively.

These children are now entitled to allotment and application therefor should be made without delay at the Creek Land Office, Muskogee, Indian Territory.

> Respectfully,
>
> Commissioner.

Applications for Enrollment of Creek Newborn
Act of 1905   Volume VI

NC-445.

Muskogee, Indian Territory, August 3, 1905.

Mary McDermott,
Fentress, Indian Territory.

Dear Madam:

In the matter of the application for the enrollment of your minor son Charlie McDermott as a citizen by blood of the Creek Nation it will be necessary for you to furnish this office with the affidavit of Kizzie Dunson, midwife, as to the birth of said child, and for that purpose a blank, which has been filled out, is inclosed herewith.

You are requested to have the same sworn to before a notary public and return to this office in the inclosed envelope.

The affidavit of the said Kizzie Dunson now on file in this office is defective inasmuch as the name of the affiant appears in the body of the affidavit as Kizzie McDermott.

Respectfully,

Commissioner.

CTD-24.
Env.

BIRTH AFFIDAVIT.
DEPARTMENT OF THE INTERIOR.
COMMISSION TO THE FIVE CIVILIZED TRIBES.

IN RE APPLICATION FOR ENROLLMENT, as a citizen of the Creek Nation, of Charlie McDermott, born on the 18th day of May, 1904

Name of Father: L. H. McDermott   a citizen of the United States Nation.
Name of Mother: Mary McDermott   a citizen of the   Creek   Nation.

Postoffice   Fentress, I.T.

Applications for Enrollment of Creek Newborn
Act of 1905 Volume VI

AFFIDAVIT OF ATTENDING PHYSICIAN OR MID-WIFE.

UNITED STATES OF AMERICA, Indian Territory, }
Western DISTRICT.

I, Kizzie Dunson, a mid-wife, on oath state that I attended on Mrs. Mary McDermott, wife of L. H. McDermott on the 18th day of Mau, 1904 ; that there was born to her on said date a male child; that said child was living March 4, 1905, and is said to have been named Charlie McDermott

Kizzie Dunson

Witnesses To Mark:
{

Subscribed and sworn to before me this 8 day of August, 1905.

J. B. Stamper
Notary Public.

BIRTH AFFIDAVIT.

DEPARTMENT OF THE INTERIOR.
COMMISSION TO THE FIVE CIVILIZED TRIBES.

IN RE APPLICATION FOR ENROLLMENT, as a citizen of the Creek Nation, of Lizzie McDermott, born on the 31st day of July, 1902

Name of Father: L.H. McDermott   a citizen of the United States Nation.
Name of Mother: Mary McDermott   a citizen of the Creek Nation ~~Nation~~.

Postoffice   Fentress, I.T.

AFFIDAVIT OF MOTHER.

UNITED STATES OF AMERICA, Indian Territory, }
Western Judicial DISTRICT.

I, Mary McDermott, on oath state that I am 30 years of age and a citizen by Blood, of the Muskokee[sic] or Creek Nation; that I am the lawful wife of L.H. McDermott, who is a citizen, ~~by the Citizen~~ of the United States ~~Nation~~; that a Female child was born to me on 31st day of July, 1902, that said child has been named Lizzie McDermott, and was living March 4, 1905.

Mary McDermott

Witnesses To Mark:
{

Applications for Enrollment of Creek Newborn
Act of 1905 Volume VI

Subscribed and sworn to before me this 22th[sic] day of March, 1905.

My Commission Expires Sept. 6th 1906.

John H. Phillips
Notary Public.

AFFIDAVIT OF ATTENDING PHYSICIAN OR MID-WIFE.

UNITED STATES OF AMERICA, Indian Territory,
Western Judicial   DISTRICT.

I, Kizzie Dunson, a Mid-Wife, on oath state that I attended on Mrs. Mary McDermott, wife of L.H. McDermott on the 31st day of July, 1902; that there was born to her on said date a Female child; that said child was living March 4, 1905, and is said to have been named Lizzie McDermott

Kizzie Dunson

Witnesses To Mark:

Subscribed and sworn to before me this 22th[sic] day of March, 1905.

My Commission Expires Sept. 6th 1906.

John H. Phillips
Notary Public.

BIRTH AFFIDAVIT.

DEPARTMENT OF THE INTERIOR.
COMMISSION TO THE FIVE CIVILIZED TRIBES.

IN RE APPLICATION FOR ENROLLMENT, as a citizen of the Creek Nation, of Charlie McDermott, born on the 18th day of May, 1904

Name of Father: L.H. McDermott   a citizen of the United States Nation.
Name of Mother: Mary McDermott   a citizen of the Creek Nation ~~Nation~~.

Postoffice   Fentress, I.T.

AFFIDAVIT OF MOTHER.

UNITED STATES OF AMERICA, Indian Territory,
Western Judicial   DISTRICT.

I, Mary McDermott, on oath state that I am 30 years of age and a citizen by Blood, of the Muskokee[sic] or Creek Nation; that I am the lawful wife of L.H. McDermott, who is a citizen, ~~by~~ *(blank)* of the United States ~~Nation~~; that a Male

Applications for Enrollment of Creek Newborn
Act of 1905   Volume VI

child was born to me on 18th day of May, 1904, that said child has been named Charlie McDermott, and was living March 4, 1905.

                                Mary McDermott

Witnesses To Mark:
{

Subscribed and sworn to before me this 22th[sic] day of March, 1905.

                                John H. Phillips
My Commission Expires Sept. 6th 1906.   Notary Public.

AFFIDAVIT OF ATTENDING PHYSICIAN OR MID-WIFE.

UNITED STATES OF AMERICA, Indian Territory, }
  Western Judicial   DISTRICT.

I, Kizzie McDermott, a Mid-Wife, on oath state that I attended on Mrs. Mary McDermott, wife of L.H. McDermott on the 18th day of May, 1904; that there was born to her on said date a Male child; that said child was living March 4, 1905, and is said to have been named Charlie McDermott

                                Kizzie Dunson

Witnesses To Mark:
{

Subscribed and sworn to before me this 22th[sic] day of March, 1905.

                                John H. Phillips
My Commission Expires Sept. 6th 1906.   Notary Public.

BIRTH AFFIDAVIT.
DEPARTMENT OF THE INTERIOR.
COMMISSION TO THE FIVE CIVILIZED TRIBES.

IN RE APPLICATION FOR ENROLLMENT, as a citizen of the Creek Nation, of Eli Tiger, born on the 16 day of June, 1904

Name of Father:	Thomas Tiger	a citizen of the	Creek	Nation.
Name of Mother:	Rose Tiger	a citizen of the	Creek	Nation.

                        Postoffice   Hanna, Ind. Ter.

Applications for Enrollment of Creek Newborn
Act of 1905   Volume VI

AFFIDAVIT OF MOTHER.

UNITED STATES OF AMERICA, Indian Territory, ⎫
   Western   DISTRICT. ⎬
                                            ⎭

    I, Rose Tiger , on oath state that I am 27 years of age and a citizen by blood , of the Creek Nation; that I am the lawful wife of Thomas Tiger , who is a citizen, by blood of the Creek Nation; that a male child was born to me on 16 day of June , 1904 , that said child has been named Eli Tiger , and was living March 4, 1905.

                                                     her
                                              Rose x Tiger
                                                  mark

Witnesses To Mark:
  {

    Subscribed and sworn to before me this   day of , 1905.

                                        (No signature given)
                                               Notary Public.

AFFIDAVIT OF ATTENDING PHYSICIAN OR MID-WIFE.

UNITED STATES OF AMERICA, Indian Territory, ⎫
   Western   DISTRICT. ⎬
          runer   ⎭

    I, Sally ~~Brown~~ , a midwife , on oath state that I attended on Mrs. Rose , wife of Thomas Tiger on the 16 day of June , 1904 ; that there was born to her on said date a *(blank)* child; that said child was living March 4, 1905, and is said to have been named Eli Tiger

                                               her
Witnesses To Mark: Sally x Bruner
  { Alex Posey   mark
    DC Skaggs

    Subscribed and sworn to before me this 23 day of March, 1905.

                                             Drennan C Skaggs
                                              Notary Public.

BIRTH AFFIDAVIT.

DEPARTMENT OF THE INTERIOR.
COMMISSION TO THE FIVE CIVILIZED TRIBES.

    IN RE APPLICATION FOR ENROLLMENT, as a citizen of the Creek Nation, of Eli Tiger , born on the 16 day of June , 1904

Applications for Enrollment of Creek Newborn
Act of 1905   Volume VI

AFFIDAVIT OF MOTHER.

UNITED STATES OF AMERICA, Indian Territory,
Western   DISTRICT.

    I, Rose Tiger , on oath state that I am 27 years of age and a citizen by blood , of the Creek Nation; that I am the lawful wife of Thomas Tiger , who is a citizen, by blood of the Creek Nation; that a male child was born to me on 16 day of June , 1904 , that said child has been named Eli Tiger , and was living March 4, 1905.

                                            her
                                    Rose x Tiger
                                      mark

Witnesses To Mark:
{

    Subscribed and sworn to before me this   day of , 1905.

                                 (No signature given)
                                          Notary Public.

AFFIDAVIT OF ATTENDING PHYSICIAN OR MID-WIFE.

UNITED STATES OF AMERICA, Indian Territory,
Western   DISTRICT.

          runer
    I, Sally B~~rown~~ , a midwife , on oath state that I attended on Mrs. Rose , wife of Thomas Tiger on the 16 day of June , 1904 ; that there was born to her on said date a *(blank)* child; that said child was living March 4, 1905, and is said to have been named Eli Tiger
                                           her
                                    Sally x Bruner
Witnesses To Mark: mark
{ Alex Posey
  DC Skaggs

    Subscribed and sworn to before me this 23 day of March, 1905.

                                    Drennan C Skaggs
                                          Notary Public.

BIRTH AFFIDAVIT.
DEPARTMENT OF THE INTERIOR.
COMMISSION TO THE FIVE CIVILIZED TRIBES.

    IN RE APPLICATION FOR ENROLLMENT, as a citizen of the Creek Nation, of Eli Tiger , born on the 16 day of June , 1904

Applications for Enrollment of Creek Newborn
Act of 1905 Volume VI

child was born to me on 18th day of May, 1904, that said child has been named Charlie McDermott, and was living March 4, 1905.

Mary McDermott

Witnesses To Mark:
{

Subscribed and sworn to before me this 22th[sic] day of March, 1905.

John H. Phillips
Notary Public.

My Commission Expires Sept. 6th 1906.

AFFIDAVIT OF ATTENDING PHYSICIAN OR MID-WIFE.

UNITED STATES OF AMERICA, Indian Territory,
Western Judicial DISTRICT.

I, Kizzie McDermott, a Mid-Wife, on oath state that I attended on Mrs. Mary McDermott, wife of L.H. McDermott on the 18th day of May, 1904; that there was born to her on said date a Male child; that said child was living March 4, 1905, and is said to have been named Charlie McDermott

Kizzie Dunson

Witnesses To Mark:
{

Subscribed and sworn to before me this 22th[sic] day of March, 1905.

John H. Phillips
Notary Public.

My Commission Expires Sept. 6th 1906.

BIRTH AFFIDAVIT.

DEPARTMENT OF THE INTERIOR.
COMMISSION TO THE FIVE CIVILIZED TRIBES.

IN RE APPLICATION FOR ENROLLMENT, as a citizen of the Creek Nation, of Eli Tiger, born on the 16 day of June, 1904

Name of Father:	Thomas Tiger	a citizen of the	Creek	Nation.
Name of Mother:	Rose Tiger	a citizen of the	Creek	Nation.

Postoffice Hanna, Ind. Ter.

Applications for Enrollment of Creek Newborn
Act of 1905 Volume VI

Name of Father: Thomas Tiger   a citizen of the   Creek   Nation.
Name of Mother: Rose Tiger   a citizen of the   Creek   Nation.

                Postoffice   Hanna, Ind. Ter.

AFFIDAVIT OF MOTHER.

UNITED STATES OF AMERICA, Indian Territory,
    Western   DISTRICT.

    I, Rose Tiger, on oath state that I am 27 years of age and a citizen by blood, of the Creek Nation; that I am the lawful wife of Thomas Tiger, who is a citizen, by blood of the Creek Nation; that a male child was born to me on 16 day of June, 1904, that said child has been named Eli Tiger, and was living March 4, 1905.

                                        her
                               Rose x Tiger
                                 mark

Witnesses To Mark:
  { Alex Posey
    DC Skaggs

    Subscribed and sworn to before me this 23 day of March, 1905.

                               Drennan C Skaggs
                               Notary Public.

AFFIDAVIT OF ATTENDING PHYSICIAN OR MID-WIFE.

UNITED STATES OF AMERICA, Indian Territory,
    Western   DISTRICT.

    I, Sally Bruner, a midwife, on oath state that I attended on Mrs. Rose Tiger, wife of Thomas Tiger on the 16 day of June, 1904; that there was born to her on said date a *(blank)* child; that said child was living March 4, 1905, and is said to have been named Eli Tiger

                                        her
                              Sally x Bruner
Witnesses To Mark: mark
  { Alex Posey
    DC Skaggs

    Subscribed and sworn to before me this 23 day of March, 1905.

                               Drennan C Skaggs
                               Notary Public.

Applications for Enrollment of Creek Newborn
Act of 1905 Volume VI

BIRTH AFFIDAVIT.

DEPARTMENT OF THE INTERIOR.
COMMISSION TO THE FIVE CIVILIZED TRIBES.

IN RE APPLICATION FOR ENROLLMENT, as a citizen of the Creek Nation, of Eli Tiger, born on the 16 day of June, 1904

Name of Father: Tom Tiger   a citizen of the   Creek   Nation. Creek Cd Field #2791
Name of Mother: Rose Tiger (nee Fish) a citizen of the   Creek   Nation. Cussehtah[sic]Town Cr Roll #8336
                        Postoffice   Hanna, I.T.

AFFIDAVIT OF MOTHER.

UNITED STATES OF AMERICA, Indian Territory, ⎫
    Western   DISTRICT. ⎬

I, Rose Tiger, on oath state that I am about 28 years of age and a citizen by blood, of the Creek Nation; that I am the lawful wife of Tom Tiger, who is a citizen, by blood of the Creek Nation; that a male child was born to me on 16 day of June, 1904, that said child has been named Eli Tiger, and was living March 4, 1905 and is now.
                                      her
                                Rose x Tiger
Witnesses To Mark: mark
  { J McDermott
    Jim Cantrell

Subscribed and sworn to before me this 28 day of November, 1906.

My Commission   J. McDermott
Expires July 25" 1907   Notary Public.

AFFIDAVIT OF ATTENDING PHYSICIAN OR MID-WIFE.

UNITED STATES OF AMERICA, Indian Territory, ⎫
    Western   DISTRICT. ⎬

I, Sally Bruner, a midwife, on oath state that I attended on Mrs. Rose Tiger, wife of Tom Tiger on the 16 day of June, 1904; that there was born to her on said date a *(blank)* child; that said child was living March 4, 1905, and is said to have been named Eli Tiger and is now living   her
                                Sally x Bruner
                                  mark

Applications for Enrollment of Creek Newborn
Act of 1905 Volume VI

Witnesses To Mark:
 { J McDermott
 { Jim Cantrell

Subscribed and sworn to before me this 28 day of November, 1906.

My Commission   J. McDermott
Expires July 25" 1907   Notary Public.

NC 446.

Muskogee, Indian Territory, December 13, 1905.

Rose Tiger,
    Care Thomas Tiger,
        Hanna, Indian Territory.

Dear Madam:

    In the matter of the application for the enrollment of Eli Tiger, born June 16, 1904, you are advised that this office is unable to identify you or the father of said child on its roll of citizens by blood of the Creek Nation.

    You are requested to state the names of your parents and those of your husband and any other members of your families, the Creek Indian Town to which each of you belongs and your roll numbers as the same appear on your deeds to land in the Creek Nation.
    This matter should receive your prompt attention.

        Respectfully,

                Acting Commissioner.

                      JWH

N C 446

Muskogee, Indian Territory, March 1, 1907.

Rose Tiger,
    c/o Thomas Tiger,
        Hanna, Indian Territory.

Dear Madam :--

    You are hereby advised that on February 15, 1907, the Secretary of the Interior approved the enrollment of your minor child, Eli Tiger, as a citizen of the Creek Nation,

Applications for Enrollment of Creek Newborn
Act of 1905 Volume VI

and that the name of said child appears upon the roll of New Born citizens by blood of the Creek Nation, enrolled under the Act of Congress approved March 3, 1905, as number 1146.

This child is now entitled to allotment, and application therefor should be made without delay at the Creek Land Office, Muskogee, Indian Territory.

Respectfully,

Commissioner.

BIRTH AFFIDAVIT.

DEPARTMENT OF THE INTERIOR.
COMMISSION TO THE FIVE CIVILIZED TRIBES.

IN RE APPLICATION FOR ENROLLMENT, as a citizen of the Muskogee Nation, of Alta Hall, born on the 21 day of July, 1903

Name of Father:	Samuel Hall	a citizen of the Noncitizen Nation.
Name of Mother:	Hannah E. Hall	a citizen of the Muskogee Nation.

Postoffice   Okemah, I.T.

AFFIDAVIT OF MOTHER.

UNITED STATES OF AMERICA, Indian Territory,
Western DISTRICT.

I, Hannah E. Hall , on oath state that I am 32 years of age and a citizen by Blood , of the Muskogee Nation; that I am the lawful wife of Samuel Hall , who is a citizen, by Noncitizen of the Muskogee Nation; that a female child was born to me on 21 day of July , 1903 , that said child has been named Alta Hall , and was living March 4, 1905.

Hannah E. Hall

Witnesses To Mark:

Subscribed and sworn to before me this 22 day of March , 1905.

MY COMMISSION EXPIRES AUG. 2, 1906.

Geo. A. Harvison
Notary Public.

Applications for Enrollment of Creek Newborn
Act of 1905   Volume VI

AFFIDAVIT OF ATTENDING PHYSICIAN OR MID-WIFE.

UNITED STATES OF AMERICA, Indian Territory,
Western   DISTRICT.

I, Louisa Hall , a Midwife , on oath state that I attended on Mrs. Hannah E. Hall, wife of Samuel Hall on the 21 day of July , 1903 ; that there was born to her on said date a female child; that said child was living March 4, 1905, and is said to have been named Alta Hall

              her
           Louisa x Hall
Witnesses To Mark: mark
 { Geo. A. Harvison
  John H. Phillips

Subscribed and sworn to before me this 22 day of March , 1905.

MY COMMISSION EXPIRES AUG. 2, 1906.   Geo. A. Harvison
               Notary Public.

BIRTH AFFIDAVIT.

DEPARTMENT OF THE INTERIOR.
COMMISSION TO THE FIVE CIVILIZED TRIBES.

IN RE APPLICATION FOR ENROLLMENT, as a citizen of the Creek Nation, of Lillie Proctor , born on the 16 day of November , 1902

Name of Father:	Dave Proctor	a citizen of the	Creek	Nation.
Name of Mother:	Katie Proctor	a citizen of the	Creek	Nation.

        Postoffice Slumker, Ind. Ter.

AFFIDAVIT OF MOTHER.

UNITED STATES OF AMERICA, Indian Territory,
Western   DISTRICT.

I, Katie Proctor , on oath state that I am about 29 years of age and a citizen by blood , of the Creek Nation; that I am the lawful wife of Dave Proctor , who is a citizen, by blood of the Creek Nation; that a female child was born to me on 16 day of November , 1902 , that said child has been named Lillie Proctor , and was living March 4, 1905.

            her
         Katie x Proctor
           mark

Applications for Enrollment of Creek Newborn
Act of 1905   Volume VI

Witnesses To Mark:
{ Alex Posey
{ DC Skaggs

Subscribed and sworn to before me this 23 day of March , 1905.

Drennan C Skaggs
Notary Public.

AFFIDAVIT OF ATTENDING PHYSICIAN OR MID-WIFE.

UNITED STATES OF AMERICA, Indian Territory, }
Western   DISTRICT.

I, Mauda Proctor , a midwife , on oath state that I attended on Mrs. Katie Proctor , wife of Dave Proctor on the 16 day of November , 1902 ; that there was born to her on said date a *(blank)* child; that said child was living March 4, 1905, and is said to have been named   Lillie Proctor

her
Mauda x Proctor
mark

Witnesses To Mark:
{ Alex Posey
{ DC Skaggs

Subscribed and sworn to before me this 23 day of March , 1905.

Drennan C Skaggs
Notary Public.

BIRTH AFFIDAVIT.

DEPARTMENT OF THE INTERIOR.
COMMISSION TO THE FIVE CIVILIZED TRIBES.

IN RE APPLICATION FOR ENROLLMENT, as a citizen of the Creek Nation, of Carrie Gooden , born on the 5th day of April , 1904

Name of Father:	Henderson Gooden	a citizen of the	Creek	Nation.
Name of Mother:	Dora Gooden	a citizen of the	Creek	Nation.

Postoffice   Edna, Ind Terr.

Applications for Enrollment of Creek Newborn
Act of 1905   Volume VI

AFFIDAVIT OF MOTHER.

UNITED STATES OF AMERICA, Indian Territory, }
Western   DISTRICT.

I, Dora Gooden, nee, Ton-ta , on oath state that I am 18 years of age and a citizen by blood , of the Creek Nation; that I am the lawful wife of Henderson Gooden , who is a citizen, by blood of the Creek Nation; that a female child was born to me on Fifth day of April , 1904 , that said child has been named Carrie Gooden, and was living March 4, 1905.

Dora Gooden

Witnesses To Mark:
{ L.L. Longfellow
{ Frank Zimmermann

Subscribed and sworn to before me this 22nd day of March , 1905.

T.W. Flynn
Notary Public.

AFFIDAVIT OF ATTENDING PHYSICIAN OR MID-WIFE.

UNITED STATES OF AMERICA, Indian Territory, }
Western   DISTRICT.

I, Sina Kay , a Midwife , on oath state that I attended on Mrs. Dora Gooden , wife of Henderson on the Fifth day of April , 1904 ; that there was born to her on said date a female child; that said child was living March 4, 1905, and is said to have been named Carrie Gooden

her
Sina Kay x
mark

Witnesses To Mark:
{ Rhoda Bruner
{ Bessie Kay

Subscribed and sworn to before me this 22nd day of March , 1905.

T.W. Flynn
Notary Public.

BIRTH AFFIDAVIT.

DEPARTMENT OF THE INTERIOR.
COMMISSION TO THE FIVE CIVILIZED TRIBES.

IN RE APPLICATION FOR ENROLLMENT, as a citizen of the Creek Nation, of Sam Gooden , born on the 22nd day of March , 1903

Applications for Enrollment of Creek Newborn
Act of 1905 Volume VI

Name of Father: Henderson Gooden a citizen of the Creek Nation.
Name of Mother: Dora Gooden a citizen of the Creek Nation.

Postoffice   Edna, Ind Terr.

AFFIDAVIT OF MOTHER.

UNITED STATES OF AMERICA, Indian Territory,
Western DISTRICT.

I, Dora Gooden, on oath state that I am 18 years of age and a citizen by blood, of the Creek Nation; that I am the lawful wife of Henderson Gooden, who is a citizen, by blood of the Creek Nation; that a male child was born to me on 22nd day of March, 1903, that said child has been named Sam Gooden, ~~and was living March 4, 1905~~.

Dora Gooden

Witnesses To Mark:
{ Frank Zimmermann
{ L.L. Longfellow

Subscribed and sworn to before me this 22nd day of March, 1905.

T.W. Flynn
Notary Public.

AFFIDAVIT OF ATTENDING PHYSICIAN OR MID-WIFE.

UNITED STATES OF AMERICA, Indian Territory,
Western DISTRICT.

I, Sina Kay, a Midwife, on oath state that I attended on Mrs. Dora Gooden, wife of Henderson Gooden on the 22nd day of March, 1903; that there was born to her on said date a male child; ~~that said child was living March 4, 1905~~, and is said to have been named Sam Gooden   her
Sina Kay x
mark

Witnesses To Mark:
{ L.L. Longfellow
{ Frank Zimmermann

Subscribed and sworn to before me this 22nd day of March, 1905.

T.W. Flynn
Notary Public.

Applications for Enrollment of Creek Newborn
Act of 1905   Volume VI

BIRTH AFFIDAVIT.

DEPARTMENT OF THE INTERIOR.
COMMISSION TO THE FIVE CIVILIZED TRIBES.

IN RE APPLICATION FOR ENROLLMENT, as a citizen of the Creek Nation, of Sam Gooden, born on the 30 day of March, 1903

Name of Father:	Henderson Gooden	a citizen of the	Creek	Nation.
Name of Mother:	Dora Gooden	a citizen of the	Creek	Nation.

Postoffice   Edna, I.T.

AFFIDAVIT OF MOTHER.

UNITED STATES OF AMERICA, Indian Territory, }
    Western   DISTRICT.

I, Dora Gooden, on oath state that I am 19 years of age and a citizen by Birth, of the Creek Nation; that I am the lawful wife of Henderson Gooden, who is a citizen, by Birth of the Creek Nation; that a male child was born to me on 30th day of March, 1903, that said child has been named Sam Gooden, and was living March 4, 1905.

                                          Dora Gooden

Witnesses To Mark:
{

Subscribed and sworn to before me this 18 day of August, 1905.

Commision[sic] Ex Jan 9-1907   Albert Ewess
                                                          Notary Public.

DEPARTMENT OF THE INTERIOR.
COMMISSION TO THE FIVE CIVILIZED TRIBES.

In the matter of the death of Sam Gooden   a citizen of the Creek Nation, who formerly resided at or near Edna, Ind Terr.   , Ind. Ter., and died on the 30th day of March, 1903

Applications for Enrollment of Creek Newborn
Act of 1905 Volume VI

AFFIDAVIT OF RELATIVE.

UNITED STATES OF AMERICA, Indian Territory, }
Western DISTRICT.

I, Rhoda Bruner , on oath state that I am 26 years of age and a citizen by blood , of the Creek Nation; that my postoffice address is Edna, Ind Terr. , Ind. Ter.; that I am Aunt of Sam Gooden who was a citizen, by blood , of the Creek Nation and that said Sam Gooden died on the 30th day of March , 1903

Rhoda Bruner

Witnesses To Mark:
{ Frank Zimmermann
L.L. Longfellow

Subscribed and sworn to before me this 22nd day of March, 1905.

T.W. Flynn
Notary Public.

AFFIDAVIT OF ACQUAINTANCE.

UNITED STATES OF AMERICA, Indian Territory, }
Western DISTRICT.

I, Bessie Kay , on oath state that I am 27 years of age, and a citizen by blood of the Creek Nation; that my postoffice address is Edan[sic], Ind Terr. , Ind. Ter.; that I was personally acquainted with Sam Gooden who was a citizen, by blood , of the Creek Nation; and that said Sam Gooden died on the 30th day of March , 1903.

Bessie Kay

Witnesses To Mark:
{ Frank Zimmermann
L.L. Longfellow

Subscribed and sworn to before me this 22nd day of March, 1905.

T.W. Flynn
Notary Public.

NC 449. H.G.H.

DEPARTMENT OF THE INTERIOR,
COMMISSIONER TO THE FIVE CIVILIZED TRIBES.

In the matter of the application for the enrollment of Sam Gooden, deceased, as a citizen by blood of the Creek Nation.

Applications for Enrollment of Creek Newborn
Act of 1905   Volume VI

STATEMENT AND ORDER.

The record in this case shows that on March 24, 1905, application was made, in affidavit form, for the enrollment of Sam Gooden, deceased, as a citizen by blood of the Creek Nation, under the provisions of the Act of Congress approved March 3, 1905. Further affidavit was filed in this case August 19, 1905.

It appears from the evidence filed in this matter that said Sam Gooden, deceased, was born March 22, 1903, or March 30, 1903, and died on said latter date.

The Act of Congress approved March 3, 1905, (33 Stats., 1048), in part, provides: "That the Commission to the Five Civilized Tribes is authorized for sixty days after the date of the approval of this act to receive and consider applications for enrollment, of children, born subsequent to May twenty-fifth, nineteen hundred and one, and prior to March fourth, nineteen hundred and five, and living on said latter date, to citizens of the Creek tribe of Indians whose enrollment has been approved by the Secretary of the Interior prior to the approval of this act; and to enroll and make allotments to such children."

It is, therefore, ordered that the application for the enrollment of Sam Gooden, deceased; as a citizen by blood of the Creek Nation be, and the same is, hereby dismissed.

Tams Bixby Commissioner.

Muskogee, Indian Territory.
DEC 12 1906

Cr NC-449

Muskogee, Indian Territory, June 10, 1905.

Dora Gooden,
    Edna, Indian Territory.

Dear Madam:

In the matter of the application for the enrollment of your minor child, Sam Gooden, as a citizen of the Creek Nation, you are advised that the Commission requires your affidavit relative to its death.

There is herewith enclosed a blank form of death affidavit, and you are requested to fill out and execute before an officer authorized to administer oaths, and return it to the Commission in the enclosed envelope.

Respectfully,

Chairman.

1 D A

Applications for Enrollment of Creek Newborn
Act of 1905   Volume VI

NC 449

Muskogee, Indian Territory, December 19, 1906.

Dora Gooden,
    Care of Henderson Gooden,
        Edna, Indian Territory.

Dear Madam:

    There is herewith inclosed a copy of the statement and order dismissing the matter of the application for the enrollment of your minor child Sam Gooden, deceased, as a citizen by blood of the Creek Nation.

        Respectfully,

Enc.
JCL.-12-20   Commissioner.

NC 450

DEPARTMENT OF THE INTERIOR,
COMMISSIONER TO THE FIVE CIVILIZED TRIBES.
Muskogee, Indian Territory, January 3, 1906.

    In the matter of the application for the enrollment of Edward Salt as a citizen by blood of the Creek Nation.

    MILLOCHE being duly sworn by Jesse McDermott, a Notary Public, testifies as follows through official interpreter, Mrs. Lona Merrick:

BY THE COMMISSIONER:

Q What is your name? A Milloche.
Q What's the name of your father? A Okchun Fixico.
Q What's the name of your mother? A Youfker.
Q What Creek Indian town do you belong to? A Weogufky.
Q How old are you? A About thirty-two or three.
Q What's your postoffice address? A Hanna.

    Witness is identified as Milloche opposite Creek Indian roll No. 8156.

Q Are you married? A Yes sir.
Q What the name of your wife? A Annie.

Applications for Enrollment of Creek Newborn
Act of 1905   Volume VI

Q Annie what? A Annie Crow or Osahwa.
Q What is the name of her father? A I dont[sic] know.
Q What is the name of her mother? A I dont[sic] know.
Q What is the name of your oldest child? A Jonah.
Q What is the name of the next one? A Turner.
Q What is the name of the next one? A Katie.
Q What is the name of the next one? A Edward.
Q Was Turner ever known by the name of Freeman? A Yes sir.

Said Annie is identified under the name of Annie Crowels opposite Creek Indian roll No. 8152 as the wife of the witness.

Q Is your child Edward living? A Yes sir.
Q Under what name do you desire to have Edward enrolled? A Under the name of Edward Salt.
Q How does it come that you want to give the name of the child as Salt when you are enrolled as Milloche and your wife enrolled with three of her oldest children under the name of Crowels? A My father's name Okchun means Salt; no matter how I am enrolled by correct name should be Milloche Salt and my wife's name should be Anna Salt and I desire to have my child enrolled under the name of Edward Salt.
Q Then this affidavit, the last one furnished by your wife, and the affidavit of Tom Tiger and John Bruner, two disinterested witnesses state the correct name of the child do they, Edward Salt? A Yes sir.

Witness s very carefully instructed that in the event he changes his postoffice address or the address of said child that he should inform this office in order that he may be promptly notified should this child be placed on the roll.

WITNESS EXCUSED.

Lona Merrick, being first duly sworn, states that as stenographer to the Commissioner to the Five Civilized Tribes she reported the proceedings had in the above entitled cause on January 3, 1907, and that the above and foregoing is a true and correct transcript of her stenographic notes as taken in said cause on said date.

Lona Merrick

Subscribed and sworn to before me January 4, 1907.

Edward Merrick
Notary Public.

Applications for Enrollment of Creek Newborn
Act of 1905 Volume VI

N.C. 450.

DEPARTMENT OF THE INTERIOR,
COMMISSIONER TO THE FIVE CIVILIZED TRIBES.
Dustin, Indian Territory, December 18, 1906.

In the matter of the application for the enrollment of Edward (Saul) Salt as a citizen by blood of the Creek Nation.

MELLOCHE[sic], being duly sworn, testified as follows through Jesse McDermott, official interpreter:

BY THE COMMISSIONER:

Q What is your name? A Melehcha is my name. (The witness is identified as Melloche).
Q What is your age? A About 33.
Q What is your postoffice address? A Hanna.
Q Are you a Creek citizen? A Yes.
Q To which Creek Indian Town do you belong? A Weogufkey[sic]
Q Have you selected your allotment of land? A Yes.
Q Did you file on the land yourself? A No, the Commission alloted[sic] me.
Q Do you know where your allotment is located? A South of here.
Q South of Dustin? A Yes.
Q What is the name of your father? A Okchun Fixeco[sic].
   (The name Okchun is a Creek word meaning Salt)
Q What is the name of your mother? A Youpka.
Q Do you know under what name you are enrolled? A No, but I always thought that my name was on the roll as Melehcha Salt. I am known by that name in the neighborhood where I live.
Q Are you married? A Yes.
Q What is the name of your wife? A Annie Salt; she may be on the roll as Annie Crow or Annie Osahwa.
Q Has she a child by you? A Yes.
Q What is the name of that child? A Edward Salt is what we call him.
Q When was he born? A Last of September was two years ago.
Q He was two year[sic] old last day of last September was he? A Yes.
Q Is Edward living? A Yes. (The child is present).
Q Do you desire to have your child enrolled under the name Edward Salt? A Yes.

There is on file at the office of the Commissioner to the Five Civilized Tribes, an affidavit in the matter of an application for the enrollment of Edward Saul, in which it is stated that your name is Melicha Saul.
Q Is that your right name? A I think I said Melehcha Salt but I guess the man who made out the affidavit misunderstood me as it is very difficult for me, as an Indian, to speak an English work plain.

---oooOOOooo---

Applications for Enrollment of Creek Newborn
Act of 1905   Volume VI

I, Jesse McDermott, on oath state that the above and foregoing is a full and true transcript of my notes as taken in said cause on said date.

Jesse McDermott

Subscribed and sworn to before me this 27" day of December, 1906.

My Commission expires
29" day of June, 1908.

Wm F A Gierke
Notary Public.

AFFIDAVIT OF TWO DISINTERESTED WITNESSES.

United States of America, (
Western Judicial District, (ss
Indian Territory. (

We, the undersigned, on oath state that we are personally acquainted with Annie (Salt) the wife of Melloche (Salt), that there was born to her a male child on or about the 30 day of September, 1904, that said child has been named Edward Salt was living March 4, 1905.
We further state that we have no interest in this case.

Tom Tiger

John Bruner

Subscribed and sworn to before me this 15" day of December, 1906.

My Commission expires
July 25", 1907.

J McDermott
Notary Public.

BIRTH AFFIDAVIT.

DEPARTMENT OF THE INTERIOR.
COMMISSION TO THE FIVE CIVILIZED TRIBES.

IN RE APPLICATION FOR ENROLLMENT, as a citizen of the Creek Nation, of Edward Saul, born on the 30 day of September, 1904

Name of Father: Melicha Saul   a citizen of the   Creek   Nation.
Name of Mother: Annie Saul   a citizen of the   Creek   Nation.

Postoffice   Hanna, Ind. Ter.

Applications for Enrollment of Creek Newborn
Act of 1905 Volume VI

AFFIDAVIT OF MOTHER.

UNITED STATES OF AMERICA, Indian Territory,
Western DISTRICT.

I, Annie Saul , on oath state that I am about 25 years of age and a citizen by blood , of the Creek Nation; that I am the lawful wife of Melicha Saul , who is a citizen, by blood of the Creek Nation; that a male child was born to me on 30 day of September , 1904 , that said child has been named Edward Saul , and was living March 4, 1905. That no one attended on me as midwife or physician at the birth of the child.

                                              her
Witnesses To Mark: Annie x Saul
   Alex Posey   mark
   DC Skaggs

Subscribed and sworn to before me this 23 day of March , 1905.

                                              Drennan C Skaggs
                                              Notary Public.

BIRTH AFFIDAVIT.

DEPARTMENT OF THE INTERIOR.
COMMISSION TO THE FIVE CIVILIZED TRIBES.

IN RE APPLICATION FOR ENROLLMENT, as a citizen of the Creek Nation, of Edward Salt , born on the 30 day of Sept , 1904

Name of Father: Melloche (Salt)   a citizen of the   Creek   Nation.
    Weogufky
Name of Mother: Annie   "   a citizen of the   Creek   Nation.
    Tuckabatchee
                             Postoffice   Hanna, I.T.

AFFIDAVIT OF MOTHER.

UNITED STATES OF AMERICA, Indian Territory,
Western DISTRICT.

I, Annie (Salt) , on oath state that I am about 26 years of age and a citizen by blood , of the Creek Nation; that I am the lawful wife of Melloche , who is a citizen, by blood of the Creek Nation; that a male child was born to me on 30 day of September , 1904 , that said child has been named Edward Salt , and was living March 4, 1905.

                                              her
                                        Annie x (Salt)
                                           mark

Applications for Enrollment of Creek Newborn
Act of 1905 Volume VI

Witnesses To Mark:
- J McDermott
- JB Myers

Subscribed and sworn to before me this 14 day of December, 1906.

My Commission   J McDermott
Expires July 25' 1907   Notary Public.

(The "Saul" Birth Affidavit, above, was given again.)

JWH

N C 450

Muskogee, Indian Territory, March 1, 1907.

Annie Salt,
    c/o Melicha Salt,
        Hanna, Indian Territory.

Dear Madam :--

You are hereby advised that on February 15, 1907, the Secretary of the Interior approved the enrollment of your minor child, Edward Salt, as a citizen by blood of the Creek Nation, and that the name of said child appears upon the roll of New Born citizens by blood of the Creek Nation, enrolled under the Act of Congress approved March 3, 1905, as number 1147.

This child is now entitled to allotment and application therefor should be made without delay at the Creek Land Office, Muskogee, Indian Territory.

Respectfully,

Commissioner.

N.C. 451.

DEPARTMENT OF THE INTERIOR,
COMMISSIONER TO THE FIVE CIVILIZED TRIBES.
Okemah, Indian Territory, September 22, 1906.

In the matter of the application for the enrollment of Ida Field as a citizen by blood of the Creek Nation.

Applications for Enrollment of Creek Newborn
Act of 1905 Volume VI

WILLIAM FIELD, being duly sworn, testified as follows (through Jesse McDermott official interpreter):

BY COMMISSIONER:

Q What is your name? A William Field.
Q What is your age? A About twenty three
Q What is your postoffice address? A Okemah.
Q Are you a Creek citizen? A Yes.
Q To which Creek Indian town do you belong? A Thlopthlocco.
Q Have you a child named Ida? A I have.
Q When was Ida born? A She was born the 26th day of the Big Winder month. She will be three years old next Big Winter month.

Big Winter month is the Creek name for the month of December.

Q Are you positive that your child will be tree[sic] years old next December? A Yes, I am.
Q She is living is she? A Yes.

The mother and midwife in their affidavit signed before John H. Phillips on March 20, 1905, stated that Ida was born December 26, 1904, and that would make the child two years old next December.

Q Is the date of Ida's birth given in their affidavits correct? A No, it could not be because Ida is now going on three years.
Q Have you any record of her birth? A No, I have not.
Q What is the name of Ida's mother? A Louina.
Q What is the name of Louina's mother? A Soma.
Q What is the name of her father? A Sam Scott.
Q Have you the deeds to Louina's allotment? A No, her father has them. He lives upon Deep Fork.

CHOTKEY FOSTER, being duly sworn, testified as follows (through Jesse McDermott official interpreter):

BY COMMISSIONER:

Q What is your name? A Chotkey Foster.
Q What is your age? A About 29.
Q What is your postoffice address? A Okemah.
Q Are you a Creek citizen? A Yes.
Q Do you know William and Louina Field? A Yes.
Q Do you know a child of theirs named Ida? A Yes.
Q Do you know when she was born? A Ida was born about three mont[sic] before my child Lola was born.

Applications for Enrollment of Creek Newborn
Act of 1905   Volume VI

Q When was your child born? A Here is the record of her birth.

The witness presents a bundle of papers containing a list of notations among which appears the following in Creek writing "Lola was born March 10, 1904."

Q Are you positive that Ida was born before your child Lola? A Yes, we all live near neighbors.

      MARY AUSTIN, being duly sworn, testified as follows (through Jesse McDermott official interpreter):

Q What is your name? A Mary Austin.
Q What is your age? A About 32 I am told.
Q What is your postoffice address? A That place they call Okemah.
Q Are you a Creek citizen? A Yes.
Q Do you know William and Louina Field? A Yes, William is my broth[sic]
Q Do you know a child of theirs named Ida? A Yes, I attended on Louina when Ida was born.
Q Do you know when that was? A It was the next day after Christmas but I cannot say what year.
Q How old will Ida be next Christmas? A Let us see----- she will b[sic] three years old if she lives.
Q Are you positive that she will be three years old next Christmas? A Yes, I am.

      There is an affidavit on file at the Office of the Commissioner to the Five Civilized Tribes, signed by you on March 20, 1905, in which you state that Ida was born December 28, 1904; that would make the child two years old the coming December.

Q Is that the correct date of her birth? A No, that is incorrect.
Q Is Ida living? A Yes, there she is. (The child is present)

      Louina Field, being duly sworn testified as follows (through Jesse McDermott official interpreter)

By Commissioner:

Q What is your name? Louina Field.
Q What is your age? A About twenty.
Q What is your postoffice address? A Okemah.
Q Are you a Creek citizen? A Yes.

Q Have you filed on your land? A Yes, my father filed for me.
Q Have you the deeds to your allotment? A No, my father has them.
Q To which Creek Indian Town do you belong? A Thlopthlocco.
Q What is your mother's name? A Soma.
Q What is your father's name? Sam Scott.
Q Have you a child named Ida? A I have, there she is.

Applications for Enrollment of Creek Newborn
Act of 1905   Volume VI

Q When was Ida born? A In December.
Q What year? A I don't know that, because I am a full blood Indian and don't [sic] a thing about dates.
Q How old will she be at her next birthday? A She will be three.

There is an affidavit on file at the office of the Commissioner to the Five Civilized Tribes signed by you on March 20, 1905, in which you state that Ida was born December 26, 1904; and that would make her two years old December.

Q Is the date of her birth as given in that affidavit correct? A No, I guess not. John Phillips fixed up the papers after we had told him the age of the child and we signed them thinking that they were correct.
Q Were you lawfully married to William when you had this child by him? A Yes, we had a marriage license when we married. We sent them to Wewoka, because we were told to do so, but we never did get it back. I guess it is down there.
Q Ida is living is she? A Yes.

I, Jesse McDermott, on oath state that the above and foregoing is a full and true transcript of my notes as taken in said cause on said date.

Jesse McDermott

Subscribed and sworn to before me this 13th day of November, 1906.

My Commission expires   Dan Upten
        Jan 31-1909   Notary Public.

BIRTH AFFIDAVIT.

DEPARTMENT OF THE INTERIOR.
COMMISSION TO THE FIVE CIVILIZED TRIBES.

IN RE APPLICATION FOR ENROLLMENT, as a citizen of the Creek Nation, of Ida Field, born on the 26" day of Dec , 1903

Name of Father: William Field   a citizen of the   Creek   Nation.
Name of Mother: Louina Field (nee Scott)   a citizen of the   Creek   Nation.

Postoffice   Okemah I.T.

Applications for Enrollment of Creek Newborn
Act of 1905 Volume VI

AFFIDAVIT OF MOTHER.

UNITED STATES OF AMERICA, Indian Territory, }
Western   DISTRICT.

I, Louina Field, on oath state that I am 20 years of age and a citizen by blood, of the Creek Nation; that I am the lawful wife of William Field, who is a citizen, by blood of the Creek Nation; that a female child was born to me on 26" day of December, 1903, that said child has been named Ida Field, and was living March 4, 1905. and is now living

         her
        Louina x Field
Witnesses To Mark: mark
{ Jesse McDermott
{ J.E. Grey

Subscribed and sworn to before me this 25" day of Sept, 1906.

My Com   J McDermott
Expires July 20" 1907   Notary Public.

AFFIDAVIT OF ATTENDING PHYSICIAN OR MID-WIFE.

UNITED STATES OF AMERICA, Indian Territory, }
Western   DISTRICT.

I, Mary Austin, a midwife, on oath state that I attended on Mrs. Louina Field, wife of William Field on the 26" day of December, 1903; that there was born to her on said date a female child; that said child was living March 4, 1905, and is said to have been named Ida Field

         her
        Mary x Austin
Witnesses To Mark: mark
{ Jesse McDermott
{ J E. Grey

Subscribed and sworn to before me this 25" day of Sept, 1906.

My Com   J McDermott
Expires July 20" 1907   Notary Public.

BIRTH AFFIDAVIT.

DEPARTMENT OF THE INTERIOR.
COMMISSION TO THE FIVE CIVILIZED TRIBES.

IN RE APPLICATION FOR ENROLLMENT, as a citizen of the Creek Nation, of Ida Field, born on the 26 day of Dec, 1903

Applications for Enrollment of Creek Newborn
Act of 1905 Volume VI

Name of Father: William Field a citizen of the Creek Nation.
Thlopthlocco
Name of Mother: Louina Field (nee Scott) a citizen of the Creek Nation.
Thlopthlocco

                                       Postoffice   Okemah I.T.

AFFIDAVIT OF MOTHER.

UNITED STATES OF AMERICA, Indian Territory,
    Western   DISTRICT.

     I, William Field , on oath state that I am 30 years of age and a citizen by blood, of the Creek Nation; that I am the lawful ~~wife~~ husband of Louina Field (nee Scott), who is a citizen, by blood of the Creek Nation; that a female child was born to ~~me~~ her on 26th day of December, 1903, that said child has been named Ida Field, and was living March 4, 1905. and is now living his
                                          William x Field
                                                  mark

Witnesses To Mark:
   { Jesse McDermott
   { *(Name Illegible)*

     Subscribed and sworn to before me this 22 day of September, 1906.

     My Commission   J McDermott
     Expires July 20" 1907   Notary Public.

BIRTH AFFIDAVIT.
DEPARTMENT OF THE INTERIOR.
COMMISSION TO THE FIVE CIVILIZED TRIBES.

     IN RE APPLICATION FOR ENROLLMENT, as a citizen of the Creek Nation, of Ida Field, born on the 26th day of December, 1904

Name of Father: William Field   a citizen of the Creek Nation.
Name of Mother: Louina Field   a citizen of the Creek Nation.

                                 Postoffice   Fentress, I.T.

Applications for Enrollment of Creek Newborn
Act of 1905   Volume VI

AFFIDAVIT OF MOTHER.

UNITED STATES OF AMERICA, Indian Territory, ⎱
Western Judicial   DISTRICT. ⎰

I, Louina Field, on oath state that I am 19 years of age and a citizen by Blood, of the Muskokee[sic] or Creek Nation; that I am the lawful wife of William Field, who is a citizen, by Blood of the Muskokee[sic] or Creek Nation; that a Female child was born to me on 26th day of December, 1904, that said child has been named Ida Field, and was living March 4, 1905.

                                                               her
                                             Louina x Field

Witnesses To Mark: mark
  { M M Morton
    Jno. H. Phillips

Subscribed and sworn to before me this 20th day of March, 1905.

                                          John H. Phillips
My Commission Expires Sept. 6th 1906.   Notary Public.

AFFIDAVIT OF ATTENDING PHYSICIAN OR MID-WIFE.

UNITED STATES OF AMERICA, Indian Territory, ⎱
Western Judicial   DISTRICT. ⎰

I, Mary Austin, a Mid-Wife, on oath state that I attended on Mrs. Louina Field, wife of William Field on the 26th day of December, 1904; that there was born to her on said date a Female child; that said child was living March 4, 1905, and is said to have been named Ida Field
                                           her
                                       Mary x Austin

Witnesses To Mark: mark
  { M M Morton
    Jno. H. Phillips

Subscribed and sworn to before me this 20th day of March, 1905.

                                          John H. Phillips
My Commission Expires Sept. 6th 1906.   Notary Public.

(The above Birth Affidavit was given again.)

Applications for Enrollment of Creek Newborn
Act of 1905   Volume VI

Cr NC-451

Muskogee, Indian Territory, June 10, 1905.

Louina Field,
    Fentress, Indian Territory.

Dear Madam:

    In the matter of the application for the enrollment of your minor child, Ida Field, as a citizen of the Creek Nation you are advised that the Commission cannot identify you on its rolls of Creek Citizens.

    You are requested to furnish the Commission with your maiden name, the names of your parents, the Creek Indian Town to which you claim to belong, your roll number as same appears on your deeds to land in the Creek Nation, and any other information which will help to identify you as a citizen of said Nation.

Respectfully,

Chairman.

NC-451

Muskogee, Indian Territory, August 4, 1905.

Louina Field,
    c/o William Field,
        Fentress, Indian Territory.

Dear Madam:

    On March 24, 1905, you filed with this office application for the enrollment of your minor daughter Ida Field as a citizen by blood of the Creek Nation, from which application it appears that you are a citizen by blood of the Creek Nation.

    This office is unable to identify you upon the final roll of citizens by blood of said nation and you are, therefore, requested to immediately inform this office of the name under which you were finally enrolled, the names of your parents and other members of your family, the Creek town to which you belong and to state also your final roll number as the same appears upon your allotment certificate and deeds.

Respectfully,

Commissioner.

Applications for Enrollment of Creek Newborn
Act of 1905 Volume VI

JWH

N C 451

Muskogee, Indian Territory, March 1, 1907.

Louina Field,
    c/o William Field,
        Okemah, Indian Territory.

Dear Madam :--

    You are hereby advised that on February 15, 1907, the Secretary of the Interior approved the enrollment of your minor child, Ida Field, as a citizen by blood of the Creek Nation, and that the name of said child appears upon the roll of New Born citizens by blood of the Creek Nation, enrolled under the Act of Congress approved March 3, 1905, as number 1148.

    This child is now entitled to allotment, and application therefor should be made without delay at the Creek Land Office, Muskogee, Indian Territory.

        Respectfully,

                Commissioner.

REFER IN REPLY TO THE FOLLOWING:
NF-567

DEPARTMENT OF THE INTERIOR,
COMMISSIONER TO THE FIVE CIVILIZED TRIBES.

Muskogee, Indian Territory, September 15, 1905.

Lula T. Wright,
    Care of Walter C. Wright,
        Tulsa, Indian Territory.

Dear Madam:
    In the matter of the application for the enrollment of your minor children, Ynema B. and Ava E. Wright, as Creek Freedmen, you are advised that this office is unable to identify you on its rolls of Creek Freedmen.

    You are requested to write this Office at an early date, giving your maiden name, the names of your parents, the Creek Indian Town to which you belong, and, if possible, your name and roll number as same appear on your deeds to land in the Creek Nation.

        Respectfully,

           Wm O. Beall
                Acting Commissioner.

Applications for Enrollment of Creek Newborn
Act of 1905   Volume VI

NF-567

Muskogee, Indian Territory November 3, 1905.

Lula F[sic]. Wright,
    Care of John W. Oveestreet[sic],
        Tulsa, Indian Territory.

Dear Madam:

    In the matter of the application for the enrollment of your minor children, Ynema B. and Ava E. Wright, as Creek Freedmen, you are advised that this Office is unable to identify you on its final roll of Creek Freedmen.

    You are requested to write this Office at an early date, giving your maiden name, the names of your parents, the Creek Indian Town to which you belong, and, if possible, your name and roll number as same appear on your deeds to land in the Creek Nation. You are also requested to advise this Office as to whether you are enrolled as a Creek Freedman or as a citizen by blood of the Creek Nation.

        Respectfully,

        Commissioner.

C 452
NF-~~567~~

DEPARTMENT OF THE INTERIOR,
COMMISSIONER TO THE FIVE CIVILIZED TRIBES.

Muskogee, Indian Territory, December 8, 1905.

    In the matter of the application for the enrollment of Ynema B. and Ava E. Wright as citizens of the Creek Nation.

    Walter Clarence Wright, being duly sworn, testified as follows:

EXAMINATION BY THE COMMISSION:
Q What is your name? A Walter Clarence Wright.
Q How old are you? A 24.
Q What is your postoffice? A Bristow.
Q Are you the husband of Lula F[sic]. Wright? A Yes sir.
Q Are you the father of Ynema B. and Alva[sic] E. Wright? A Yes sir.
Q Is your wife a citizen by blood or a Freedman? A She is a citizen by blood.
Q Her name is Lula T. Wright' is it not? A Yes, Lula T. Wright.
Q Both of these children living? A Yes sir.
Q You know when they were born? A Ynema was born--

Applications for Enrollment of Creek Newborn
Act of 1905 Volume VI

Q How old is she? A She is three years, past.
Q In what month was she three years old? A She was three years old--let's see--
Q Was she born in July? A July 10.
Q 1902? A Yes sir.
Q Do you know when Ava E. was born? A Born--was born January.
Q What year? A 1904.
Q Is she living? A Yes sir.

Witness presents deed of Lula T. Self, Creek Roll No. 3029.

Q Is this deed to your wife's allotment? A Yes sir.
Q Her maiden name, then, was Lula T. Self? A Yes sir.

INDIAN TERRITORY, Western District.
    I, J. Y. Miller, a stenographer to the Commission to the Five Civilized Tribes, do hereby certify that the above and foregoing is a true and complete translation of my notes as same appear in my stenographic report of this case.
                        JY Miller
Sworn to and subscribed before me
this the 8th day of December, 1905.   J McDermott
                                         Notary Public.

DEPARTMENT OF THE INTERIOR

COMMISSION TO THE FIVE CIVILIZED TRIBES.

    In re application for enrollment, as a citizen of the creek[sic] Nation of Ynema B Wright born on the 10th day of July, 1902
                                          no
name of the Father   Walter C Wright   a ^ citizen of the Creek Nation.
name of the Mother   Lula T Wright   a citizen of the Creek Nation.
                                Postoffice Tulsa I.T.

Affidavit of Mother

United States of America Indian Territory
    Western   District

    I Lula T. Wright on oath state that I am - 25 - years of age and a citizen by Birth of the Creek Nation that I am the lawful wife of Walter C Wright who is a non citizen by (blank) of the Creek Nation; that a female   child was born to me on 10th day of July   1902 that said child has been named Ynema B Wright , and was living March 4, 1905
                                        Lula T Wright
Must be two : John W Overstreet
  witnesses   : C C *(Illegible)*

Applications for Enrollment of Creek Newborn
Act of 1905 Volume VI

Subscribed and sworn to before me this 6th day of April 1905.

                                                John W Overstreet
                                                Notary Public.

Affidavit of attending phician[sic] or Mid wife,

United States of America Indian Territory
    Western   District

        I Martha A Self a midwife on oath state that I attendid[sic] on Mrs. Lula T Wright wife of Walter C Wright on the 10th day of July , 1902 ; that there was born to her on said date a female child; that said child was living march[sic] 4, 1905 and is said to have been named Ynema B Wright

                                                Martha A Self

Witness to Mark : John W Overstreet
  must be two   : C C *(Illegible)*
  witnesses

Subscribed and sworn to before me this 6th day of April 1905.

                                                John W Overstreet
                                                Notary Public.

DEPARTMENT OF THE INTERIOR

COMMISSION TO THE FIVE CIVILIZED TRIBES.

        In re application for enrollment, as a citizen of the creek[sic] Nation of Ava E Wright born on the 15th day of January, 1904

                                      no
name of the Father Walter C Wright   a ^ citizen of the Creek Nation.
name of the Mother Lula T Wright   a citizen of the Creek Nation.

                                Postoffice Tulsa I.T.

                                  Affidavit of Mother

United States of America Indian Territory
    Western   District

        I Lula T. Wright on oath state that I am - 25 - years of age and a citizen by Birth of the Creek Nation that I am the lawful wife of Walter C Wright who is a non citizen ~~by~~ *(blank)* of the Creek Nation; that a female child was born to me on 15th day of January 1904 that said child has been named Ava E Wright , and was living March 4, 1905

Applications for Enrollment of Creek Newborn
Act of 1905   Volume VI

                                              Lula T Wright

Must be two : John W Overstreet
witnesses   : C C *(Illegible)*

Subscribed and sworn to before me this 6th day of April   1905.

                                                   John W Overstreet
                                                 Notary Public.

                Affidavit of attending phician[sic] or Mid wife,

United States of America Indian Territory
     Western   District

      I Martha A Self a midwife on oath state that I attendid[sic] on Mrs. Lula T Wright wife of Walter C Wright on the 15th day of January , 1904 ; that there was born to her on said date a female child; that said child was living march[sic] 4, 1905 and is said to have been named Ava E Wright

                                              Martha A Self

Witness to Mark :   John W Overstreet
  must be two   :   C C *(Illegible)*
  witnesses

Subscribed and sworn to before me this 6th day of April   1905.

                                                 John W Overstreet
                                                 Notary Public.

                    453
W. W. WINSTON
   MERCHANT
 HANNA, OKLAHOMA

                                      HANNA, OKLAHOMA   3/12 - 15

The U P Indian Superintendent
    Muskogee Okla -
        My Dear Sir:
                in[sic] reply to your inquiry of the 8th *(illegible)* as to Peggie Harper daughter Sarah Gown # 457

You will find that by looking up Roll there is two Peggie Harpers not related in any way. Peggie Harper mother of Sarah Gown #457 - Roll No is 8136. Peggie Harper mother of Hiawatha Gains Roll No 8130 which I made proof of heir[sic] info for W W Winston *(illegible)* for her child Hiawatha Gains only had one child as stated in proof herewith shown

                                         Jack Smith

Applications for Enrollment of Creek Newborn
Act of 1905   Volume VI

BIRTH AFFIDAVIT.

DEPARTMENT OF THE INTERIOR.
COMMISSION TO THE FIVE CIVILIZED TRIBES.

IN RE APPLICATION FOR ENROLLMENT, as a citizen of the Creek Nation, of Sarah Gown, born on the 23 day of March, 1902

Name of Father: Bud Gown   a citizen of the United States Nation.
Name of Mother: Peggie Harper   a citizen of the   Creek   Nation.

Postoffice   Carson Ind. Ter.

AFFIDAVIT OF MOTHER.

UNITED STATES OF AMERICA, Indian Territory, ⎫
     Western   DISTRICT.   ⎬

I, Peggie Harper, on oath state that I am over 20 years of age and a citizen by blood, of the Creek Nation; that I am not the lawful wife of Bud Gown, who is a citizen, ~~by~~ *(blank)* of the United States Nation; that a female child was born to me on 23 day of March, 1902, that said child has been named Sarah Gown, and was living March 4, 1905.

Peggie Harper

Witnesses To Mark:
{

Subscribed and sworn to before me this 21 day of March, 1905.

Drennan C Skaggs
Notary Public.

AFFIDAVIT OF ATTENDING PHYSICIAN OR MID-WIFE.

UNITED STATES OF AMERICA, Indian Territory, ⎫
     Western   DISTRICT.   ⎬

I, Fayeche Yahola, a midwife, on oath state that I attended on Mrs. Peggie Harper, ~~wife of~~ *(blank)* on the 23 day of March, 1902; that there was born to her on said date a female child; that said child was living March 4, 1905, and is said to have been named Sarah Gown
                                           her
                              Fayeche x Yahola
                                          mark

Applications for Enrollment of Creek Newborn
Act of 1905   Volume VI

Witnesses To Mark:
- Alex Posey
- DC Skaggs

Subscribed and sworn to before me this 23 day of March, 1905.

Drennan C Skaggs
Notary Public.

HGH

REFER IN REPLY TO THE FOLLOWING:

NC-454.

DEPARTMENT OF THE INTERIOR,
COMMISSIONER TO THE FIVE CIVILIZED TRIBES.

Muskogee, Indian Territory, August 4, 1905.

Myrtle Harris,
   c /o Walter Harris,
      Jennings, Oklahoma.

Dear Madam:

    In the matter of the application for the enrollment of your minor children Lulu May Harris and Theodore Quincy Harris as citizens by blood of the Creek Nation, it will be necessary, before the rights of said children as citizens of the Creek Nation can be finally determined, for you to furnish this office with the original or a certified copy of the marriage license and certificate between yourself and Walter Harris, the father of said children.

Respectfully,

Tams Bixby
Commissioner.

Muskogee, Indian Territory, August 14, 1905.

Walter Harris,
   Jennings, Oklahoma.

Dear Sir:

    Receipt is acknowledged of your letter of August 9, 1905 enclosing a copy of your marriage license and certificate.

Applications for Enrollment of Creek Newborn
Act of 1905   Volume VI

You ask if this is all that will be needed to complete the enrollment of your child and also request information as to when you will be able to file for this child.

In reply you are advised that said marriage license has been filed in the matter of the application for the enrollment of said child and that no further proof will be needed in said case.

When the enrollment of this child has been finally approved by the Secretary of the Interior you will be given an opportunity to file for it.

    Respectfully,

    Acting Commissioner.

Territory of Oklahoma,
    SS.
Pawnee County,

Personally appeared before me, G S Van Eman, a Notary Public in and for said County and Territory, Annie Gross, who being of legal age and by me first duly sworn, on her oath says; That she was present and acted as Mid-wife at the birth of Luly[sic] May Harris, on Jan the 23rd 1903 and that said Lulu May Harris, is the daughter of Walter Harris and Myrtle Harris his wife and that the said Walter Harris is a Creek Citizen.

    Annie Gross

Subscribed and sworn to before me this 21st day of March 1905.

    G.S. Van Eman
My Com expires Jan 22 1907   Notary Public.

BIRTH AFFIDAVIT.

DEPARTMENT OF THE INTERIOR.
COMMISSION TO THE FIVE CIVILIZED TRIBES.

IN RE APPLICATION FOR ENROLLMENT, as a citizen of the Creek Nation, of Lulu May Harris, born on the 23rd day of January, 1903

Name of Father:	Walter Harris	a citizen of the Creek	Nation.
Name of Mother:	Myrtle Harris	a citizen of the *(blank)*	Nation.

    Postoffice   Jennings, Pawnee County, Oklahoma Ter.

Applications for Enrollment of Creek Newborn
Act of 1905   Volume VI

AFFIDAVIT OF MOTHER.

UNITED STATES OF AMERICA, ~~Indian~~ Territory, Oklahoma
Pawnee County, ~~DISTRICT.~~

I, Myrtle Harris, on oath state that I am (20) Twenty years of age and a citizen by marriage, of the Creek Nation; that I am the lawful wife of Walter Harris, who is a citizen, by birth of the Creek Nation; that a female child was born to me on the 23rd day of January, 1903, that said child has been named Lulu May Harris, and was living March 4, 1905.

Myrtle Harris

Witnesses To Mark:

Subscribed and sworn to before me this 29th day of March, 1905.

G.S. Van Eman
Notary Public.

My Com expires Jan 22nd 1907.

AFFIDAVIT OF ATTENDING PHYSICIAN OR MID-WIFE.

UNITED STATES OF AMERICA, ~~Indian~~ Territory, Oklahoma
Pawnee County, ~~DISTRICT.~~

I, Annie Gross, a midwife, on oath state that I attended on Mrs Myrtle Harris, wife of Walter Harris on the 23rd day of January, 1903; that there was born to her on said date a female child; that said child was living March 4, 1905, and is said to have been named Lulu May Harris

Annie Gross
mid wife

Witnesses To Mark:

Subscribed and sworn to before me this 29th day of March, 1905.

G.S. Van Eman
Notary Public.

My Com expires Jan 22nd 1907.

Applications for Enrollment of Creek Newborn
Act of 1905 Volume VI

CERTIFICATE OF TRUE COPY.

United States of America, ⎫
Indian Territory, ⎬ ss.
Western District. ⎭

I, *R. P. HARRISON*, Clerk of the United States Court in the Western District, Indian Territory, do hereby certify that the instrument hereto attached is a full, true and correct copy of a Marriage License *as the same appears from the records of my office.*

WITNESS my hand and seal of said Court at Muskogee *in said Territory, this* 9" *day of* August *A. D. 190*5

By John Harlan
Deputy Clerk

R. P. Harrison
Clerk and Ex-Officio Recorder.

Book M page 142

❋ MARRIAGE LICENSE ❋

UNITED STATES OF AMERICA ⎫
Indian Territory ⎬ ss.   No. 685
Northern ~~Western~~ District ⎭

To Any Person Authorized by Law to Solemnize Marriage---Greeting:

You are *Hereby* *C*ommanded to Solemnize the Rite and Publish the Banns of Matrimony between Mr. Walter Harris of Jennings Okla. ~~in the Indian~~ Territory, aged 21 years and *M*iss Myrtle Gross of Bristow in the Indian Territory aged 18 years according to law, and do you officially sign and return this license to the parties therein named.

(Seal)

WITNESS my hand and official seal ~~at Muskogee Indian Territory~~ this 15 day of Feby A.D. 1902

Chas. A. Davidson
Clerk of the U S Court.

By Wm R. Shackleford Deputy.

Applications for Enrollment of Creek Newborn
Act of 1905 Volume VI

| ?~ ?~ | CERTIFICATE OF MARRIAGE | ~? ~? |

UNITED STATES OF AMERICA ⎫
    Indian Territory   ⎬ ss.
Northern ~~Western~~ District ⎭

I, E.W. Sims Mayor of Bristow, I.T. , a ~~Minister of the Gospel~~, DO HEREBY CERTIFY that on the 16 day of Feby A. D. 1902 did duly and according to law as commanded in the foregoing License, solemnize the Rite and Publish the Banns of Matrimony between the parties therein named.

WITNESS my hand this 17 day of Feby A. D. 1902

(Seal)

My credentials are recorded in the office of the Clerk of the United States Court, Indian Territory ~~Western~~ District Book   Page

                                          E.W. Sims   Mayor
                                          ~~A Minister of the Gospel~~

Note This license and certificate of marriage must be returned to the office of the Clerk of the United States court in the Western District Indian Territory from whence it was issued within sixty days from the date thereof of the party to whom the license was issued will be liable in the amount of the one hundred dollars ($100.00)

    Filed and duly recorded this 1" day of Mch, 1902.
        Book M   page 148   Chas. A. Davidson
                                            Clerk of the United States Court.

Territory of Oklahoma,
                         SS.
    Pawnee County.

Personally appeared before me, G S Van Eman, Notary Public in and for said County and Territory, J.Z. Nell, M. D. who being by me first duly sworn, on his oath says; That he is a regular practicing Physician and that he was the attending physician at the birth of a child on Jan 28th 1905, Walter Harris and Myrtle Harris his wife being the parents of the said child and the said Walter Harris being an Indian. The said affiant further testifies that said child has been named Theodore Quincy Harris, and that the said Walter Harris is a citizen of the Creek Nation and on the rolls as such. And deponent further saith not.

                                              J.O. Newell M.D.

Subscribed and sworn to before me this 21st day of March A D 1905.

                                              G.S. Van Eman
                                              Notary Public.

My Com Expires
Jan 22nd 1907.

Applications for Enrollment of Creek Newborn
Act of 1905 Volume VI

Territory of Oklahoma,
                   SS.
Pawnee County.

Personally appeared before me, G S Van Eman, Notary Public in and for said County and Territory, Annie Gross, who being of proper age and by me first duly sworn, on her oath says; That she was present and assisted at the birth of a child to Mrs Myrtle Harris on the 28th day of January 1905, said Mrs Myrtle Harris being the wife of Walter Harris, who is a Citizen of the Creek Nation (an Indian) and that said child has been named Theodore Quincy Harris.

                                                          Annie Gross

Subscribed and sworn to before me this 21st day of March 1905.

My Com Expires Jan   G. S. Van Eman
22nd 1907   Notary Public.

BIRTH AFFIDAVIT.

DEPARTMENT OF THE INTERIOR.
COMMISSION TO THE FIVE CIVILIZED TRIBES.

IN RE APPLICATION FOR ENROLLMENT, as a citizen of the Creek Nation, of Theodore Quincy Harris, born on the 28th day of January, 1905

Name of Father:	Walter Harris	a citizen of the	Creek	Nation.
Name of Mother:	Myrtle Harris	a citizen of the	*(blank)*	Nation.

                             Postoffice   Jennings, Pawnee Co, O. T.

AFFIDAVIT OF MOTHER.

Oklahoma
UNITED STATES OF AMERICA, ~~Indian~~ Territory,
Pawnee County,   ~~DISTRICT.~~

I, Myrtle Harris, on oath state that I am Twenty years of age and a citizen by marriage, of the Creek Nation; that I am the lawful wife of Walter Harris, who is a citizen, by birth of the Creek Nation; that a male child was born to me on the 28th day of January, 1905, that said child has been named Theodore Quincy Harris, and was living March 4, 1905.

                                              Myrtle Harris

Witnesses To Mark:

Applications for Enrollment of Creek Newborn
Act of 1905   Volume VI

Subscribed and sworn to before me this 29th day of March, 1905.

G.S. Van Eman
Notary Public.

My Com expires Jan 22nd 1907.

AFFIDAVIT OF ATTENDING PHYSICIAN OR MID-WIFE.

Oklahoma
UNITED STATES OF AMERICA, ~~Indian~~ Territory,
Pawnee County,   ~~DISTRICT.~~

I, J. Q. Newell, a physician, on oath state that I attended on Mrs. Myrtle Harris, wife of Walter Harris on the 28th day of January, 1905; that there was born to her on said date a male child; that said child was living March 4, 1905, and is said to have been named Theodore Quincy Harris

J Q Newell M.D.

Witnesses To Mark:
{

Subscribed and sworn to before me this 29th day of March, 1905.

G.S. Van Eman
Notary Public.

My Com expires Jan 22nd 1907.

NC-455.

Muskogee, Indian Territory, August 4, 1905.

William Stoddard,
    Morse, Indian Territory.

Dear Sir:

In the matter of the application for the enrollment of your minor son Joseph Stoddard, born July 1, 1903, as a citizen by blood of the Creek Nation it will be necessary for you to furnish this office with the affidavits of two disinterested persons relative to the birth of said child; said affidavits to set forth the name of said child, when he was born, the names of his parents and whether or not he was living on March 4, 1905.

Respectfully,

Commissioner.

Applications for Enrollment of Creek Newborn
Act of 1905 Volume VI

BIRTH AFFIDAVIT.

DEPARTMENT OF THE INTERIOR.
COMMISSION TO THE FIVE CIVILIZED TRIBES.

IN RE APPLICATION FOR ENROLLMENT, as a citizen of the Creek Nation, of Joseph Stoddard, born on the 1 day of July, 1903

Name of Father:	William Stoddard	a citizen of the	Creek	Nation.
Name of Mother:	Lousanna Stoddard	a citizen of the	Creek	Nation.

Postoffice   Morse I. T.

AFFIDAVIT OF ~~MOTHER~~. Acquaintance

UNITED STATES OF AMERICA, Indian Territory,
Western DISTRICT.

I, Ramsey Knight, on oath state that I am 26 years of age and a citizen by Blood, of the Creek Nation; that I am ~~the lawful wife of~~ Personally Acquaintaned[sic] with Lousanna Stoddard wife of William Stoddard, who is a citizen, by Blood of the Creek Nation; that a Male child was born to ~~me on~~ Her on or about 1 day of July, 1903, that said child has been named Joseph Stoddard, and was living March 4, 1905.

My Commission Expires March 5th, 1908.[sic]   Ramsey Knight

Witnesses To Mark:

Subscribed and sworn to before me this 8 day of August, 1905.

C. C. Eskridge
Notary Public.

Acquaintance
AFFIDAVIT OF ~~ATTENDING PHYSICIAN OR MID-WIFE~~.

UNITED STATES OF AMERICA, Indian Territory,
Western DISTRICT.

I, Palissa Key, a *(blank)*, on oath state that I ~~attended on Mrs.~~ am personally acquainted with Lousanna Stoddard, wife of William Stoddard on the *(blank)* day of *(blank)*, 1*(blank)*; that there was born to her ~~on said date~~ a Male child; on or about the 1 Day of July 1903 that said child was living March 4, 1905, and is said to have been named Joseph Stoddard.

Palissa Key

Witnesses To Mark:

Applications for Enrollment of Creek Newborn
Act of 1905   Volume VI

Subscribed and sworn to before me this 8 day of August, 1905.

C. C. Eskridge
Notary Public.

Sworn Statement

United States of America, Indian Territory }
Western District

We, William Stoddard and Lousanna Stoddard do solemnly swear that there was no one present on July 1st, 1903, when our child (Joseph Stoddard) was born except ourselves.

William Stoddard
Lousanna Stoddard

Subscribed and sworn to before me this 23rd day of March 1905

My Commission Expires March 5th, 1908.   C. C. Eskridge
Notary Public.

BIRTH AFFIDAVIT.

DEPARTMENT OF THE INTERIOR.
COMMISSION TO THE FIVE CIVILIZED TRIBES.

IN RE APPLICATION FOR ENROLLMENT, as a citizen of the Muskogee Nation, of Joseph Stoddard, born on the 1 day of July, 1903

Name of Father: William Stoddard   a citizen of the Muskogee   Nation.
Name of Mother: Lousanna Stoddard   a citizen of the Muskogee   Nation.

Postoffice   Morse I.T.

AFFIDAVIT OF MOTHER.

UNITED STATES OF AMERICA, Indian Territory, }
Western   DISTRICT.

I, Lousanna Stoddard, on oath state that I am 28 years of age and a citizen by Blood, of the Muskogee Nation; that I am the lawful wife of William Stoddard, who is a citizen, by Blood of the Muskogee Nation; that a Male child was born to me on 1 day of July, 1903, that said child has been named Joseph Stoddard, and was living March 4, 1905.

Applications for Enrollment of Creek Newborn
Act of 1905 Volume VI

Lousanna Stoddard

Witnesses To Mark:
{

Subscribed and sworn to before me this 23 day of March , 1905.

My Commission Expires March 5th, 1908.   C. C. Eskridge
Notary Public.

AFFIDAVIT OF ATTENDING PHYSICIAN OR MID-WIFE.

UNITED STATES OF AMERICA, Indian Territory,
    Western   DISTRICT.

I, William Stoddard , a *(blank)* , on oath state that I attended on Mrs. Lousanna Stoddard , wife of Myself on the 1 day of July , 1903 ; that there was born to her on said date a male child; that said child was living March 4, 1905, and is said to have been named Joseph Stoddard

William Stoddard

Witnesses To Mark:
{

Subscribed and sworn to before me this 23 day of March , 1905.

My Commission Expires March 5th, 1908.   C. C. Eskridge
Notary Public.

BIRTH AFFIDAVIT.

DEPARTMENT OF THE INTERIOR.
COMMISSION TO THE FIVE CIVILIZED TRIBES.

IN RE APPLICATION FOR ENROLLMENT, as a citizen of the Muskogee Nation, of Abraham Yahola , born on the 27 day of May , 1903

Name of Father:	Billy Yahola	a citizen of the Muskogee Nation.
Name of Mother:	Winey Yahola	a citizen of the Muskogee Nation.

Postoffice   Morse I.T.

Applications for Enrollment of Creek Newborn
Act of 1905   Volume VI

AFFIDAVIT OF MOTHER.

UNITED STATES OF AMERICA, Indian Territory,　}
　　Western　　　　　　DISTRICT.

    I, Winey Yahola, on oath state that I am 33 years of age and a citizen by Blood, of the Muskogee Nation; that I am the lawful wife of Billy Yahola, who is a citizen, by Blood of the Muskogee Nation; that a male child was born to me on 27 day of May, 1903, that said child has been named Abraham Yahola, and was living March 4, 1905.

                                                   Her
                                      Winey x Yahola

Witnesses To Mark: Mark
{ W. W. Green
  William Stoddard

    Subscribed and sworn to before me this 23 day of March, 1905.

My Commission Expires March 5th, 1908.   C. C. Eskridge
                                               Notary Public.

AFFIDAVIT OF ATTENDING PHYSICIAN OR MID-WIFE.

UNITED STATES OF AMERICA, Indian Territory,　}
　　Western　　　　　　DISTRICT.

    I, Lousanna Stoddard, a Mid-Wife, on oath state that I attended on Mrs. Winey Yahola, wife of Billy Yahola on the 27 day of May, 1903 ; that there was born to her on said date a Male child; that said child was living March 4, 1905, and is said to have been named Abraham Stoddard

                                        Lousanna Stoddard

Witnesses To Mark:

{

    Subscribed and sworn to before me this 23 day of March, 1905.

My Commission Expires March 5th, 1908.   C. C. Eskridge
                                               Notary Public.

Applications for Enrollment of Creek Newborn
Act of 1905 Volume VI

NC-457.

Muskogee, Indian Territory, August 4, 1905.

Dora Grayson,
   c/o Joe Grayson,
      Beggs, Indian Territory.
Dear Madam:

    In the matter of the application for the enrollment of your minor daughter Panzie May Grayson as a citizen by blood of the Creek Nation it will be necessary, before the rights of said child as such citizen can be finally determined, for you to furnish this office with the original or a certified copy of the marriage license and certificate showing the marriage between you and Joe Grayson, the father of said child.

                        Respectfully,

                        Commissioner.

CERTIFICATE OF TRUE COPY.

United States of America,
   Indian Territory,   } ss.
   Western District.   *I, R. P. HARRISON, Clerk of the United States Court in the Western District, Indian Territory, do hereby certify that the instrument hereto attached is a full, true and correct copy of* a Marriage License *as the same appears from the records of my office.*

          WITNESS my hand and seal of said Court at   Muskogee
          in said Territory, this 12" *day of* Aug   *A. D. 1*905

By   John Harlan   R. P. Harrison
        Deputy Clerk   *Clerk and Ex-Officio Recorder.*

                      Book N.   page 303.

❋   MARRIAGE LICENSE   ❋

UNITED STATES OF AMERICA
   Indian Territory   } ss.   No. 283
   Western District

To Any Person Authorized by Law to Solemnize Marriage---Greeting:

Applications for Enrollment of Creek Newborn
Act of 1905 Volume VI

You are Hereby Commanded to Solemnize the Rite and Publish the Banns of Matrimony between Mr. Joe Grayson of Beggs in the Indian Territory, aged 36 years and Miss Dora Fish of Beggs in the Indian Territory aged 21 years according to law, and do you officially sign and return this license to the parties therein named.

WITNESS my hand and official seal ~~at Muskogee Indian Territory~~ this 25 day of Oct A.D. 1902

(Seal)

R.P. Harrison
Clerk of the U S Court.

By A. Z. English Deputy.

| CERTIFICATE OF MARRIAGE |

UNITED STATES OF AMERICA
    Indian Territory } ss.
    Western District

I, W. R. Baker, a Minister of the Gospel, DO HEREBY CERTIFY that on the 25 day of Sept A. D. 1902 did duly and according to law as commanded in the foregoing License, solemnize the Rite and Publish the Banns of Matrimony between the parties therein named.

WITNESS my hand this 25 day of Sept A. D. 1902

My credentials are recorded in the office of the Clerk of the United States Court, Indian Territory Western District Book B Page 12

W. R. Baker
A Minister of the Gospel

Note This license and certificate of marriage must be returned to the office of the Clerk of the United States court in the Western District Indian Territory from whence it was issued within sixty days from the date thereof of the party to whom the license was issued will be liable in the amount of the one hundred dollars ($100.00).

Filed and duly recorded this 27 day of Oct. 1902
By R. A. *(Illegible)* Deputy

R.P. Harrison Clerk
Book N at Page 303.

BIRTH AFFIDAVIT.

DEPARTMENT OF THE INTERIOR.
COMMISSION TO THE FIVE CIVILIZED TRIBES.

IN RE APPLICATION FOR ENROLLMENT, as a citizen of the Creek Nation, of Panzie May Grayson, born on the 2nd day of April, 1904

Applications for Enrollment of Creek Newborn
Act of 1905 Volume VI

Name of Father: Joe Grayson   a citizen of the Creek Nation.
Name of Mother: Dora Grayson   a citizen of the Creek Nation.

Postoffice Beggs I.T.

AFFIDAVIT OF MOTHER.

UNITED STATES OF AMERICA, Indian Territory,
Western   DISTRICT.

 I, Dora Grayson , on oath state that I am 24 years of age and a citizen by marriage , of the Creek Nation; that I am the lawful wife of Joe Grayson , who is a citizen, by blood of the Creek Nation; that a female child was born to me on 2nd day of April , 1904 , that said child has been named Panzie May Grayson , and was living March 4, 1905.

             Dora Grayson

Witnesses To Mark:
{ Wm F A Gierke
{ James K. Kepley

 Subscribed and sworn to before me this 21st day of March , 1905.

             Wm FA Gierke
             Notary Public.

AFFIDAVIT OF ATTENDING PHYSICIAN OR MID-WIFE.

UNITED STATES OF AMERICA, Indian Territory,
Western   DISTRICT.

 I, Mary Nash , a mid wife , on oath state that I attended on Mrs. Dora Grayson , wife of Joe Grayson on the 2nd day of April , 1904 ; that there was born to her on said date a female child; that said child was living March 4, 1905, and is said to have been named Panzie May Grayson

             Mary Nash

Witnesses To Mark:
{ Wm F A Gierke
{ James K. Kepley

 Subscribed and sworn to before me this 21st day of March , 1905.

             Wm FA Gierke
             Notary Public.

Applications for Enrollment of Creek Newborn
Act of 1905 Volume VI

BIRTH AFFIDAVIT.

DEPARTMENT OF THE INTERIOR.
COMMISSION TO THE FIVE CIVILIZED TRIBES.

IN RE APPLICATION FOR ENROLLMENT, as a citizen of the Creek Nation, of Ewell Durant Newton, born on the 30 day of July, 1901

Name of Father: Eugene Newton   a citizen of the United States Nation.
Name of Mother: Sarah Elizabeth Newton   a citizen of the Creek Nation.

                 Postoffice   Oktaha Ind Ter
                              formerly Summit I.T.

AFFIDAVIT OF MOTHER.

UNITED STATES OF AMERICA, Indian Territory,
    Western   DISTRICT.

    I, Sarah Elizabeth Newton, on oath state that I am (30) thirty years of age and a citizen by blood, of the Creek Nation; that I am the lawful wife of Eugene Newton, who is a citizen, by ----- of the United States ~~Nation~~; that a male child was born to me on 30th day of July, 1901, that said child has been named Ewell Durant Newton, and is now living.

                              Sarah Elizabeth Newton

Witnesses To Mark:
    { W M Calmes
    { J Walter Rankin
    AJ Snelson
Subscribed and sworn to before me this 24th day of March, 1905.

                              W M Calmes
                                  Notary Public.

AFFIDAVIT OF ATTENDING PHYSICIAN OR MID-WIFE.

UNITED STATES OF AMERICA, Indian Territory,
    Western   DISTRICT.

    I, Nannie Grayson, a midwife, on oath state that I attended on Mrs. Sarah Elizabeth Newton, wife of Eugene Newton on the 30th day of July, 1901; that there was born to her on said date a male child; that said child is now living and is said to have been named Ewell Durant Newton
                                her
                         Nannie x Grayson
                             mark

Applications for Enrollment of Creek Newborn
Act of 1905 Volume VI

Witnesses To Mark:
- W M Calmes
- J Walter Rankin

AJ Snelson

Subscribed and sworn to before me this 24th day of March, 1905.

W M Calmes
Notary Public.

BIRTH AFFIDAVIT.

DEPARTMENT OF THE INTERIOR.
COMMISSION TO THE FIVE CIVILIZED TRIBES.

IN RE APPLICATION FOR ENROLLMENT, as a citizen of the Creek Nation, of Guy Jackson Newton, born on the 1st day of Feb, 1904

Name of Father: Eugene Newton — a citizen of the United States Nation.
Name of Mother: Sarah Elizabeth Newton — a citizen of the Creek Nation.

Postoffice   Oktaha
See other aff.

AFFIDAVIT OF MOTHER.

UNITED STATES OF AMERICA, Indian Territory,
Western   DISTRICT.

I, Sarah Elizabeth Newton, on oath state that I am thirty years of age and a citizen by blood, of the Creek Nation; that I am the lawful wife of Eugene Newton, who is a citizen, by *(blank)* of the United States Nation; that a male child was born to me on 1st day of Feby, 1904, that said child has been named Guy Jackson Newton, and is now living.

Sarah Elizabeth Newton

Witnesses To Mark:
- W M Calmes
- J Walter Rankin

AJ Snelson

Subscribed and sworn to before me this 24th day of March, 1905.

W M Calmes
Notary Public.

Applications for Enrollment of Creek Newborn
Act of 1905 Volume VI

AFFIDAVIT OF ATTENDING PHYSICIAN OR MID-WIFE.

UNITED STATES OF AMERICA, Indian Territory,
Western DISTRICT.

I, Nannie Grayson, a midwife, on oath state that I attended on Mrs. Sarah Elizabeth Newton, wife of Eugene Newton on the 1st day of Feby, 1904; that there was born to her on said date a male child; that said child is now living and is said to have been named Guy Jackson Newton

her
Nannie x Grayson
mark

Witnesses To Mark:
{ W M Calmes
{ J Walter Rankin
AJ Snelson

Subscribed and sworn to before me this 24th day of March, 1905.

W M Calmes
Notary Public.

DEPARTMENT OF THE INTERIOR,
COMMISSIONER TO THE FIVE CIVILIZED TRIBES.
MUSKOGEE, INDIAN TERRITORY.
May 10, 1906.

In the matter of the application for the enrollment of Henry and Lula (Field) Foster, as citizens by blood of the Creek Nation.

Chotka Foster, being duly sworn, testified as follows, through Official Interpreter, Lona Merrick.

Q What is your name? A Chotka Foster.
Q What is the name of your father? A Dick Field.
Q Was he ever known by any other name? A Yes sir, Parhose.
Q What is the name of your mother? A Montarley.
Q What Creek Indian town do you belong to? A Thlopthlocco.
Q Have you a sister named Mary Foster? A Yes sir.
Q How old are you? A About 30.
Q What is your post office address? A Okemah.
Q Are you sometimes called Foster Field? A Yes sir.
Q Have you two children named Henry and Lula? A Yes sir.
Q Are they living? A Yes sir.
Q If you[sic] name is foster, their names must be Henry and Lula Foster? A Yes sir.
Q Is Henry about four years old? A Over four years old.
Q And is Lula little over two years old? A Yes sir.
Q What is the name of the mother of these children? A Mary Micco.

Applications for Enrollment of Creek Newborn
Act of 1905   Volume VI

Q Is she living? A Yes sir.
Q Is she your wife? A Yes sir.
Q Are you married to her? A Yes sir.
Q Her name must be Mary Foster then, isn't it? A Yes sir.
Q What was her name before she married you? A Mary Micco.
Q Do you know what town she belong[sic] to? A Thlopthlocco.
Q Did she have a child named Tiger? A Yes sir.
Q George Tiger? A Yes sir.

Witness is identified as Chotka Foster opposite Creek Indian Roll No. 4583, and the mother of his two children herein is identified as Mary Micco, opposite Creek Indian Roll No. 5090.

Witness is advised that this office has affidavits, as he has been notified by letter, of the mother and of the midwife in these cases, in these cases, in which the mother's name is signed by mark, Mary Field, and the children are called Henry and Lula Field, and the witness' name is given as Foster Field.

Lona Merrick, being duly sworn, states that the above and foregoing is a true and correct transcript of her stenographic notes as taken in said cause on said date.

Lona Merrick

Subscribed and sworn to before me this 10th day of May, 1906.

HGHains
Notary Public.

BIRTH AFFIDAVIT.
DEPARTMENT OF THE INTERIOR.
COMMISSION TO THE FIVE CIVILIZED TRIBES.

IN RE APPLICATION FOR ENROLLMENT, as a citizen of the Creek Nation, of Lula Foster, born on the 10 day of March, 1904

Name of Father: Chotka Foster   a citizen of the   Creek   Nation.
Name of Mother: Mary   "   a citizen of the   "   Nation.
                  called Mary Micco
                           Postoffice   Okemah I.T.

Applications for Enrollment of Creek Newborn
Act of 1905 Volume VI

AFFIDAVIT OF MOTHER.

UNITED STATES OF AMERICA, Indian Territory,
Western DISTRICT.

I, Mary Foster, on oath state that I am 31 years of age and a citizen by blood, of the Creek Nation; that I am the lawful wife of Chotka Foster, who is a citizen, by blood of the Creek Nation; that a female child was born to me on 10 day of March, 1904, that said child has been named Lula Foster, and was living March 4, 1905.

                                    her
                          Mary x Foster

Witnesses To Mark: mark
  { John D Richards
    W. N. Barry

Subscribed and sworn to before me this 12 day of May, 1906.

My Commission Expires Sept. 6th 1906.   John H. Phillips
                                                Notary Public.

AFFIDAVIT OF ATTENDING PHYSICIAN OR MID-WIFE.

UNITED STATES OF AMERICA, Indian Territory,
Western DISTRICT.

I, Mary Austln, a midwife, on oath state that I attended on Mrs. Mary Foster, wife of Chotka Foster on the 10 day of March, 1904; that there was born to her on said date a female child; that said child was living March 4, 1905, and is said to have been named Lula Foster

                                   her
                        Mary x Austin
                           mark

Witnesses To Mark:
  { John D Richards
    W. N. Barry

Subscribed and sworn to before me this 12 day of May, 1906.

My Commission Expires Sept. 6th 1906.   John H. Phillips
                                                Notary Public.

Applications for Enrollment of Creek Newborn
Act of 1905   Volume VI

BIRTH AFFIDAVIT.

DEPARTMENT OF THE INTERIOR.
COMMISSION TO THE FIVE CIVILIZED TRIBES.

IN RE APPLICATION FOR ENROLLMENT, as a citizen of the Creek Nation, of Lula Field, born on the 10th day of March, 1904

Name of Father:	Foster Field	a citizen of the	Creek	Nation.
Name of Mother:	Mary Field	a citizen of the	Creek	Nation.

Postoffice   Fentress, I.T.

AFFIDAVIT OF MOTHER.

UNITED STATES OF AMERICA, Indian Territory,
Western Judicial   DISTRICT.

I, Mary Field, on oath state that I am 30 years of age and a citizen by Blood, of the Muskokee[sic] or Creek Nation; that I am the lawful wife of Foster Field, who is a citizen, by Blood of the Muskokee[sic] or Creek Nation; that a Female child was born to me on 10th day of March, 1904, that said child has been named Lula Field, and was living March 4, 1905.

Witnesses To Mark:
{ M M Morton
  John H. Phillips

her
Mary x Field
mark

Subscribed and sworn to before me this 20th day of March, 1905.

My Commission Expires Sept. 6th 1906.

John H. Phillips
Notary Public.

AFFIDAVIT OF ATTENDING PHYSICIAN OR MID-WIFE.

UNITED STATES OF AMERICA, Indian Territory,
Western Judicial   DISTRICT.

I, Mary Austin, a Mid-Wife, on oath state that I attended on Mrs. Mary Field, wife of Foster Field on the 10th day of March, 1904 ; that there was born to her on said date a Female child; that said child was living March 4, 1905, and is said to have been named Lula Field

her
Mary x Austin
mark

Applications for Enrollment of Creek Newborn
Act of 1905 Volume VI

Witnesses To Mark:
 { M M Morton
 { John H. Phillips

Subscribed and sworn to before me this 20th day of March, 1905.

My Commission Expires Sept. 6th 1906.

John H. Phillips
Notary Public.

BIRTH AFFIDAVIT.

DEPARTMENT OF THE INTERIOR.
COMMISSION TO THE FIVE CIVILIZED TRIBES.

IN RE APPLICATION FOR ENROLLMENT, as a citizen of the Creek Nation, of Henry Foster, born on the 24 day of January, 1902

Name of Father:	Chotka Foster	a citizen of the	Creek	Nation.
Name of Mother:	Mary "	a citizen of the	"	Nation.

called Mary Micco
Postoffice Okemah I.T.

AFFIDAVIT OF MOTHER.

UNITED STATES OF AMERICA, Indian Territory, }
 Western DISTRICT. }

I, Mary Foster, on oath state that I am 31 years of age and a citizen by blood, of the Creek Nation; that I am the lawful wife of Chotka Foster, who is a citizen, by blood of the Creek Nation; that a male child was born to me on 24 day of January, 1902, that said child has been named Henry Foster, and was living March 4, 1905.

 her
 Mary x Foster
Witnesses To Mark: mark
 { John D Richards
 { W. N. Barry

Subscribed and sworn to before me this 12 day of May, 1906.

My Commission Expires Sept. 6th 1906.

John H. Phillips
Notary Public.

Applications for Enrollment of Creek Newborn
Act of 1905 Volume VI

AFFIDAVIT OF ATTENDING PHYSICIAN OR MID-WIFE.

UNITED STATES OF AMERICA, Indian Territory,
Western DISTRICT.

I, Mary Austin , a midwife , on oath state that I attended on Mrs. Mary Foster , wife of Chotka Foster on the 24" day of January , 1902 ; that there was born to her on said date a male child; that said child was living March 4, 1905, and is said to have been named Henry Foster

                              her
                        Mary x Austin
                          mark

Witnesses To Mark:
- John D Richards
- W. N. Barry

Subscribed and sworn to before me this 12 day of May , 1906.

My Commission Expires Sept. 6th 1906.   John H. Phillips
                                          Notary Public.

BIRTH AFFIDAVIT.
DEPARTMENT OF THE INTERIOR.
COMMISSION TO THE FIVE CIVILIZED TRIBES.

IN RE APPLICATION FOR ENROLLMENT, as a citizen of the Creek Nation, of Henry Field , born on the 24th day of January , 1902

| Name of Father: | Foster Field | a citizen of the | Creek | Nation. |
| Name of Mother: | Mary Field | a citizen of the | Creek | Nation. |

Postoffice   Fentress, I.T.

AFFIDAVIT OF MOTHER.

UNITED STATES OF AMERICA, Indian Territory,
Western Judicial DISTRICT.

I, Mary Field , on oath state that I am 30 years of age and a citizen by Blood , of the Muskokee[sic] or Creek Nation; that I am the lawful wife of Foster Field , who is a citizen, by Blood of the Muskokee[sic] or Creek Nation; that a Male child was born to me on 24th day of January, 1902 , that said child has been named Henry Field, and was living March 4, 1905.   her
                        Mary x Field
                        mark

Applications for Enrollment of Creek Newborn
Act of 1905 Volume VI

Witnesses To Mark:
- M M Morton
- John H. Phillips

Subscribed and sworn to before me this 20th day of March, 1905.

My Commission Expires Sept. 6th 1906.

John H. Phillips
Notary Public.

AFFIDAVIT OF ATTENDING PHYSICIAN OR MID-WIFE.

UNITED STATES OF AMERICA, Indian Territory,
Western Judicial **DISTRICT.**

I, Mary Austin, a Mid-Wife, on oath state that I attended on Mrs. Mary Field, wife of Foster Field on the 24th day of January, 1902; that there was born to her on said date a Male child; that said child was living March 4, 1905, and is said to have been named Henry Field

her
Mary x Austin
mark

Witnesses To Mark:
- M M Morton
- John H. Phillips

Subscribed and sworn to before me this 20th day of March, 1905.

My Commission Expires Sept. 6th 1906.

John H. Phillips
Notary Public.

NC-459.

Muskogee, Indian Territory, August 4, 1905.

Mary Field,
    c/o Foster Field,
        Fentress, Indian Territory.

Dear Madam:

In the matter of the application for the enrollment of your minor children Lula Field and Henry Field, as citizens by blood of the Creek Nation, you are advised that, before the rights of said children can be finally determined, it will be necessary for you and your husband Foster Field to appear in person before this office at Muskogee, Indian Territory for the purpose of being examined under oath.

Such appearance should be made at once.

Applications for Enrollment of Creek Newborn
Act of 1905   Volume VI

Respectfully,

Commissioner.

HGH

REFER IN REPLY TO THE FOLLOWING:

DEPARTMENT OF THE INTERIOR,
COMMISSIONER TO THE FIVE CIVILIZED TRIBES.

Muskogee, Indian Territory, October 23, 1906.

Mary Foster,
 c/o Chotka Foster,
  Fentress, Indian Territory.

Dear Madam:

  You are hereby advised that the names of your minor children, Henry and Lula Foster, are contained in the partial list of citizens by blood of the Creek Nation, approved by the Secretary of the Interior October 15, 1906, and that selections of land in the Creek Nation May now be made for them at the Creek Land Office in Muskogee, Indian Territory.
  This matter should receive your prompt attention.

Respectfully,

Tams Bixby Commissioner

NC 460.

DEPARTMENT OF THE INTERIOR,
COMMISSIONER TO THE FIVE CIVILIZED TRIBES,
Near Morse, Indian Territory, October 5, 1906.

  In the matter of the application for the enrollment of Wallace (Hicks) Long as a citizen by blood of the Creek Nation.
  YUSIE LONG, being duly sworn, testified as follows through Jesse McDermott, official interpreter.

BY COMMISSIONER:

Q What is your name? A Yusie Long.
Q What is your age? A About 20.
Q What is your postoffice address? A Morse, I.T.
Q Are you a Creek citizen? A Yes.
Q Have you a child named Wallace? A Yes.

Applications for Enrollment of Creek Newborn
Act of 1905   Volume VI

Q When was he born? A February 21, 1905.
Q Is he living? A Yes, here he is.
Q What is the name of his father? A Simmer.
Q Simmer what? A I don't know.
Q Do you know under what name he might be enrolled? A No.
Q Were you lawfully married to the father of this child when you had this child by him? A No
Q Had you ever lived together as a man and wife prior to the birth of the birth[sic] of Wallace? A No, never had.
Q Does Simmer contribute anything toward the support of this child?   No, he hasn't anything to contribute.
Q Under what name do you desire this child enrolled? A Wallace Long. I have him in custody anyway.

Winey Yarhola, being duly sworn, testified as follows through Jesse McDermott official interpreter.

BY COMMISSIONER:

Q State your name, age and postoffice address? Winey Yarhola; 35; Okfuskee.
Q Are you a Creek citizen? A Yes.
Q Do you know Yusie Hicks? A Yes, I know her but that is not her right name.
Q What is her right name? A Yusie Long. Her allotment joins the town of Okemah.
Q Do you know a child of hers named Wallace? A Yes, I attended on her when the child was born.
Q You attended on the mother did you? A Yes.
Q When was the child born? A February of last year.
Q What day of the month do you know? A About 10th.
Q Do you know who the father of this child is? A The mother says that Simmer is the father.
Q Do you know his other name besides Simmer.[sic] A They call him Simmer, Simmer Hicks and sometimes Simmer Ahfonoke.
Q Is Wallace living? A Yes.

----oooOOOooo----

I, Jesse McDermott, on oath state that the above and foregoing is a full and true transcript of my notes as taken in said cause on said date.

Jesse McDermott

Subscribed and sworn to before me this 19th day of December, 1906.

Alex Posey
Notary Public.

Applications for Enrollment of Creek Newborn
Act of 1905   Volume VI

BIRTH AFFIDAVIT.

DEPARTMENT OF THE INTERIOR.
COMMISSION TO THE FIVE CIVILIZED TRIBES.

IN RE APPLICATION FOR ENROLLMENT, as a citizen of the Muskogee Nation, of Wallace Hicks, born on the 21 day of Feb, 1905

Name of Father:	Seamen Hicks	a citizen of the	Muskogee Nation.
Name of Mother:	Usey Hicks	a citizen of the	Muskogee Nation.

Postoffice   Morse, I.T.

AFFIDAVIT OF MOTHER.

UNITED STATES OF AMERICA, Indian Territory, }
Western   DISTRICT.

I, Usey Hicks, on oath state that I am 19 years of age and a citizen by Blood, of the Muskogee Nation; that I am the lawful wife of Seamen Hicks, who is a citizen, by Blood of the Muskogee Nation; that a Male child was born to me on 21 day of Feb, 1905, that said child has been named Wallace Hicks, and was living March 4, 1905.

Witnesses To Mark:
{ H. L. Young
{ William Stoddard

her
Usey x Hicks
mark

Subscribed and sworn to before me this 23 day of March, 1905.

My Commission Expires March 5th, 1908.

C. C. Eskridge
Notary Public.

AFFIDAVIT OF ATTENDING PHYSICIAN OR MID-WIFE.

UNITED STATES OF AMERICA, Indian Territory, }
Western   DISTRICT.

I, Winey Yahola, a Mid-Wife, on oath state that I attended on Mrs. Usey Hicks, wife of Seamen Hicks on the 21 day of Feb, 1905; that there was born to her on said date a male child; that said child was living March 4, 1905, and is said to have been named Wallace Hicks

Witnesses To Mark:
{ Joseph Herberger
{ William Stoddard

her
Winey x Yahola
mark

Applications for Enrollment of Creek Newborn
Act of 1905 Volume VI

Subscribed and sworn to before me this 23 day of March, 1905.

My Commission Expires March 5th, 1908.
C. C. Eskridge
Notary Public.

BIRTH AFFIDAVIT.

DEPARTMENT OF THE INTERIOR.
COMMISSION TO THE FIVE CIVILIZED TRIBES.

IN RE APPLICATION FOR ENROLLMENT, as a citizen of the Creek Nation, of Wallace Hicks, born on the 21 day of Feb, 1905

Name of Father: Simmer Ahfonoke   a citizen of the   Creek   Nation.
Name of Mother: Yusie Long   a citizen of the   Creek   Nation.

Postoffice   Okfuskee, I.T.
c/o Billy Yahola

AFFIDAVIT OF MOTHER.

UNITED STATES OF AMERICA, Indian Territory,
Western DISTRICT.

I, Yusie Long, on oath state that I am 20 years of age and a citizen by blood, of the Creek Nation; that I am the lawful wife of Simmer Ahfonoke, who is a citizen, by blood of the Creek Nation; that a Male child was born to me on 21" day of February, 1905, that said child has been named Wallace Long, and was living March 4, 1905.

her
Yusie x Long
Witnesses To Mark: mark
  Jesse McDermott
  J.E. Guy

Subscribed and sworn to before me this 5 day of October, 1906.

J McDermott
Notary Public.

Illegitimate child

Applications for Enrollment of Creek Newborn
Act of 1905 Volume VI

AFFIDAVIT OF ATTENDING PHYSICIAN OR MID-WIFE.

UNITED STATES OF AMERICA, Indian Territory,
Western DISTRICT.

I, Winey Yahola , a midwife , on oath state that I attended on Mrs. Yusie Long , not the wife of *(blank)* on the 21st day of Feb , 1905 ; that there was born to her on said date a male child; that said child was living March 4, 1905, and is said to have been named Wallace Long

                                       her
Witnesses To Mark: Winey x Yahola
    { Jesse McDermott   mark
     J.E. Guy

Subscribed and sworn to before me this 2^d day of October , 1906.

My Commission   J McDermott
    Expires July 25" 1907   Notary Public.

BIRTH AFFIDAVIT.

DEPARTMENT OF THE INTERIOR.
COMMISSION TO THE FIVE CIVILIZED TRIBES.

IN RE APPLICATION FOR ENROLLMENT, as a citizen of the Muskogee Nation, of Wallace Hicks , born on the 21 day of Feb , 1905

Name of Father: Seamen Hicks   a citizen of the Muskogee   Nation.
Name of Mother: Usey Hicks   a citizen of the   Muskogee   Nation.

                        Postoffice   Morse. I.T.

AFFIDAVIT OF MOTHER.

UNITED STATES OF AMERICA, Indian Territory,
Western DISTRICT.

I, Usey Hicks , on oath state that I am 19 years of age and a citizen by Blood , of the Muskogee Nation; that I am the lawful wife of Seamen Hicks , who is a citizen, by Blood of the Muskogee Nation; that a Male child was born to me on 21 day of Feb , 1905 , that said child has been named Wallace Hicks , and ~~is now~~ was living March 4, 1905.

                                     her
Witnesses To Mark: Usey x Hicks
                        mark
  { H.L. Young
    William Stoddard

Applications for Enrollment of Creek Newborn
Act of 1905 Volume VI

Subscribed and sworn to before me this 23 day of March, 1905.

My Commission Expires   (Signed)   C C Eskridge
March 5th 1905   Notary Public.

AFFIDAVIT OF ATTENDING PHYSICIAN OR MID-WIFE.

UNITED STATES OF AMERICA, Indian Territory,
     Western   DISTRICT.

I, Winey Yahola, a midwife, on oath state that I attended on Mrs. Usey Hicks, wife of Seamen Hicks on the 21 day of Feb., 1905; that there was born to her on said date a male child; that said child is now was living March 4, 1905 and is said to have been named Wallace Hicks

                                         her
                               Winey x Yahola
Witnesses To Mark: mark
     Joseph Herberger
     William Stoddard

Subscribed and sworn to before me this 23 day of March, 1905.

My Commission Expires   C C Eskridge
March 5" 1905   Notary Public.

REFER IN REPLY TO THE FOLLOWING:
NC-460.

DEPARTMENT OF THE INTERIOR,   HGH
COMMISSIONER TO THE FIVE CIVILIZED TRIBES.

Muskogee, Indian Territory, August 4, 1905.

Seamen Hicks,
     Morse, Indian Territory.

Dear Sir:

     In the matter of the application for the enrollment of your minor son Wallace Hicks as a citizen by blood of the Creek Nation this office is unable to identify either you or your wife Usey Hicks upon the final roll of citizens by blood of the Creek Nation.

     You are, therefore, requested to state the names under which you were enrolled, the names of your parents and other members of your families and your roll numbers as the same appear from your allotment certificates and deeds.

     Please give this matter your prompt attention.

Applications for Enrollment of Creek Newborn
Act of 1905   Volume VI

Respectfully,

Tams Bixby   Commissioner.

N C 460

JWH

Muskogee, Indian Territory, March 1, 1907.

Yusie Long,
    c/o Simmer Ahfonoke,
    Morse, Indian Territory.

Dear Madam :--

    You are hereby advised that on February 15, 1907, the Secretary of the Interior approved the enrollment of your minor child, Wallace Long, as a citizen by blood of the Creek Nation, and that the name of said child appears upon the roll of New Born citizens by blood of the Creek Nation, enrolled under the Act of Congress approved March 3, 1905, as number 1149.

    This child is now entitled to allotment, and application therefor should be made without delay at the Creek Land Office, Muskogee, Indian Territory.

Respectfully,

Commissioner.

BIRTH AFFIDAVIT.

DEPARTMENT OF THE INTERIOR.
COMMISSION TO THE FIVE CIVILIZED TRIBES.

    IN RE APPLICATION FOR ENROLLMENT, as a citizen of the Creek Nation, of Jesse Barnett, born on the 21th[sic] day of January, 1905

Name of Father:	Daniel Barnett	a citizen of the	Creek	Nation.
Name of Mother:	Cookie Barnett	a citizen of the	Creek	Nation.

Postoffice   Okemah, I.T.

Applications for Enrollment of Creek Newborn
Act of 1905   Volume VI

AFFIDAVIT OF MOTHER.

UNITED STATES OF AMERICA, Indian Territory, }
Western Judicial   DISTRICT.

    I, Cookie Barnett , on oath state that I am 20 years of age and a citizen by Blood , of the Muskokee[sic] or Creek   Nation; that I am the lawful wife of Daniel Barnett , who is a citizen, by Blood of the Muskokee[sic] or Creek   Nation; that a Male child was born to me on 21st   day of January , 1905 , that said child has been named Jesse Barnett , and was living March 4, 1905.

                              her
                      Cookie x Barnett
Witnesses To Mark: mark
  { M M Morton
    John H. Phillips

Subscribed and sworn to before me this 20th day of January , 1905.

My Commission Expires Sept. 6th 1906.   John H. Phillips
                                          Notary Public.

AFFIDAVIT OF ATTENDING PHYSICIAN OR MID-WIFE.

UNITED STATES OF AMERICA, Indian Territory, }
Western Judicial   DISTRICT.

    I, Mary Austin , a Mid-Wife , on oath state that I attended on Mrs. Cookie Barnett , wife of Daniel Barnett on the 21st day of January , 1905 ; that there was born to her on said date a Male   child; that said child was living March 4, 1905, and is said to have been named Jesse Barnett

                              her
                      Mary x Austin
Witnesses To Mark: mark
  { M M Morton
    John H. Phillips

Subscribed and sworn to before me this 20th day of January , 1905.

My Commission Expires Sept. 6th 1906.   John H. Phillips
                                          Notary Public.

Applications for Enrollment of Creek Newborn
Act of 1905   Volume VI

BIRTH AFFIDAVIT.

DEPARTMENT OF THE INTERIOR.
COMMISSION TO THE FIVE CIVILIZED TRIBES.

IN RE APPLICATION FOR ENROLLMENT, as a citizen of the Creek Nation, of James Barnett, born on the 14th day of June, 1903

Name of Father:	Daniel Barnett	a citizen of the	Creek	Nation.
Name of Mother:	Cookie Barnett	a citizen of the	Creek	Nation.

Postoffice   Okemah, I.T.

AFFIDAVIT OF MOTHER.

UNITED STATES OF AMERICA, Indian Territory,
Western Judicial   DISTRICT.

I, Cookie Barnett, on oath state that I am 20 years of age and a citizen by Blood, of the Muskokee[sic] or Creek Nation; that I am the lawful wife of Daniel Barnett, who is a citizen, by Blood of the Muskokee[sic] or Creek Nation; that a Male child was born to me on 14th day of June, 1903, that said child has been named James Barnett, and was living March 4, 1905.

         her
      Cookie x Barnett
         mark

Witnesses To Mark:
 { M M Morton
  Jno H. Phillips   Okemah I.T.

Subscribed and sworn to before me this 20th day of January, 1905.

My Commission Expires Sept. 6th 1906.   John H. Phillips
            Notary Public.

AFFIDAVIT OF ATTENDING PHYSICIAN OR MID-WIFE.

UNITED STATES OF AMERICA, Indian Territory,
Western Judicial   DISTRICT.

I, Mary Field, a Mid-Wife, on oath state that I attended on Mrs. Cookie Barnett, wife of Daniel Barnett on the 14th day of June, 1903; that there was born to her on said date a Male child; that said child was living March 4, 1905, and is said to have been named James Barnett

         her
      Mary x Field
         mark

Applications for Enrollment of Creek Newborn
Act of 1905   Volume VI

Witnesses To Mark:
{ M M Morton
{ Jno H. Phillips Okemah I.T.

Subscribed and sworn to before me this 20th day of January, 1905.

My Commission Expires Sept. 6th 1906.

John H. Phillips
Notary Public.

NC 462.

Muskogee, Indian Territory, August 4, 1905.

Sawyer Hicks,
    Morse, Indian Territory.

Dear Sir:

    In the matter of the application for the enrollment of your minor daughter Lowiny Hicks, as a citizen by blood of the Creek Nation, this office is unable to identify either you or your wife Janie Hicks upon the final roll of citizens by blood of the Creek Nation.

    You are therefore requested to inform this office of the names under which you and your wife were enrolled, the names of your parents, and other members of your families, the Creek Indian Town to which you belong and you should also state your final roll numbers as the same appear upon your allotment certificates and deeds.

    Please give this matter your prompt attention.

Respectfully,

Commissioner.

NC 462.

Muskogee, Indian Territory, December 13, 1905.

Janie Hicks,
    Care Sawyer Hicks,
        Morse, Indian Territory.

Dear Madam:

Applications for Enrollment of Creek Newborn
Act of 1905 Volume VI

In the matter of the application for the enrollment of your minor daughter Lowiny Hicks, as a citizen by blood of the Creek Nation, this office is unable to identify you or your husband, Sawyer Hicks, on its final rolls of citizens by blood of the Creek Nation.

You are therefore requested to inform this office of the names under which you and your said husband were enrolled, the names of your respective parents and other members of your families, the Creek Indian Town to which you belong and your final roll numbers as the same appears upon your allotment certificates and deeds.

Please give this matter your prompt attention.

Respectfully,

Commissioner.

NC462.

DEPARTMENT OF THE INTERIOR,
COMMISSIONER TO THE FIVE CIVILIZED TRIBES,
Near Morse, Indian Territory, October 5, 1906.

In the matter of the application for the enrollment of Lowiney Foster as a citizen by blood of the Creek Nation.

JANIE FOSTER, being duly sworn, testified as follows through Jesse McDermott official interpreter:

BY COMMISSIONER:

Q What is your name? A Janie Foster.
Q What is your age? A About 25.
Q What is your postoffice address? A Okfuskee.
Q Are you a Creek citizen? A Yes.
Q Have you a child named Lowiney? A I did have but she is now dead.
Q When did she die? A She died in about two weeks after we made out the affidavits about her enrollment.
Q Do you know what date? A No, I do not.
Q When was she born? A September two years ago.
Q Do you know what date in September? A It was about the middle of the month.
Q We have your affidavit stating that Lowiney was born Setpember[sic] 17, 1904. Is that the correct date about her birth? A Yes.
Q What is the name of the father of this child? A He has three different names. Sayochee, Siah Hicks and Sayochee Ahfonoke.
Q Do you know under what name he is enrolled? A No, I do not.
Q Were you lawfully married to him when you had this child by him? A No.
Q Had you and he ever live[sic] together as a man and wife prior to the birth of Lowiney? A No, never had.

Applications for Enrollment of Creek Newborn
Act of 1905   Volume VI

Q Do you live with the faher[sic] of this child at the present time? A No.
Q Did he contribute anything toward the support of Lowiney during her lifetime? A No, not a nickel.
Q Who had the custody of the child when it died? A I had.
Q Under which name do you desire her enrolled? A Lowiney Foster.

Lousianna Stoddard, being duly sworn, testified as follows through Jesse McDermott official interpreter.

BY COMMISSIONER:

Q What is your name? Lousianna Stoddard.
Q What is your age? A About 28.
Q What is your postoffice address? A Morse, I.T.
Q Are you a Creek citizen? A I am.
Q Do you know Janie Hicks? A Yes, I think she is enrolled as Janie Foster, because her husband was a Foster.
Q Do you know a child of hers named Lowiney? A I do.
Q Do you know when that child was born? A The child was born two years ago last month.
Q September? A Yes.
Q Do you know what day of the month is[sic] was? A It was about the middle
Q We have your affidavit stating that Lowiney was born September 17, 1904. Is that the date? A Yes.
Q Who is the father of the child? A They call him Sayochee. He is also known as Siah Hicks. Others call him Sayochee Ahfonokee.
Q Do you know whether Janie was ever married to the father of this child? A No, I was living March 4, 1905 in that neighborhood before and after the child was born but never had heard of them being married.
Q Is Lowiney living? A No, she died sometime after we made out the affidavits about mer[sic] enrollment. Possibly the mother could furnish you the date of her death. The mother had the child with her when we executed the affidavits at Morse.
Q You were the midwife at the birth of this child were you not? A Yes.

The father had but little to do with the child during its lifetime.

---oooOOOooo---

I, Jesse McDermott, on oath state that the above and foregoing is a full and true transcript of my notes as taken in said cause on said date.

Jesse McDermott

Subscribed and sworn to before me this ?th day of December, 1906.

Alex Posey
Notary Public.

Applications for Enrollment of Creek Newborn
Act of 1905 Volume VI

BIRTH AFFIDAVIT.

DEPARTMENT OF THE INTERIOR.
COMMISSION TO THE FIVE CIVILIZED TRIBES.

IN RE APPLICATION FOR ENROLLMENT, as a citizen of the Creek Nation, of Lowiney Foster, born on the 17" day of Sept , 1904

Name of Father:	Sayochee Ahfonoke	a citizen of the	Creek	Nation.
Name of Mother:	Janie Foster	a citizen of the	Creek	Nation.

Postoffice   Okfuskee, I.T.

AFFIDAVIT OF MOTHER.

UNITED STATES OF AMERICA, Indian Territory,
Western   DISTRICT.

I, Janie Foster , on oath state that I am about 25 years of age and a citizen by blood , of the Creek Nation; that I am not the lawful wife of Sayochee Ahfonoke , who is a citizen, by blood of the Creek Nation; that a female child was born to me on 17 day of September , 1904 , that said child has been named Lowiney Foster , and was living March 4, 1905.

              her
            Janie x Foster
Witnesses To Mark: mark
 { Jesse McDermott
   J.E. Guy

Subscribed and sworn to before me this 5" day of October , 1906.

  Illegitimate child   J McDermott
               Notary Public.

AFFIDAVIT OF ATTENDING PHYSICIAN OR MID-WIFE.

UNITED STATES OF AMERICA, Indian Territory,
Western   DISTRICT.

I, Lousanna Stoddard , a midwife , on oath state that I attended on Mrs. Janie Foster not the , wife of *(blank)* on the 17" day of Sept , 1904 ; that there was born to her on said date a female child; that said child was living March 4, 1905, and is said to have been named Lowiney Foster

              Lousanna Stoddard

Applications for Enrollment of Creek Newborn
Act of 1905 Volume VI

Witnesses To Mark:
{

Subscribed and sworn to before me this 2^d day of October, 1906.

My Com   J McDermott
Exp July 25" 1907   Notary Public.

BIRTH AFFIDAVIT.

DEPARTMENT OF THE INTERIOR.
COMMISSION TO THE FIVE CIVILIZED TRIBES.

IN RE APPLICATION FOR ENROLLMENT, as a citizen of the Muskogee Nation, of Lowiney Foster, born on the 17 day of Sept, 1904

Name of Father:	Sawyer Hicks	a citizen of the	Muskogee Nation.
Name of Mother:	Janie Hicks	a citizen of the	Muskogee Nation.

Postoffice   Morse, I.T.

AFFIDAVIT OF MOTHER.

UNITED STATES OF AMERICA, Indian Territory, }
Western   DISTRICT.

I, Janie Hicks, on oath state that I am 25 years of age and a citizen by Blood, of the Muskogee Nation; that I am the lawful wife of Sawyer Hicks, who is a citizen, by Blood of the Muskogee Nation; that a Female child was born to me on 17 day of Sept, 1904, that said child has been named Lowiney Hicks, and is now living.

                                her
                        Janie x Hicks
Witnesses To Mark: mark
{ Joseph Herberger
  William Stoddard

Subscribed and sworn to before me this 23 day of March, 1905.

My Commission Expires March 5th, 1908.   C. C. Eskridge
                                          Notary Public.

Applications for Enrollment of Creek Newborn
Act of 1905   Volume VI

AFFIDAVIT OF ATTENDING PHYSICIAN OR MID-WIFE.

UNITED STATES OF AMERICA, Indian Territory, }
   Western   DISTRICT.

I, Lousanna Stoddard , a Mid-Wife , on oath state that I attended on Mrs. Janie Hicks , wife of Sawyer Hicks on the 17 day of Sept , 1904 ; that there was born to her on said date a Female child; that said child is now living and is said to have been named Lowiney Hicks

Lousanna Stoddard

Witnesses To Mark:
{

Subscribed and sworn to before me this 2^d day of October, 1906.

My Commission Expires March 5th, 1908.   C. C. Eskridge
                                                               Notary Public.

(The above Birth Affidavit given again.)

JWH

N C 462

Muskogee, Indian Territory, March 1, 1907.

Janie Foster,
   c/o Sayochee Ahfornoke[sic],
      Morse, Indian Territory.

Dear Madam :--

You are hereby advised that on February 15, 1907, the Secretary of the Interior approved the enrollment of your minor child, Lowiney Foster, as a citizen by blood of the Creek Nation, and that the name of said child appears upon the roll of New Born citizens by blood of the Creek Nation, enrolled under the Act of Congress approved March 3, 1905, as number 1150.

This child is now entitled to allotment and application therefor should be made without delay at the Creek Land Office, Muskogee, Indian Territory.

Respectfully,

Commissioner.

Applications for Enrollment of Creek Newborn
Act of 1905 Volume VI

HGH

COMMISSIONERS:
TAMS BIXBY,
THOMAS B. NEEDLES,
C.R. BRECKINBRIDGE.

DEPARTMENT OF THE INTERIOR,
COMMISSIONER TO THE FIVE CIVILIZED TRIBES.

REFER IN REPLY TO THE FOLLOWING:

NC 463.

WM. O. BEALL
Secretary

ADDRESS ONLY THE
COMMISSION TO THE FIVE CIVILIZED TRIBES.

Muskogee, Indian Territory, June 5, 1905.

Adella Gooch,
    Choska, Indian Territory.

Dear Madam:

    In the matter of the application for the enrollment of your minor children, Maudie and Claudie Gooch, who it is presumed are twins, you are advised that there are on file with the Commission affidavits stating that they were born January 9 and January 19, 1902, and you are requested to advise the Commission as to which of these dates is correct.

                  Respectfully,
                    (Name Illegible)
                    Commissioner in Charge.

N C 463   COPY   HGH

Muskogee, Indian Territory, June 30, 1905.

Ed Gooch,
    Choska, Indian Territory.

Dear Sir:

    In the matter of the application for the enrollment of your minor children, Maudie and Claudie Gooch, who it is presumed are twins, you are advised that there are on file with the Commission affidavits stating that they were born January 9, and January 19, 1902.

    You are requested to advise the Commission as to the correct date.

                  Respectfully,

Dentlemen[sic]:

    Replying to above will say that the correct date of birth of Maudie and Claudie Gooch is January 19. They are twins and were were--[sic] born on 19th of January, 1902. Chairman

Applications for Enrollment of Creek Newborn
Act of 1905 Volume VI

                                                      Yores[sic] very truly

                              his
                         Ed x Gooch

Witness   mark

E C Gillard

J. L Ussery

BIRTH AFFIDAVIT.

                         DEPARTMENT OF THE INTERIOR.
             COMMISSION TO THE FIVE CIVILIZED TRIBES.

    IN RE APPLICATION FOR ENROLLMENT, as a citizen of the CREEK Nation, of Claudy, born on the 9 day of ~~Feb~~ Jan, 1902

Name of Father: Ed Gooch   a citizen of the   Creek   Nation.
Name of Mother: Adella "   not a citizen of the   Creek   Nation.

                         Postoffice   Choska, I.T.

                     AFFIDAVIT OF ~~MOTHER~~. Father

UNITED STATES OF AMERICA, Indian Territory,
      WESTERN   DISTRICT.

    I, Ed Gooch, on oath state that I am 27 years of age and a citizen by blood, of the Creek Nation; that I am the lawful ~~wife~~ husband of Adella Gooch, who is not a citizen, by *(blank)* of the Creek Nation; that a male child was born to me on 9" day of ~~Feb~~ Jan, 1902, that said child has been named Claudy Gooch, and is now living.

                                       His
                                 Ed x Gooch
Witnesses To Mark: mark
   { Jesse McDermott
     EC Griesel

    Subscribed and sworn to before me this 25" day of Mar, 1905.

                                Edw C Griesel
                                    Notary Public.

Applications for Enrollment of Creek Newborn
Act of 1905   Volume VI

BIRTH AFFIDAVIT.

DEPARTMENT OF THE INTERIOR.
COMMISSION TO THE FIVE CIVILIZED TRIBES.

IN RE APPLICATION FOR ENROLLMENT, as a citizen of the CREEK Nation, of Claudy Gooch , born on the 9 day of ~~February~~ January, 1902

Name of Father: Ed Gooch   a citizen of the   Creek   Nation.
Name of Mother: Adella Gooch   a citizen of the   U.S.   Nation.

Postoffice   Choska, I.T.

Child present

AFFIDAVIT OF MOTHER.

UNITED STATES OF AMERICA, Indian Territory, }
    Western   DISTRICT.   }

I, Adella Gooch , on oath state that I am 29 years of age and a citizen by ----- , of the United States Nation; that I am the lawful wife of Ed Gooch , who is a citizen, by blood of the Creek Nation; that a male child was born to me on 9th day of ~~F~~ January , 1902 , that said child has been named Claudy Gooch , and is now living.

                              her
                     Adella x Gooch
                        mark

Witnesses To Mark.
  { Irwin Donovan
    Ed Merrick

Subscribed and sworn to before me this 29 day of April , 1905.

                            Edward Merrick
                            Notary Public.

BIRTH AFFIDAVIT.

DEPARTMENT OF THE INTERIOR.
COMMISSION TO THE FIVE CIVILIZED TRIBES.

IN RE APPLICATION FOR ENROLLMENT, as a citizen of the Creek Nation, of Claudie Gooch, born on the 19th day of January , 1902

Name of Father: Ed Gooch   a citizen of the   Creek   Nation.
Name of Mother: Adella Gooch   a citizen of the *(big smudge)* Nation.

Postoffice   Choska Ind Ter

Applications for Enrollment of Creek Newborn
Act of 1905 Volume VI

AFFIDAVIT OF MOTHER.

UNITED STATES OF AMERICA, Indian Territory, }
Western DISTRICT.

I, Adella Gooch, on oath state that I am 29 years of age and a citizen by U. S, of the Creek Nation; that I am the lawful wife of Ed Gooch, who is a citizen, by blood of the Creek Nation; that a male child was born to me on 19th day of January, 1902, that said child has been named Claudie Gooch, and is now living.

                              Her
                         Adella x Gooch
                             mark

Witnesses To Mark:
{ Linn D Gaines
{ *(Illegible)* Todd

Subscribed and sworn to before me this 1st day of May, 1905.

My Commission Expires July 9th, 1906.   J O Cravens
                                              Notary Public.

AFFIDAVIT OF ATTENDING PHYSICIAN OR MID-WIFE.

UNITED STATES OF AMERICA, Indian Territory, }
Western DISTRICT.

I, Rebecka Ussery, a midwife, on oath state that I attended on Mrs. Adella Gooch, wife of Ed Gooch on the 19th day of January, 1902; that there was born to her on said date a male child; that said child is now living and is said to have been named Claudie Gooch

                             her
                       Rebecka x Ussery
Witnesses To Mark: mark
{ Linn D Gaines
{ *(Illegible)* Todd

Subscribed and sworn to before me this 1st day of May, 1905.

My Commission Expires July 9th, 1906.   J O Cravens
                                              Notary Public.

Applications for Enrollment of Creek Newborn
Act of 1905   Volume VI

BIRTH AFFIDAVIT.

DEPARTMENT OF THE INTERIOR.
COMMISSION TO THE FIVE CIVILIZED TRIBES.

IN RE APPLICATION FOR ENROLLMENT, as a citizen of the CREEK Nation, of James A Gooch, born on the 19" day of May, 1904

Name of Father:	Ed Gooch	a citizen of the	Creek	Nation.
Name of Mother:	Adella "	not a citizen of the	Creek	Nation.

Postoffice   Choska, I.T.

AFFIDAVIT OF ~~MOTHER~~. Father

UNITED STATES OF AMERICA, Indian Territory, }
WESTERN   DISTRICT.

I, Ed Gooch, on oath state that I am 27 years of age and a citizen by blood, of the Creek Nation; that I am the lawful ~~wife~~ husband of Adella Gooch, who is not a citizen, by ~~blood~~ of the Creek Nation; that a male child was born to me on 19" day of May, 1904, that said child has been named James A Gooch, and ~~is now living~~. died in Sept. 1904

His
Ed x Gooch
mark

Witnesses To Mark:
{ Jesse McDermott
{ EC Griesel

Subscribed and sworn to before me this 25" day of Mar, 1905.

(No Signature)
Notary Public.

NC 463.   JLD

DEPARTMENT OF THE INTERIOR,
COMMISSIONER TO THE FIVE CIVILIZED TRIBES.

In the matter of the application for the enrollment of James A. Gooch, deceased, as a citizen by blood of the Creek Nation.

. . . .

STATEMENT AND ORDER.

The record in this case shows that on March 22, 1905, application was made, in

Applications for Enrollment of Creek Newborn
Act of 1905   Volume VI

affidavit form, for the enrollment of James A. Gooch, deceased, as a citizen by blood of the Creek Nation, under the act of Congress approved March 3, 1905.

It appears that the evidence filed in this matter that said James A. Gooch, deceased, was born May 19, 1904, and died in September 1904.

The act of Congress approved March 3, 1905, (33 Stats., 1048), provides:

"That the Commission to the Five Civilized Tribes is authorized for sixty days after the date of the approval of this act to receive and consider applications for enrollment, of children, <u>born subsequent to May twenty-fifth, nineteen hundred and one, and prior to March fourth, nineteen hundred and five, and living on said latter date, to c</u>itizens of the Creek tribe of Indians whose enrollment has been approved by the Secretary of the Interior prior to the approval of this act; and to enroll and make allotments to such children."

It is, therefore, ordered that the application for the enrollment of James A. Gooch, deceased, as a citizen by blood of the Creek Nation be, and the same is, hereby dismissed.

Tams Bixby Commissioner.

Muskogee, Indian Territory.
JAN 4 – 1907

BIRTH AFFIDAVIT.

DEPARTMENT OF THE INTERIOR.
COMMISSION TO THE FIVE CIVILIZED TRIBES.

IN RE APPLICATION FOR ENROLLMENT, as a citizen of the Creek Nation, of Maudie Gooch, born on the 19th day of January, 1902

Name of Father:	Ed Gooch	a citizen of the	Creek	Nation.
Name of Mother:	Adella Gooch	a citizen of the	U.S.	Nation.

Postoffice   *(blank)*

AFFIDAVIT OF MOTHER.

UNITED STATES OF AMERICA, Indian Territory, ⎫
  Western   DISTRICT. ⎭

I, Adella Gooch, on oath state that I am 29 years of age and a citizen by U. S , of the *(blank)* Nation; that I am the lawful wife of Ed Gooch, who is a citizen, by Blood of the Creek Nation; that a Female child was born to me on 19th day of January, 1902, that said child has been named Maudie Gooch, and is now living.

                    Her
         Adella x Gooch
                    mark

Applications for Enrollment of Creek Newborn
Act of 1905   Volume VI

Witnesses To Mark:
{ Linn D Gaines
{ *(Illegible)* Todd

Subscribed and sworn to before me this 1st day of May, 1905.

My Commission Expires July 9th, 1906.   J O Cravens
                                                     Notary Public.

AFFIDAVIT OF ATTENDING PHYSICIAN OR MID-WIFE.

UNITED STATES OF AMERICA, Indian Territory, }
    Western   DISTRICT.   }

I, Rebecka Ussery, a midwife, on oath state that I attended on Mrs. Adella Gooch, wife of Ed Gooch on the 19th day of January, 1902; that there was born to her on said date a Female child; that said child is now living and is said to have been named Maudie Gooch

                                    Her
                            Rebecka x Ussery
Witnesses To Mark: mark
{ Linn D Gaines
{ *(Illegible)* Todd

Subscribed and sworn to before me this 1st day of May, 1905.

My Commission Expires July 9th, 1906.   J O Cravens
                                                     Notary Public.

BIRTH AFFIDAVIT.

DEPARTMENT OF THE INTERIOR.
COMMISSION TO THE FIVE CIVILIZED TRIBES.

IN RE APPLICATION FOR ENROLLMENT, as a citizen of the CREEK Nation, of Maudy, born on the 9 day of ~~Feb~~ Jan, 1902

Name of Father: Ed Gooch   a citizen of the   Creek   Nation.
Name of Mother: Adella "   not a citizen of the   "   Nation.

                        Postoffice   Choska, I.T.

Applications for Enrollment of Creek Newborn
Act of 1905   Volume VI

AFFIDAVIT OF ~~MOTHER~~. Father

UNITED STATES OF AMERICA, Indian Territory,
WESTERN   DISTRICT.

    I, Ed Gooch , on oath state that I am 27 years of age and a citizen by blood, of the Creek Nation; that I am the lawful ~~wife~~ husband of Adella Gooch , who is not a citizen, by *(blank)* of the Creek   Nation; that a female   child was born to me on 9" day of ~~Feb~~ Jan , 1902 , that said child has been named   Maudy Gooch , and is now living.

                                     His
                              Ed x Gooch
Witnesses To Mark: mark
  { Jesse McDermott
    EC Griesel

Subscribed and sworn to before me this 25" day of Mar, 1905.

                                 Edw C Griesel
                                        Notary Public.

BIRTH AFFIDAVIT.

DEPARTMENT OF THE INTERIOR.
COMMISSION TO THE FIVE CIVILIZED TRIBES.

IN RE APPLICATION FOR ENROLLMENT, as a citizen of the Creek Nation, of Maudy Gooch, born on the 9 day of January, 1902

Name of Father:	Ed Gooch	a citizen of the	Creek	Nation.
Name of Mother:	Adella Gooch	a citizen of the	U.S.	Nation.

                          Postoffice   Choska

Child present

AFFIDAVIT OF MOTHER.

UNITED STATES OF AMERICA, Indian Territory,
    Western   DISTRICT.

    I, Adella Gooch , on oath state that I am 29 years of age and a citizen by ----- , of the U.S.   Nation; that I am the lawful wife of Ed Gooch , who is a citizen, by blood of the Creek   Nation; that a female   child was born to me on 9th day of January , 1902 , that said child has been named Maudy Gooch , and is now living.

                                         her
                                Adella x Gooch
                                    mark

Applications for Enrollment of Creek Newborn
Act of 1905 Volume VI

Witnesses To Mark:
{ Irwin Donovan
{ Ed Merrick

    Subscribed and sworn to before me this 29 day of April, 1905.

                                      Edward Merrick
                                      Notary Public.

NC 464.

                            Muskogee, Indian Territory, August 4, 1905.

Mollie King,
    c/o Peter King,
        Senora, Indian Territory.

Dear Madam:

    On March 28, 1905, you filed with this office application for the enrollment of your minor daughter Sullie[sic] King, born April 26, 1904, as a citizen by blood of the Creek Nation. It is stated in said application that you are a citizen by blood of the Creek Nation.

    This office is unable to identify you upon the final roll of citizens by blood of said nation and you are therefore requested to state the name under which you were enrolled, the names of your parents and other members of your family, the Creek town to which you belong and your final roll number as the same appears on your allotment certificate and deeds.

    It is also stated in said application that there was no physician or midwife present when said child was born. In lieu of the affidavit of such physician or midwife it will be necessary for you to furnish this office, in the matter of the enrollment of said child, the affidavits of two disinterested persons relative to her birth; said affidavits to set forth the date of the birth of said child, her name, the names of her parents and whether or not she was living March 4, 1905.

                          Respectfully,

                                        Commissioner.

Applications for Enrollment of Creek Newborn
Act of 1905   Volume VI

NC 1076[sic].

Muskogee, Indian Territory, October 23, 1905.

Millie[sic] King,
    c/o Peter King,
        Senora, Indian Territory.

Dear Madam:

    In the matter of the application for the enrollment of your minor child, Sallie King, born April 26, 1904, as a citizen by blood of the Creek Nation, you are advised that it will be necessary for you to furnish this office with the affidavits of two disinterested witnesses relative to the birth of said child. Said affidavits to set forth said child's name, the date of her birth, the names of her parents and whether or not she was living March 4, 1905.

        Respectfully,

                Commissioner.

NC 1076.

Muskogee, I T July 25, 1906.

Millie King
    c/o Peter King
        Henryetta I T

Dear Madam:

    In the matter of the application for the enrollment of your minor children Luila and Sallie King, you are advised that you should appear at this office at an early date with the midwife or physician who attended you at the birth of these children for the purpose of being examined under oath
        respy

            Comr

NC 464   JWH

Muskogee, Indian Territory, March 1, 1907.

Mollie King,
    c/o Peter King,
        Senora, Indian Territory.

Applications for Enrollment of Creek Newborn
Act of 1905 Volume VI

Dear Madam :--

You are hereby advised that on February 15, 1907, the Secretary of the Interior approved the enrollment of your minor child, Sallie King, as a citizen by blood of the Creek Nation, and that the name of said child appears upon the roll of New Born citizens by blood of the Creek Nation, enrolled under the Act of Congress approved March 3, 1905, as number 1151.

This child is now entitled to allotment and application therefor should be made without delay at the Creek Land Office, Muskogee, Indian Territory.

Respectfully,

Commissioner.

AFFIDAVIT OF TWO DISINTERESTED WITNESSES.

United States of America, (
Western Judicial District, (ss
Indian Territory. (

We, the undersigned, on oath state that we are personally acquainted with Mollie King the wife of Peter King , that there was born to her a male child on or about the 26 day of April 1904, that said child has been named Sallie King and was living March 4, 1905.

We further state that we have no interest in this case.

Witnesses to mark.	Edward Starr
J. McDermott	her
	Lea x Starr
Thomas Hays	mark

Subscribed and sworn to before me this 5' day of Dec 1906.

My Commission expires J McDermott
July 25", 1907.

BIRTH AFFIDAVIT.

DEPARTMENT OF THE INTERIOR.
COMMISSION TO THE FIVE CIVILIZED TRIBES.

IN RE APPLICATION FOR ENROLLMENT, as a citizen of the Creek Nation, of Sullie King , born on the 26th day of April, 1904

Applications for Enrollment of Creek Newborn
Act of 1905   Volume VI

Name of Father: Peter King   a citizen of the   Creek   Nation.
Name of Mother: Mollie King   a citizen of the   Creek   Nation.

Postoffice   Senora I.T.

AFFIDAVIT OF MOTHER.

UNITED STATES OF AMERICA, Indian Territory, ⎫
  Western   DISTRICT.   ⎬
                                             ⎭

I, Mollie King, on oath state that I am twenty three years of age and a citizen by Blood, of the Creek Nation; that I am the lawful wife of Peter King, who is a citizen, by blood of the Creek Nation; that a female child was born to me on 26th day of April, 1904, that said child has been named Sullie King, and was living March 4, 1905.

Mollie King

Witnesses To Mark:
⎰ Edward Starr
⎱ C M Osborn

Subscribed and sworn to before me this 24th day of March, 1905.

There was no physician   J W Fowler
or midwife present   Notary Public.

(The above Birth Affidavit was given again.)

BIRTH AFFIDAVIT.
DEPARTMENT OF THE INTERIOR.
COMMISSION TO THE FIVE CIVILIZED TRIBES.

IN RE APPLICATION FOR ENROLLMENT, as a citizen of the Creek Nation, of Sallie King, born on the 26 day of April, 1904

Name of Father: Peter King   a citizen of the   Creek   Nation.
  Arbeka Tuladega[sic] Town   Starr)
Name of Mother: Mullie (Mollie) King (nee   a citizen of the   Creek   Nation.
  Arbeka Tuladega[sic] Town

Postoffice   Senora, Ind. Ter.

Applications for Enrollment of Creek Newborn
Act of 1905 Volume VI

AFFIDAVIT OF MOTHER.

UNITED STATES OF AMERICA, Indian Territory, }
Western DISTRICT.

I, Mullie King, on oath state that I am about 22 years of age and a citizen by blood, of the Creek Nation; that I am the lawful wife of Peter King, who is a citizen, by blood of the Creek Nation; that a female child was born to me on 26 day of April, 1904, that said child has been named Sallie King, and was living March 4, 1905.

              her
            Mullie x King
Witnesses To Mark: mark
 { DC Skaggs
  Alex Posey

Subscribed and sworn to before me this 26 day of June, 1905.

            Drennan C Skaggs
            Notary Public.

AFFIDAVIT OF ATTENDING PHYSICIAN OR MID-WIFE.

UNITED STATES OF AMERICA, Indian Territory, }
Western DISTRICT.

                my wife
I, Peter King, a ~~(blank)~~, on oath state that I attended on ^ Mrs. Mullie King, ~~wife of (blank)~~ on the 26 day of April, 1904; that there was born to her on said date a female child; that said child was living March 4, 1905, and is said to have been named Sallie King
            his
          Peter x King
Witnesses To Mark: mark
 { DC Skaggs
  Alex Posey

Subscribed and sworn to before me this 26 day of June, 1905.

            Drennan C Skaggs
            Notary Public.

BIRTH AFFIDAVIT.

DEPARTMENT OF THE INTERIOR.
COMMISSION TO THE FIVE CIVILIZED TRIBES.

IN RE APPLICATION FOR ENROLLMENT, as a citizen of the Creek Nation, of Sallie King, born on the 26 day of April, 1904

Applications for Enrollment of Creek Newborn
Act of 1905 Volume VI

Name of Father:	Peter King	a citizen of the Creek	Nation.
			nee Starr
Name of Mother: Mullie (Mollie) King	a citizen of the	Creek	Nation.

Postoffice	Senora, Ind. Ter.

AFFIDAVIT OF MOTHER.

Child is present

UNITED STATES OF AMERICA, Indian Territory,　}
　Western　　　　DISTRICT.

I, Mullie King , on oath state that I am about 22 years of age and a citizen by blood , of the Creek   Nation; that I am the lawful wife of Peter King , who is a citizen, by blood of the Creek   Nation; that a female   child was born to me on 26   day of April , 1904 , that said child has been named Sallie King , and was living March 4, 1905.

　　　　　　　　　　　　　　　　　　　　　　her
　　　　　　　　　　　　　　　　Mullie x King
Witnesses To Mark:　　　　　　　　mark
　{ DC Skaggs
　 Alex Posey

Subscribed and sworn to before me this 26 day of June , 1905.

　　　　　　　　　　　　　Drennan C Skaggs
　　　　　　　　　　　　　　Notary Public.

AFFIDAVIT OF ATTENDING PHYSICIAN OR MID-WIFE.

UNITED STATES OF AMERICA, Indian Territory,　}
　Western　　　　DISTRICT.

　　　　　　　　　　　　　　　　　　　　　　　　　my wife
I, Peter King , a *(blank)* , on oath state that I attended on ^ Mrs. Mullie King , ~~wife of~~ *(blank)* on the 26 day of April , 1904 ; that there was born to her on said date a female child; that said child was living March 4, 1905, and is said to have been named Sallie King　　　　　　　　　　　　　　　　　　his
　　　　　　　　　　　　　　　　Peter x King
Witnesses To Mark:　　　　　　　　mark
　{ DC Skaggs
　 Alex Posey

Subscribed and sworn to before me this 26 day of June , 1905.

　　　　　　　　　　　　　Drennan C Skaggs
　　　　　　　　　　　　　　Notary Public.

Applications for Enrollment of Creek Newborn
Act of 1905 Volume VI

BIRTH AFFIDAVIT.

DEPARTMENT OF THE INTERIOR.
COMMISSION TO THE FIVE CIVILIZED TRIBES.

IN RE APPLICATION FOR ENROLLMENT, as a citizen of the Creek Nation, of Sallie King, born on the 26 day of April, 1904.

Name of Father: Peter King   a citizen of the   Creek   Nation.
Name of Mother: Mollie King (nee Starr)   a citizen of the   Creek   Nation.
Tulledega Town
                              Postoffice   Senora, I.T.

AFFIDAVIT OF MOTHER.
Child is present

UNITED STATES OF AMERICA, Indian Territory, ⎫
Western   DISTRICT.   ⎬

I, Mollie King, on oath state that I am about 22 years of age and a citizen by blood, of the Creek Nation; that I am the lawful wife of Peter King, who is a citizen, by blood of the Creek Nation; that a female child was born to me on 26 day of April, 1904, that said child has been named Sallie King, and was living March 4, 1905. and is now living

                                  her
                          Mollie x King
Witnesses To Mark;   mark
{ J McDermott
{ Thomas Harjo

Subscribed and sworn to before me this 5th day of December, 1906.

My Commission   J McDermott
Expires July 25" 1907   Notary Public.

BIRTH AFFIDAVIT.

DEPARTMENT OF THE INTERIOR.
COMMISSION TO THE FIVE CIVILIZED TRIBES.

IN RE APPLICATION FOR ENROLLMENT, as a citizen of the CREEK Nation, of Romie Loundine White, born on the 27th day of July, 1904.

Name of Father: J. P. White   a citizen of the   *(blank)*   Nation.
Name of Mother: Mary White   a citizen of the   Creek   Nation.

Applications for Enrollment of Creek Newborn
Act of 1905 Volume VI

Postoffice   Oktaha, Ind. Ter.

AFFIDAVIT OF MOTHER.

UNITED STATES OF AMERICA, Indian Territory, }
WESTERN DISTRICT.

I, Mary White, on oath state that I am 19 years of age and a citizen by birth, of the Creek Nation; that I am the lawful wife of J.P. White, who is not a citizen, by *(blank)* of the *(blank)* Nation; that a female child was born to me on 27th day of July, 1904, that said child has been named Romie Loundine White, and is now living.

Mary White

Witnesses To Mark:
{

Subscribed and sworn to before me this 23rd day of March, 1905.

A. M. Darling
Notary Public.

AFFIDAVIT OF ATTENDING PHYSICIAN OR MID-WIFE.

UNITED STATES OF AMERICA, Indian Territory, }
Western DISTRICT.

I, Wm L. Lett, a physician, on oath state that I attended on Mrs. Mary White, wife of J.P. White on the 27th day of July, 1904; that there was born to her on said date a female child; that said child is now living and is said to have been named Romie Loundine White

Wm L. Lett M.D.

Witnesses To Mark:
{

Subscribed and sworn to before me this 20th day of March, 1905.

A. M. Darling
Notary Public.

Applications for Enrollment of Creek Newborn
Act of 1905 Volume VI

BIRTH AFFIDAVIT.

DEPARTMENT OF THE INTERIOR.
COMMISSION TO THE FIVE CIVILIZED TRIBES.

IN RE APPLICATION FOR ENROLLMENT, as a citizen of the Creek Nation, of Elgie Fox, born on the 8 day of August, 1903

Name of Father: John Fox   a citizen of the   Creek   Nation.
Name of Mother: Lenie Fox   a citizen of the   Creek   Nation.

Postoffice   Brushhill I T

AFFIDAVIT OF MOTHER.

UNITED STATES OF AMERICA, Indian Territory, ⎫
    Western   DISTRICT. ⎭

I, Lenie Fox, on oath state that I am 31 years of age and a citizen by Blood, of the Creek Nation; that I am the lawful wife of John Fox, who is a citizen, by Blood of the Creek Nation; that a male child was born to me on 8th day of August, 1903, that said child has been named Elgie Fox, and is now living.

                                  her
                           Lenie x Fox
Witnesses To Mark: mark
   { D C Skaggs Russell
    M J Byers

Subscribed and sworn to before me this 23 day of March, 1905.

                        M. Y. Killingsworth
                           Notary Public.

AFFIDAVIT OF ATTENDING PHYSICIAN OR MID-WIFE.

UNITED STATES OF AMERICA, Indian Territory, ⎫
    Western   DISTRICT. ⎭

I, M A Dobbs, a midwife, on oath state that I attended on Mrs. Lenie Fox, wife of John Fox on the 8 day of August, 1903; that there was born to her on said date a male child; that said child is now living and is said to have been named Elgie Fox

                        M A Dobbs

Witnesses To Mark:
   { D C Skaggs Russell
    M J Byers

Applications for Enrollment of Creek Newborn
Act of 1905   Volume VI

Subscribed and sworn to before me this 23   day of March , 1905.

M. Y. Killingsworth
Notary Public.

CERTIFICATE OF RECORD.

𝔘nited 𝔖tates of 𝔄merica,
   INDIAN TERRITORY, } ss.
   Western District.

I, **ROBERT P. HARRISON**, Clerk of the United States Court in the Western District, Indian Territory, do hereby certify that the instrument hereto attached was filed for record in my office the   14   day of   Aug   1902 at -----   M., and duly recorded in Book   N , Marriage Record, Page   156

WITNESS my hand and seal of said Court at Muscogee, in said Territory, this   11ˢᵗ[sic]   day of   Aug   A. D. 1902

R P Harrison   Clerk.

By   J L Peacock   Deputy.

𝔐ARRIAGE 𝔏ICENSE.

𝔘nited 𝔖tates of 𝔄merica,
   Indian Territory, } ss.   No. **46**
   Western District.

To Any Person Authorized by Law to Solemnize Marriage---Greeting:

𝔜ou are 𝔥ereby 𝔠ommanded to Solemnize the Rite and Publish the Banns of Matrimony between Mr.   Andy Posey   of   Wagoner , in the Indian Territory, aged   23   years and Miss Minnie Miller   of   Wagoner   in the Indian Territory aged   18   years according to law, and do you officially sign and return this License to the parties therein named.

WITNESS my hand and official seal at Muscogee Indian Territory this   19ᵗʰ   day of   July   A.D. 190 2

R.P. Harrison
Clerk of the U.S. Court

By   A.Z. English   Deputy

Applications for Enrollment of Creek Newborn
Act of 1905 Volume VI

CERTIFICATE OF MARRIAGE.

••••••

United States of America,
INDIAN TERRITORY, } ss.
Western District.

I, H.W. Bowman , a Minister of the Gospel, DO HEREBY CERTIFY that on the 25 day of July A. D. 1902, I did duly and according to law as commanded in the foregoing License, solemnize the Rite and Publish the Banns of Matrimony between the parties therein named.

WITNESS my hand this 20 day of July A. D. 1902

My credentials are recorded in the office of the Clerk of the United States Court, Indian Territory, Northern District, Book C , Page 106 .

HW Bowman
A Minister of the Gospel

Note—This License and Certificate of Marriage must be returned to the Office of the Clerk of the United States Court in the Northern District, Indian Territory, from whence it was issued, within sixty days from the date thereof, or the party to whom the license was issued will be liable in the amount of the One Hundred Dollars ($100.00)

BIRTH AFFIDAVIT.

DEPARTMENT OF THE INTERIOR.
COMMISSION TO THE FIVE CIVILIZED TRIBES.

IN RE APPLICATION FOR ENROLLMENT, as a citizen of the Creek Nation, of Thomas Owen Posey , born on the 12 day of May , 1903

Name of Father:	Andy W Posey	a citizen of the	Creek	Nation.
Name of Mother:	Minnie Posey	a citizen of the	U.S.	Nation.

Postoffice Wagoner I.T.

AFFIDAVIT OF MOTHER.

UNITED STATES OF AMERICA, Indian Territory, }
Western Judicial DISTRICT.

I, Minnie Posey , on oath state that I am 20 years of age and a citizen by ----- , of the United States ~~Nation~~; that I am the lawful wife of Andy W Posey , who is a

Applications for Enrollment of Creek Newborn
Act of 1905   Volume VI

citizen, by Blood of the Creek Nation; that a Male child was born to me on 12th day of May , 1903 , that said child has been named Thomas Owen Posey , and was living March 4, 1905.

Minnie Poset

Witnesses To Mark:
{

Subscribed and sworn to before me this 25th day of March , 1905.

H R Bonner
Notary Public.

AFFIDAVIT OF ATTENDING PHYSICIAN OR MID-WIFE.

UNITED STATES OF AMERICA, Indian Territory,
Western Judicial   DISTRICT.

I, G W Jobe , a Physician , on oath state that I attended on Mrs. Minnie Posey , wife of Andy W Posey on the 12th day of May , 1903 ; that there was born to her on said date a male child; that said child was living March 4, 1905, and is said to have been named Thomas Owen Posey

G W Jobe M.D.

Witnesses To Mark:
{

Subscribed and sworn to before me this 25th day of March , 1905.

H R Bonner
My Com Ex July 1st 1906   Notary Public.

BIRTH AFFIDAVIT.

DEPARTMENT OF THE INTERIOR.
COMMISSION TO THE FIVE CIVILIZED TRIBES.

IN RE APPLICATION FOR ENROLLMENT, as a citizen of the Creek Nation, of Jimmy Lewis, born on the 8th day of August , 1903

Name of Father:	Thomas Lewis	a citizen of the	Creek	Nation.
Name of Mother:	Lucy Baker	a citizen of the	Creek	Nation.

Child present   Postoffice   Oktaha IT.

Applications for Enrollment of Creek Newborn
Act of 1905 Volume VI

AFFIDAVIT OF MOTHER.

UNITED STATES OF AMERICA, Indian Territory,
Western DISTRICT.

    I, Lucy Baker , on oath state that I am 25 years of age and a citizen by blood , of the Creek Nation; that I am not the lawful wife of Thomas Lewis , who is a citizen, by blood of the Creek Nation; that a male child was born to me on 8" day of August , 1902[sic] , that said child has been named Jimmy Lewis , and was living March 4, 1905.

                                                Lucy Baker

Witnesses To Mark:
{

    Subscribed and sworn to before me this 25 day of Mar , 1905.

                                                J McDermott
                                               Notary Public.

AFFIDAVIT OF ATTENDING PHYSICIAN OR MID-WIFE.

UNITED STATES OF AMERICA, Indian Territory,
Western DISTRICT.

    I, Louisa Simmons , a mid-wife , on oath state that I attended on ~~Mrs.~~ Lucy Baker , ~~wife of~~ *(blank)* on the 8th day of August , 1903 ; that there was born to her on said date a male child, that said child was living March 4, 1905, and is said to have been named Jimmy Lewis
                                                     her
                                             Louisa x Simmons
Witnesses To Mark: mark
{ Daniel N. Bard
  Wash Collins

    Subscribed and sworn to before me this 20th day of March, 1905.

My commission expires July 3rd 1906.   Charles Buford
                                                        Notary Public.

NC-469.

                                        Muskogee, Indian Territory, August 4, 1905.

Callie Island,
        c/o George Island,
                Sapulpa, Indian Territory.

Applications for Enrollment of Creek Newborn
Act of 1905   Volume VI

Dear Madam:

On March 28, 1905 you appeared before the Commission to the Five Civilized Tribes and made application for the enrollment of your minor daughter Louisa Island as a citizen by blood of the Creek Nation and at that time submitted your affidavit which sets forth that sad child was born on July 25, 1903. Subsequently you and Aggie Fisher, midwife, appeared before said Commission and made affidavit to the effect that said child was born on July 20, 1904.

For the purpose of correcting this discrepancy as to the date of the birth of your daughter Louisa Island there is inclosed herewith blank for proof of birth which has been filled out, except as to the date of the birth of said child. You are requested to insert the correct date of the birth of your said daughter, have the affidavit properly executed and return the same to this office in the inclosed envelope.

Respectfully,

CTD-25.   Commissioner.
Env.

BIRTH AFFIDAVIT.

DEPARTMENT OF THE INTERIOR.
COMMISSION TO THE FIVE CIVILIZED TRIBES.

IN RE APPLICATION FOR ENROLLMENT, as a citizen of the Creek Nation, of Louisa Island, born on the 25" day of July, 1903

Name of Father: George Island   a citizen of the   Creek   Nation.
Name of Mother: Callie Island   a citizen of the   Creek   Nation.
                        Postoffice   Sapulpa, I.T

AFFIDAVIT OF MOTHER.

UNITED STATES OF AMERICA, Indian Territory,
    Western   DISTRICT.

I, Callie Island, on oath state that I am 24 years of age and a citizen by blood, of the Creek Nation; that I am the lawful wife of George Island, who is a citizen, by blood of the Creek Nation; that a female child was born to me on 25" day of July, 1903, that said child has been named Louisa Island, and was living March 4, 1905.

                            her
                    Callie x Island
                            mark

Applications for Enrollment of Creek Newborn
Act of 1905   Volume VI

Witnesses To Mark:
{ Frank Weeks
{ L. S. Scott

Subscribed and sworn to before me this 9" day of September, 1905.

John W. Weeks
My Commission Expires July 8th, 1906.   Notary Public.

AFFIDAVIT OF ATTENDING PHYSICIAN OR MID-WIFE.

UNITED STATES OF AMERICA, Indian Territory,
    Western   DISTRICT.

I, Aggie Fisher, a mid-wife, on oath state that I attended on Mrs. Callie Island, wife of George Island on the 25" day of July, 1903; that there was born to her on said date a female child; that said child was living March 4, 1905, and is said to have been named Louisa Island

Aggie Fisher

Witnesses To Mark:
{

Subscribed and sworn to before me this 9" day of September, 1905.

John W. Weeks
My Commission Expires July 8th, 1906.   Notary Public.

BIRTH AFFIDAVIT.

DEPARTMENT OF THE INTERIOR.
COMMISSION TO THE FIVE CIVILIZED TRIBES.

IN RE APPLICATION FOR ENROLLMENT, as a citizen of the CREEK Nation, of Louisa Island, born on the 25" day of July, 1903

Name of Father:	George Island	a citizen of the	Creek	Nation.
Name of Mother:	Callie "	a citizen of the	Creek	Nation.

(Child present)   Postoffice   Sapulpa, I.T

Applications for Enrollment of Creek Newborn
Act of 1905   Volume VI

AFFIDAVIT OF MOTHER.

UNITED STATES OF AMERICA, Indian Territory, }
WESTERN   DISTRICT.

I, Callie Island , on oath state that I am 24 years of age and a citizen by blood , of the Creek Nation; that I am the lawful wife of George Island , who is a citizen, by blood of the Creek Nation; that a female child was born to me on 25" day of July , 1903 , that said child has been named Louisa Island , and was living March 4, 1905.

                her
                Callie x Island
Witnesses To Mark: mark
{ EC Griesel
  Jesse McDermott

Subscribed and sworn to before me this 28" day of Mar , 1905.

                J McDermott
                Notary Public.

BIRTH AFFIDAVIT.

DEPARTMENT OF THE INTERIOR.
COMMISSION TO THE FIVE CIVILIZED TRIBES.

IN RE APPLICATION FOR ENROLLMENT, as a citizen of the Creek Nation, of Louisa Island, born on the 20 day of July , 1904

Name of Father: (Cussehta)	George Island	a citizen of the	Creek	Nation.
Name of Mother: (Tuskegee)	Callie Island	a citizen of the	Creek	Nation.

            Postoffice   Sapulpa, I.T

AFFIDAVIT OF MOTHER.
                Child Present

UNITED STATES OF AMERICA, Indian Territory, }
   Western   DISTRICT.

I, Callie Island , on oath state that I am 30 years of age and a citizen by blood , of the Creek Nation; that I am the lawful wife of George Island , who is a citizen, by blood of the Creek Nation; that a female child was born to me on 20 day of July , 1904 , that said child has been named Louisa Island , and was living March 4, 1905.

                Her
                Callie x Island
                mark

Applications for Enrollment of Creek Newborn
Act of 1905   Volume VI

Witnesses To Mark:
{ David Shelby
{ Jesse McDermott

Subscribed and sworn to before me this 26 day of April , 1905.

(Seal)   Edw C Griesel
   Notary Public.

AFFIDAVIT OF ATTENDING PHYSICIAN OR MID-WIFE.

UNITED STATES OF AMERICA, Indian Territory,
   Western   DISTRICT.

I, Aggie Fisher , a Mid wife , on oath state that I attended on Mrs. Callie Island, wife of George Island on the 20 day of July , 1904 ; that there was born to her on said date a female child; that said child was living March 4, 1905, and is said to have been named Louisa Island

Aggie Fisher

Witnesses To Mark:
{

Subscribed and sworn to before me this 26 day of April , 1905.

(Seal)   Edw C Griesel
   Notary Public.

BIRTH AFFIDAVIT.

DEPARTMENT OF THE INTERIOR.
COMMISSION TO THE FIVE CIVILIZED TRIBES.

IN RE APPLICATION FOR ENROLLMENT, as a citizen of the CREEK Nation, of Louvinna Island, born on the 28" day of Feb , 1905

Name of Father:	George Island	a citizen of the Creek	Nation.
Name of Mother:	Callie "	a citizen of the Creek	Nation.

(Child present)   Postoffice   Sapulpa, I.T

Applications for Enrollment of Creek Newborn
Act of 1905 Volume VI

AFFIDAVIT OF MOTHER.

UNITED STATES OF AMERICA, Indian Territory, }
WESTERN DISTRICT. }

I, Callie Island , on oath state that I am 24 years of age and a citizen by blood , of the Creek Nation; that I am the lawful wife of George Island , who is a citizen, by blood of the Creek Nation; that a female child was born to me on 28" day of Feb , 1905 , that said child has been named Louvinna Island , and is now living.

                          her
                    Callie x Island
Witnesses To Mark: mark
  { EC Griesel
    Jesse McDermott

Subscribed and sworn to before me this 28" day of Mar , 1905.

                    J McDermott
                    Notary Public.

BIRTH AFFIDAVIT.

DEPARTMENT OF THE INTERIOR.
COMMISSION TO THE FIVE CIVILIZED TRIBES.

IN RE APPLICATION FOR ENROLLMENT, as a citizen of the Creek Nation, of Luvena Island, born on the 28 day of Feb , 1905

Name of Father: (Cussehta)	George Island	a citizen of the	Creek	Nation.
Name of Mother: (Tuskegee)	Callie Island	a citizen of the	Creek	Nation.

                Postoffice   Sapulpa

AFFIDAVIT OF MOTHER.

                                Chi<u>ld Present</u>

UNITED STATES OF AMERICA, Indian Territory, }
  Western   DISTRICT. }

I, Callie Island , on oath state that I am 30 years of age and a citizen by blood , of the Creek Nation; that I am the lawful wife of George Island , who is a citizen, by blood of the Creek Nation; that a female child was born to me on 28 day of February , 1905 , that said child has been named Luvena Island , and was living March 4, 1905.   Her
                    Callie x Island
                       mark

Applications for Enrollment of Creek Newborn
Act of 1905   Volume VI

Witnesses To Mark:
{ David Shelby
{ Jesse McDermott

Subscribed and sworn to before me this 26 day of April , 1905.

(Seal)   Edw C Griesel
                                                Notary Public.

AFFIDAVIT OF ATTENDING PHYSICIAN OR MID-WIFE.

UNITED STATES OF AMERICA, Indian Territory, }
      Western   DISTRICT.

I, Mary Grayson , a Mid wife , on oath state that I attended on Mrs. Callie Island, wife of George Island on the   28 day of Feb , 1905 ; that there was born to her on said date a female child; that said child was living March 4, 1905, and is said to have been named   Luvena Island

                                        Her
                              Mary x Grayson
Witnesses To Mark: mark
{ David Shelby
{ Jesse McDermott

Subscribed and sworn to before me this 27 day of April , 1905.

(Seal)   Edw C Griesel
                                                Notary Public.

BA- 1269-B.

DEPARTMENT OF THE INTERIOR,
COMMISSION TO THE FIVE CIVILIZED TRIBES.
MUSKOGEE, INDIAN TERRITORY, MARCH 28, 1905.

-ooOoo-

In the matter of the application for the enrollment of Levorne Sudduth, as a citizen by blood of the Creek Nation.

PHOEBE SUDDUTH, being duly sworn, testified as follows through Jesse McDermott, Official Interpreter:

Applications for Enrollment of Creek Newborn
Act of 1905 Volume VI

EXAMINATION BY COMMISSION:
Q What is your name? A Phoebe Sudduth.
Q How old are you? A Twenty-two.
Q What is your postoffice address? A Wagoner.
Q Are you a citizen of the Creek Nation? A Yes.
Q What was your maiden name? A Phoebe Anderson.

Witness is identified on Creek Indian Card as Phoebe Anderson, Field Number 229, and her name is contained in the partial list of citizens by blood, approved by the Secretary of the Interior March 13, 1902, Roll Number 776.

Q Have you a child named Levorne Sudduth? A Yes.
Q What is the name of the father of that child? A Bob Sudduth.
Q Is he living? A No.
Q When did he die? A I do not know.
Q When was Levorne born? A I do not know.
Q When did he die? A I do not know.
Q How long did he live? A Two weeks.
Q Are you sure that he only lived two weeks? A Yes.
Q Did he live longer that two weeks? He lived two weeks; that is all I know.
Q How many days did he live? A I do not know that.
Q Did you have a doctor in attendance when Levorne was born? A Yes.
Q What is his name? A Dr. Walker.
Q Where does he live? A Coweta.
Q Who else was present when Levorne was born? A Ella Flowers.
Q Where does she live? A She now lives at Wagoner.
Q Was there any record made of the birth of Levorne---did any one set down the date of his birth in a book or anywhere? A It might have been, but I do not know.
Q Was that child born in this new year? A Yes.
Q That is 1905? A Yes.
Q Do you know when Washington's birthday comes? A No, I never did study it.

WILLIAM SUDDUTH, being duly sworn, testified as follows:

EXAMINATION BY COMMISSION:
Q What is your name? A William Sudduth.
Q How old are you? A 27 February 20th, last.
Q What is your postoffice address? A Wagoner.
Q Do you know a child of Bob and Phoebe Sudduth's by the name of Levorne? A Yes.
Q When was that child born? A February 20th.
Q What year? A 1905.
Q Why do you remember that date so well? A Because my mother was sitting up with her (Phoebe) and I was sick in another room--all was sick but one.
Q Is that the reason you remember that date so well just because she was sick and your mother was sitting up with her and you were sick in another room, and all were sick but one? A No, because that was when it was born.
Q Did you ever see the date of this child's birth written down anywhere? A Yes.

185

Applications for Enrollment of Creek Newborn
Act of 1905   Volume VI

Q What date did you see written down? A February 20th.
Q Who wrote that down? A Me---I did.
Q When did you write that down? A The day it was born.
Q The very same day it was born? A Yes.
Q What did you write that with, pen or pencil? A Pencil--the very one that I have now I wrote it down with---it is an indelible.
Q Do you live at the same place with this woman? A Yes.
Q Are you any kin to her? A Indeed not.
Q What do you mean by "indeed not", you say she married your brother? [sic] Yes, she married my brother Bob.
Q Then she is your sister-in-law? A Yes, by marriage.
Q Is your brother living? A No.
Q When did he die? A The last of April or first of May in last year.
Q 1904? A Yes.
Q Is Levorne Sudduth living? A No.
Q How long did he live--Levorne? A About two weeks.
Q What do you mean by about two weeks--do you mean that he lived more or less than two weeks? A When I said about two weeks I meant that he did not live much more than two weeks.
Q Were you present when he died? A No.
Q Then you did not write that down? A No.
Q Did they have a doctor when he died? A I do not know.
Q Did they put the date of Levorne's death on a tombstone? A No.
Q Did they have a funeral? A They had not funeral but they had a burying.
Q Were you at the burying? A No.
Q When did you come back-- how many days after that child's death? A Just a few days.
Q Well, about how many? A About three days.
Q What day did you get back there? A I do not remember now. I went to Claremore March the third and then I----then the next day I came back to Wagoner.
Q So you came back to Wagoner about the 5th of March? A Yes, I expect so. The child had been buried about three days.
Q Did they tell you he had been buried three days? A They did not say.
Q But you said you got back about three days after the burying? A Yes
Q Did you get back on the 5th of March? A I expect so.
Q You went to Claremore March 3rd and came back to Wagoner on the 4th or 5th of March, is that right? A I came back to Wagoner March 4th and I went home on the 5th of March.
Q You remember that distinctly? A Yes.
Q You got back to Wagoner on the 5th of March? A Yes.
Q And when you got back they told you that Levorne had been buried about three days? A Yes.
Q Was that child living when you left home on that trip? A Yes.
Q How long were you away--were you away as long as a week? A No.
Q Are you positive that you arrived in Wagoner after that trip on the 5th of March? A I arrived at Wagoner on March 4th and left Wagoner on the 5th on that 5?45 Flyer, and then I came here to Muskogee---

Applications for Enrollment of Creek Newborn
Act of 1905 Volume VI

Q You say this child was born February 20th, 1905, that is not so long off that you aught[sic] to get mixed up--how many days after the birth of this child did you start there? A I do not know the very day I left home.
Q How many trips did you make from home after the birth of this child until its death? A Just one.
Q When did you begin that trip--what day? The reason I ask you this is because a while ago I asked you how you remembered the date of the child's birth and you said you remembered it by a certain trip, now I ask you what day of the month did you start on that trip? A I left home March 1st, but I am not positive about it being March 1st because I did not look at the calender[sic].
Q After the 1st where did you go? A To Claremore.
Q Was that child living when you left home? [sic] Yes.
Q How long did you stay at Claremore? A I went there one night and came back next day to Wagoner. I just moved to Wagoner last Saturday.
Q Where did you go then? A I went to Coweta March 5th.
Q When you got back home there was no Levorne Sudduth there? A No.
Q Are you positive that you left home on March 1? A Yes.
Q Are you positive that Levorne was living March 4, 1905 then? A Yes.
Q When you got back home on the 5th of March what time of the day was it--was it morning, evening or night? A I arrived back at Coweta in the morning.
Q Early in the morning? A Suppose so; it was about nine o'clock.
Q Did you inquire then about where that child Levorne was? A I met my little brother when I got off the train---he is eight years old---and I asked about all the people, how they were, and he said that they were all well but Levorne he was dead. I asked him and then he told me.
Q Did he tell you what day? A Yes, but I took no note of it then.
Q Did he say the child had been dead one, two or three days? A I cannot remember exactly.
Q But he was dead and buried when you got there March 5th? A Yes.
Q What did he die of? A I do not know--Doctor Walton would know.
Q Dr. who? A Dr. Willie W. Walton.
Q Where does he live? A Coweta.
Q Would he know the date of the birth and death of this child? A Yes he is our family physician.
Q Do you know how long they kept the child after it died until it was buried? A No.
Q You do not know whether the funeral was the day before you got back? A It had been buried longer than that.
Q According to that the child could not have been living on the 3rd of March could it? A No, because I came back on the 5th.
A And it was dead and buried then? A Yes.

PHOEBE SUDDUTH, recalled, testifies as follows:

Q What was the matter with Levorne when he died? A I do not know.
Q He just died? A Yes.
Q How long did you keep him after he died--did you keep him as much as a day or did you keep him as much as two days? A Just one half day.

Applications for Enrollment of Creek Newborn
Act of 1905 Volume VI

Q When did he die, morning, evening or night? A In the morning.
Q Do you remember when this man, William Sudduth, came back after Levorne died? A Yes.
Q How long had it been dead and buried when he came back? A I do not know.
Q Do you know whether he had been buried two days? A No answer.
Q Was that child buried the day before this man came back? A do not know.
Q When did they bury him, morning, noon or night--you said they buried him a half day after he died? A They burid[sic] him the same day.

WILLIAM SUDDUTH, recalled, testified as follows:
Q Are you positive that Levorne was not buried the day before you came back? A I remember now, since I have been thinking--I left home March 1, and mama said that it died the night that I stayed at Wagoner, Indian Territory, which was the 2nd; it died in the morning, and they could not get a new coffin to fit and so they had some one to make one, and I am satisfied that they buried it the same day.
Q What makes you think it was the 2nd of March? A I was at Wagoner the 2nd of March and my mother said that it died the night I was at Wagoner.
Q What is your mother's name? A Ella Flowers.
Q Is she at Coweta? A No, I moved to Wagoner; we were living at Coweta at that time.
Q You say you remember getting home on the 5th of March--what day of the week was that? A I do not remember that.
Q Don't you remember whether it was Friday, Saturday or Sunday? A I do not remember now, I will be positive.
Q When did your mother tell you that the child died the night you were in Wagoner on that trip? A I came home and gave them a scolding for not telephoning me to Wagoner how the child was getting along. I asked them when I left to telephone or let me know if any of them got sick and I would come back, and if I couldn't get back on the train, couldn't make the time, I would come through by land anyhow, but mother said that I could not do any good and that she had enough money to have the coffin made and thought that they could do just as well without me as if I was there. I could not have got there in time to see the child die anyway.
Q Then that trip to Wagoner was the first trip you made after you left home? A Yes.

Zera Ellen Parrish, being sworn on her oath states that as a stenographer to the Commission to the Five Civilized Tribes she reported the above case and that this is a full, true and correct transcript of her stenographic notes in same.

Zera Ellen Parrish

Subscribed and sworn to
before me this 29th day of
March, 1905.

Edw C Griesel
Notary Public.

Applications for Enrollment of Creek Newborn
Act of 1905 Volume VI

N.C. 470.

DEPARTMENT OF THE INTERIOR,
COMMISSIONER TO THE FIVE CIVILIZED TRIBES.
MUSKOGEE, I.T. December 16, 1905.

In the matter of the application for the enrollment of Ida, Rosetta and Levorn Suddath[sic] as citizens by blood of the Creek Nation.

Phoebe Suddath, being duly sworn, testified as follows:

Q What is your name? A Phoebe Suddath.
Q You have testified in this case before haven't you? A Yes, sir
Q Give the names of your children? [sic] Ida Suddath, Rosetta Suddath and Levorn Suddath.
Q Which one of these children was born first? A Ida
Q What year was she born in? A April 20th
Q I asked you what year? A 1902.
A And she died in the same year didn't she? A No, sir
Q What day and month can you tell? A No answer.
Q January, February March or April? A April
Q Are you sure it was born April 1903[sic] A Yes, sir
Q Do you know the date? A April 15
Q Are you sure it was April 15, 1903? A Yes, sir
Q We have an affidavit executed by you in which you state that Rosetta was born---day of April 1902 and another in which----an earlier affidavit-- you state Rosetta was born 18 of March 1902
Q Now 1902 was wrong was it? A Yes, sir
Q That was the year Ida was born and this one was not her twin? A Yes, sir
Q And the March was wrong? A Yes, sir
Q The affidavit giving April is correct is it? A Yes, sir
Q Later on we also received the affidavit of Willie Suddath and Mary Spann and they testified that Rosetta was born in 1902. This child Rosetta is living? A Yes, sir
Q Where is she? A Right here.
Q You don't remember dates very well do you? [sic] No answer
Q Now this third child Levorn, you have testified and the others have testified it lived about two weeks, do you remember when it was born? A No, sir
Q Wasn't born long ago was it? A No, sir
Q Was it before or after last Christmas? A It was after Christmas.
Q Was it after the first of the year? Do you remember the month in which he was born? A No, sir
Q You have testified before about Levorn and your testimony gave the impression that he was born and died before March 4, 1905 is that correct as you now remember it or do you remember when March 4, 1905 was? A No, sir
Q You are positive of that? A Yes, sir

Applications for Enrollment of Creek Newborn
Act of 1905   Volume VI

Q You received a letter from this office telling you to appear with the midwife who attended at the birth of Rosetta and at least one other witness, you didn't bring any witness did you? A Yes, sir
Q you[sic] signed one affidavit Sudduth and another Suddath, which is correct? A I don't remember.

William Sudduth being duly sworn, testified as follows:

Q What is your name, how do you spell it? [sic] William Sudduth
Q Was Bob Sudduth your brother? A Yes, sir
Q And that is the way he spelled his name was it? A Yes, sir
Q What is the name of the child in your arms? A Rosetta Sudduth
Q You have testified about the child Levorn, your dead brothers[sic] child, and you said you thought that he died and was buried March 2, do you remember saying that? A Yes, sir
Q Ida Sudduth what year was she born in? A 1902
Q And died the same year? A Yes, sir
Q Was Ida Sudduth a twin of Rosetta, you have in your arms? [sic] No, sir
Q Then how came[sic] you to make out an affidavit that Rosetta was born in 1902? A Just a mistake.
Q When was Rosetta born? A 1903, April 15
Q You are sure of that now? A Yes, sir

Phoebe Sudduth is advised that under the testimony, Ida Sudduth is not entitled to enrollment because she died too soon. Levorn Sudduth is not entitled because he died before March 4th. Rosetta Sudduth will require further proof because you have given conflicting dates besides you had no physician did you? A Yes, sir
Q What was his name? A Dicey Gibson.
Q Can you get her affidavit? A No answer.

Witness is advised that if she can secure the affidavit of the midwife setting forht[sic] the date of this child's birth, and whether or not it was living March 4, 1905 March 4, 1905, it should be done at once. If the affidavit of the midwife can be procured do so if not two disinterested witnesses will be required to make affidavit.
Q What is your post office address? A Wagoner.

I, Anna Garrigues, on oath state that the above and foregoing is a true and correct copy of my stenographic notes taken in said case on said date.

Anna Garrigues

Subscribed and sworn to before
me this 16 day of December 1905.

J McDermott
Notary Public.

Applications for Enrollment of Creek Newborn
Act of 1905 Volume VI

N.C. 470.　　　　　　　　　　　　　　　　　　　　　　　　　　　　J.L.De.
DEPARTMENT OF THE INTERIOR,
COMMISSIONER TO THE FIVE CIVILIZED TRIBES.

In the matter of the application for the enrollment of Ida Sudduth, deceased, and Levorn Sudduth, deceased, as citizens by blood of the Creek Nation.

STATEMENT AND ORDER.

The record in this case shows that on March 28, 1905, applications were made, in affidavit form, supplemented by testimony taken March 28, 1905 and December 16, 1905, for the enrollment of Ida Sudduth, deceased, and Levorn Sudduth, deceased, as citizens by blood of the Creek Nation, under the provisions of the act of Congress approved March 3, 1905.

It appears from the evidence filed in this matter that said Ida Sudduth was born April 20, 1902, and died in the month of June of the same year.

The evidence as to the dates of birth and death of said Levorn Sudduth is conflicting but the weight of evidence shows that he was born February 20, 1905, and died March 2 of the same year.

The act of Congress approved March 3, 1905, (33 Stats., 1048), in part provides:

"That the Commission to the Five Civilized Tribes is authorized for sixty days after the date of the approval of this act to receive and consider applications for enrollment, of children, born subsequent to May twenty-fifth, nineteen hundred and one, and prior to March fourth, nineteen hundred and five, and living on said latter date, to citizens of the Creek tribe of Indians whose enrollment has been approved by the Secretary of the Interior prior to the approval of this act; and to enroll and make allotments to such children."

It is, therefore, ordered that the applications for the enrollment of Ida Sudduth, deceased, and Levorn Sudduth, deceased, as citizens by blood of the Creek Nation, be, and the same are, hereby dismissed.

　　　　　　　　　　　　　　　　　　　　Tams Bixby Commissioner.
Muskogee, Indian Territory.
JAN 18 1907

BIRTH AFFIDAVIT.
DEPARTMENT OF THE INTERIOR.
COMMISSION TO THE FIVE CIVILIZED TRIBES.

IN RE APPLICATION FOR ENROLLMENT, as a citizen of the CREEK Nation, of Levorn Suddath, born on the *(blank)* day after of Christmas in , 1904

Applications for Enrollment of Creek Newborn
Act of 1905   Volume VI

Name of Father: Bob Suddath   a citizen of the   U. S.   Nation.
Name of Mother: Phoebe   "   a citizen of the   Creek   Nation.

Postoffice   Wagoner

AFFIDAVIT OF MOTHER.

UNITED STATES OF AMERICA, Indian Territory, ⎫
   Western   DISTRICT. ⎭

I, Phoebe Suddath , on oath state that I am 22 years of age and a citizen by blood , of the Creek Nation; that I am the lawful wife of Bob Suddath (dc'd) , who is a citizen, by ----- of the U.S. Nation; that a male child was born to me on -- after X-mas in , 1904 , that said child has been named Levorn Suddath , and ~~is now living~~. died 2 weeks after birth

                                    Phoebe Suddethe[sic]

Witnesses To Mark:
{

Subscribed and sworn to before me this 28" day of March , 1905.

                          J McDermott
                            Notary Public.

BIRTH AFFIDAVIT.
DEPARTMENT OF THE INTERIOR.
COMMISSION TO THE FIVE CIVILIZED TRIBES.

IN RE APPLICATION FOR ENROLLMENT, as a citizen of the CREEK Nation, of Ida Suddath, born on the ----- day of Feb. , 1902

Name of Father: Bob Suddath (d)   a citizen of the   U.S.   Nation.
Name of Mother: Phoebe   "   a citizen of the   Creek   Nation.

Postoffice   Wagoner

AFFIDAVIT OF MOTHER.

UNITED STATES OF AMERICA, Indian Territory, ⎫
   WESTERN   DISTRICT. ⎭

I, ~~Ida~~ Phoebe Suddath , on oath state that I am 22 years of age and a citizen by blood , of the Creek   Nation; that I am the lawful wife of Bob Suddath , who is a citizen, by ----- of the U.S. Nation; that a female child was born to me on ----- day

Applications for Enrollment of Creek Newborn
Act of 1905   Volume VI

of Feb. , 1902 , that said child has been named Ida Suddath , and is now living. died June 1902.

                                                    Phoebe Suddeth[sic]

Witnesses To Mark:
{

Subscribed and sworn to before me this 28" day of March , 1905.

                                                    J McDermott
                                                    Notary Public.

BIRTH AFFIDAVIT.
DEPARTMENT OF THE INTERIOR.
COMMISSION TO THE FIVE CIVILIZED TRIBES.

IN RE APPLICATION FOR ENROLLMENT, as a citizen of the CREEK Nation, of Rosetta Suddath , born on the 18" day of March, 1902

Name of Father:	Bob Suddath	a citizen of the	U.S.	Nation.
Name of Mother:	Phoebe "	a citizen of the	Creek	Nation.

                                    Postoffice   Wagoner

AFFIDAVIT OF MOTHER.

UNITED STATES OF AMERICA, Indian Territory, }
       WESTERN   **DISTRICT.**

I, Phoebe Suddath , on oath state that I am 22 years of age and a citizen by blood , of the Creek Nation; that I am the lawful wife of Bob Suddath , who is a citizen, by ----- of the U. S. Nation; that a female child was born to me on 18" day of March , 1902 , that said child has been named Rosetta Suddath , and is now living.

                                                  Phoebe Suddeth[sic]

Witnesses To Mark:
{

Subscribed and sworn to before me this 28" day of March , 1905.

                                                  J McDermott
                                                Notary Public.

Applications for Enrollment of Creek Newborn
Act of 1905 Volume VI

BIRTH AFFIDAVIT.

DEPARTMENT OF THE INTERIOR.
COMMISSION TO THE FIVE CIVILIZED TRIBES.

IN RE APPLICATION FOR ENROLLMENT, as a citizen of the Creek Nation, of Rosetta Sudduth, born on the 15" day of April, 1903

Name of Father:	Bob Sudduth	a citizen of the	U.S.	Nation.
Name of Mother:	Phoebe Sudduth	a citizen of the	Creek	Nation.

Postoffice   Wagoner

AFFIDAVIT OF MOTHER.

UNITED STATES OF AMERICA, Indian Territory,
Western   DISTRICT.

I, Phoebe Sudduth, on oath state that I am 23 years of age and a citizen by blood, of the Creek Nation; that I am the lawful wife of Bob Sudduth, who is a citizen, by ----- of the U.S. Nation; that a female child was born to me on 15" day of April, 1903, that said child has been named Rosetta Sudduth, and was living March 4, 1905.

Phoebe Sudduth

Witnesses To Mark:

Subscribed and sworn to before me this 16" day of December, 1905.

Henry G. Hains
Notary Public.

BIRTH AFFIDAVIT.

DEPARTMENT OF THE INTERIOR.
COMMISSION TO THE FIVE CIVILIZED TRIBES.

IN RE APPLICATION FOR ENROLLMENT, as a citizen of the Creek Nation, of Rosetta Sudduth, born on the *(blank)* day of April, 1902

Name of Father:	Bob Sudduth	a citizen of the	----	Nation.
Name of Mother:	Phoebe Sudduth	a citizen of the	Creek	Nation.

Postoffice   Wagoner, I.T.

Applications for Enrollment of Creek Newborn
Act of 1905   Volume VI

AFFIDAVIT OF MOTHER.

UNITED STATES OF AMERICA, Indian Territory,
Western   DISTRICT.

    I, Phoebe Sudduth , on oath state that I am 23 years of age and a citizen by blood , of the Creek   Nation; that I am the lawful wife of Bob Sudduth (now deceased) , who is a citizen, by ----- of the ------   Nation; that a female child was born to me on *(blank)* day of April , 1902 , that said child has been named Rosetta Sudduth , and was living March 4, 1905.

                                                        Phoebe Sudduth

Witnesses To Mark:

    Subscribed and sworn to before me this 29th day of August , 1905.

                                                  Howard Searcy
                                                Notary Public.

AFFIDAVIT
• • • •

United States of America)
    Indian Territory   (ss:
Western Judicial District)

    Willie Sudduth and Mary Spann, of lawful age, being first duly sworn, each for himself, states:

    That they are well and personally acquainted with Phoebe Sudduth, and have been for more than five years last past; that on the *(blank)* day of April, 1902, a female child was born to said Phoebe Sudduth, which was afterwards named Rosetta Sudduth; that said child is still living.
    Affiants further state that the only person who attended o said Phoebe Sudduth at the birth of said child, was one Dicey Gipson, a mid-wife who resided three miles south of the Town of Coweta, I.T., and that said Dicey Gipson died in the month of August, 1904.

                                                  Willie Sudduth

                                                  Mary Spann

    Subscribed in my presence and sworn to before me this 29th day of August, 1905.

                                                  Howard Searcy
                                                Notary Public

My commission expires Dec. 16, 1907.

Applications for Enrollment of Creek Newborn
Act of 1905 Volume VI

Western District
Indian Territory   SS

    We, the undersigned, on oath state that we are personally acquainted with Phoebe Sudduth wife of Bob Sudduth; that on ~~or about~~ on the 15" day of April, 1903, a female child was born to them and has been named Rosetta Sudduth; and that said child was living March 4, 1905.

    We further state that we have no interest in the above case.

                                          her
                                    Melvina x Rogers
                                        mark
                                        her
                                    Rose x *(Illegible)*
Witness to mark: mark
  J F Hall
  M. J. Phillips

Subscribed and sworn to before
  me this 4th day of January 1906

                                        H R Bonner
                                          Notary Public

My com ex July 1st 1906

NC-470.

                              Muskogee, Indian Territory, August 4, 1905.

Phoebe Suddath,
    Wagoner, Indian Territory.

Dear Madam:

    On March 28, 1905 you appears[sic] before the Commission to the Five Civilized Tribes and made application for the enrollment of your minor daughter Rosetta Suddath and at that time submitted your affidavit only as to the birth of said child stating that no one attended you when he was born of said child.

    You are advised that it will be necessary, in the matter of the enrollment of said child, for you to furnish the affidavit of the attending physician or midwife as to her birth and for that purpose a blank for proof of birth is inclosed herewith.

    In having the same executed be careful to see that all blank spaces are properly filled, all names written in full and that the notary public, before whom the affidavits are

Applications for Enrollment of Creek Newborn
Act of 1905   Volume VI

sworn to, attaches his name and seal to each affidavit. In case any signature if by mark the same must be attest[sic] by two disinterested witnesses.

Respectfully,

B C
Env.
Commissioner.

NC 470.

Muskogee, Indian Territory, January 19, 1907.

Phoebe Sudduth,
    General Delivery,
        Muskogee, Indian Territory.

Dear Madam:

There is herewith enclosed one copy of the statement and order of the Commissioner to the Five Civilized Tribes, dated January 18, 1907, dismissing the application made by you for the enrollment of your minor children, Ida and Levorn Suddth[sic], both deceased, as citizens of the Creek Nation.

Respectfully,

Commissioner.

Register.
LM-1110.

BIRTH AFFIDAVIT.

DEPARTMENT OF THE INTERIOR,
COMMISSIONER TO THE FIVE CIVILIZED TRIBES.

IN RE APPLICATION FOR ENROLLMENT, as a citizen of the Creek Nation, of Richard Roy Hooks , born on the 25 day of Dec , 1904

Name of Father:	Lem P. Hooks	a citizen of the	U.S.	Nation.
Name of Mother:	Alice Hooks	a citizen of the	Creek	Nation.

Postoffice   Broken Arrow I.T.

Applications for Enrollment of Creek Newborn
Act of 1905 Volume VI

AFFIDAVIT OF MOTHER.

UNITED STATES OF AMERICA, Indian Territory, }
Western District.

I, Alice Hooks, on oath state that I am 34 years of age and a citizen by Blood, of the Creek Nation; that I am the lawful wife of Lem P. Hooks, who is a citizen, by Birth of the U.S. Nation; that a Male child was born to me on 25 day of December, 1904, that said child has been named Richard Roy Hooks, and was living March 4, 1905.

Alice Hooks

Witness to Mark: }

Subscribed and sworn to before me this 24" day of March, 1905.

Com Ex 7/3/1906   Robert E. Lynch
                                   Notary Public.

AFFIDAVIT OF ATTENDING PHYSICIAN OR MID-WIFE.

UNITED STATES OF AMERICA, Indian Territory, }
Western District.

I, R.S. Plumblee[sic], a Physician, on oath state that I attended on Mrs. Alice Hooks, wife of Lem P. Hooks on the 25 day of December, 1904; that there was born to her on said date a *(blank)* child; that said child was living March 4, 1905, and is said to have been named Richard Roy Hooks

R.S. Plumlee. M.D.

Witness to Mark: }

Subscribed and sworn to before me this 25 day of March, 1905.

My Commission Expires January 13, 1907   F.S. Aurd
                                                              Notary Public.

BIRTH AFFIDAVIT.

DEPARTMENT OF THE INTERIOR.
COMMISSION TO THE FIVE CIVILIZED TRIBES.

IN RE APPLICATION FOR ENROLLMENT, as a citizen of the Muskogee Nation, of Edward Benson, born on the 11 day of March, 1904

Applications for Enrollment of Creek Newborn
Act of 1905   Volume VI

Name of Father: William Benson   a citizen of the Muskogee   Nation.
Name of Mother: Katie Benson   a citizen of the Muskogee   Nation.

Postoffice   Morse I.T.

AFFIDAVIT OF MOTHER.

UNITED STATES OF AMERICA, Indian Territory,
Western   DISTRICT.

I, Katie Benson , on oath state that I am 35 years of age and a citizen by Blood, of the Muskogee Nation; that I am the lawful wife of William Benson , who is a citizen, by Blood of the Muskogee Nation; that a Male child was born to me on 11 day of March , 1904 , that said child has been named Edward Benson , and was living March 4, 1905.

Katie Benson

Witnesses To Mark:

Subscribed and sworn to before me this 24 day of March , 1905.

C. C. Eskridge
My Commission Expires March 5th, 1908.   Notary Public.

AFFIDAVIT OF ATTENDING PHYSICIAN OR MID-WIFE.

UNITED STATES OF AMERICA, Indian Territory,
Western   DISTRICT.

I, J.A. Kennedy , a Physician , on oath state that I attended on Mrs. Katie Benson , wife of William Benson on the 11 day of March , 1904 ; that there was born to her on said date a male child; that said child was living March 4, 1905, and is said to have been named Edward Benson

J A Kennedy M.D.

Witnesses To Mark:

Subscribed and sworn to before me this 24 day of March , 1905.

C. C. Eskridge
My Commission Expires March 5th, 1908.   Notary Public.

Applications for Enrollment of Creek Newborn
Act of 1905 Volume VI

DEPARTMENT OF THE INTERIOR,
COMMISSION TO THE FIVE CIVILIZED TRIBES.

IN RE Application for Enrollment, as a citizen of the Muskogee Nation, of Billie Benson, born on the 1 day of Nov , 1901

Name of Father: William Benson   a citizen of the Muskogee Nation.
Name of Mother: Katie Benson   a citizen of the Muskogee Nation.
on roll as Katie Watson

Post-office: Morse I.T.

AFFIDAVIT OF MOTHER.

UNITED STATES OF AMERICA, }
   INDIAN TERRITORY. }
   Western   District. }

I, Katie Benson , on oath state that I am 35 years of age and a citizen by Blood , of the Muskogee Nation; that I am the lawful wife of William Benson , who is a citizen, by Blood of the Muskogee Nation; that a male child was born to me on 1 day of Nov , 1901 , that said child has been named Billie Benson , and is now living.

                                Katie Benson

WITNESSES TO MARK:
{

Subscribed and sworn to before me this 24 *day of* March , *1905*.

                                C. C. Eskridge
My Commission Expires March 5th, 1908.   *NOTARY PUBLIC.*

AFFIDAVIT OF ATTENDING PHYSICIAN OR MID-WIFE.

UNITED STATES OF AMERICA, }
   INDIAN TERRITORY. }
   Western   District. }

I, Bettie Carr , a Mid-wife , on oath state that I attended on Mrs. Katie Benson , wife of William Benson on the 1 day of Nov. , 1901 ; that there was born to her on said date a Male child; that said child is now living and is said to have been named Billie Benson

                                        her
                              Bettie Carr x
WITNESSES TO MARK: mark
{ J. E. Tiger
  A. V. Seller

Applications for Enrollment of Creek Newborn
Act of 1905 Volume VI

Subscribed and sworn to before me this 1st *day of* April, *1905*.

BB Chitwood
NOTARY PUBLIC.

NC-473.

Muskogee, Indian Territory, August 4, 1905.

Nancy Cooper,
    c/o Sam Cooper,
        Bixby, Indian Territory.

Dear Madam:

    On March 25, 1905 you filed with the Commission to the Five Civilized Tribes an application for the enrollment of your daughter Nellie Cooper as a citizen by blood of the Creek Nation. From the information contained in said application this office is unable to identify you upon the final roll of citizens by blood of the Creek Nation.

    In order that you May be properly identified you are requested to immediately inform this office as to the name under which you were finally enrolled, the names of your parents and other members of your family, the Creek Indian town to which you belong and your final roll number as the same appears upon your allotment certificate and deeds.

                Respectfully,

                              Commissioner.

BIRTH AFFIDAVIT.
DEPARTMENT OF THE INTERIOR.
COMMISSION TO THE FIVE CIVILIZED TRIBES.

    IN RE APPLICATION FOR ENROLLMENT, as a citizen of the CREEK Nation, of Nellie Cooper, born on the 3rd day of Feby., 1903

Name of Father: Sam Cooper   a citizen of the   Creek   Nation. Euchee Town
Name of Mother: Nancy Cooper (nee Littlehead) a citizen of the   Creek   Nation. Euchee Town

                        Postoffice   Bixby Ind. Ter.

Applications for Enrollment of Creek Newborn
Act of 1905   Volume VI

AFFIDAVIT OF MOTHER.

UNITED STATES OF AMERICA, Indian Territory,
WESTERN   DISTRICT.

I, Nancy Cooper, on oath state that I am about 29 years of age and a citizen by blood, of the Creek Nation; that I am the lawful wife of Sam Cooper, who is a citizen, by blood of the Creek Nation; that a female child was born to me on third day of February, 1903, that said child has been named Nellie Cooper, and is now living.

                 her
              Nancy x Cooper
Witnesses To Mark: mark
 { Sam Cooper
   Albert Cooper

Subscribed and sworn to before me this 23rd day of March, 1905.

             J. F. *(Illegible)*
               Notary Public.
            My Commission Expires July 2nd, 1906.

AFFIDAVIT OF ATTENDING PHYSICIAN OR MID-WIFE.

UNITED STATES OF AMERICA, Indian Territory,
WESTERN   DISTRICT.

            acting as midwife

I, Lucy Wolf, a Creek citizen, on oath state that I attended on Mrs. Nancy Cooper, wife of Sam Cooper on the third day of Feb, 1903; that there was born to her on said date a female child; that said child is now living and is said to have been named Nellie Cooper

                her
             Lucy x Wolfe
Witnesses To Mark: mark
 { Sam Cooper
   Albert Cooper

Subscribed and sworn to before me this 23rd day of March, 1905.

             J. F. *(Illegible)*
               Notary Public.
            My Commission Expires July 2nd, 1906.

Applications for Enrollment of Creek Newborn
Act of 1905   Volume VI

N.C. 393[sic].

Muskogee, Indian Territory, August 3, 1905.

Annie Watson,
    Care Sandy Watson,
        Dustin, Indian Territory.

Dear Madam:

    March 28, 1905 there was filed at this office, an affidavit executed by you relative to the birth of your child, Dave Watson. You state that the father of said child is Sandy Watson.

    This office cannot identify you on its rolls of citizens of the Creek Nation and you are requested to state your maiden name, the names of your parents, the Creek Indian Town to which you belong and if possible the numbers which appear on your deeds to land in the Creek Nation.

    This matter should receive your prompt attention.

Respectfully,

Commissioner.

N C 474

Brush Hill Ind Ter Sept 8, 1905

Commissioner

    Muskogee, Ind Ter

Dear Sir

    Received your letter of August 25, 1905 in reply which you asked me to give my maiden name The childs[sic] is Dave Watson born Sept 26, 1904 and his father is Sandy Watson of Dustin Ind Ter and my maiden name was Annie Howell my creek[sic] town is Tuskegee and also Dave Watson is my child was the reason I enrolled him and I gave my number of land in the other letter or I can give my numbers again

E 1/2 of S E 1/4 Sec 11 town 11 range 11
N E 1/4 of N E 1/4   14   11   11
W 1/2 of N W 1/4 of N W 1/4 and
W 1/2 E 1/2 of N W 1/4 of N W 1/2 13-11-11

Applications for Enrollment of Creek Newborn
Act of 1905   Volume VI

This contain[sic] 150 acres which I have no certificate for the other land So this is all I think you have asked me

Respectfully

Annie Watson nee Howell

BIRTH AFFIDAVIT.

DEPARTMENT OF THE INTERIOR.
COMMISSION TO THE FIVE CIVILIZED TRIBES.

IN RE APPLICATION FOR ENROLLMENT, as a citizen of the Creek Nation, of Lela Watson, born on the 2 day of September, 1903

Name of Father:	Sandy Watson	a citizen of the	Creek	Nation.
Name of Mother:	Annie Watson	a citizen of the	Creek	Nation.

Postoffice   Dustin, Ind. Ter.

AFFIDAVIT OF MOTHER.

UNITED STATES OF AMERICA, Indian Territory,
Western   DISTRICT.

I, Annie Watson, on oath state that I am 22 years of age and a citizen by blood, of the Creek Nation; that I am the lawful wife of Sandy Watson, who is a citizen, by blood of the Creek Nation; that a female child was born to me on 2 day of September, 1903, that said child has been named Lela Watson, and was living March 4, 1905. That the midwife (Sally Watson) who attended on me at the time the child was born is unable to appear to execute an affidavit on account of illness.

Annie Watson

Witnesses To Mark:

{

Subscribed and sworn to before me this 24 day of March, 1905.

Drennan C Skaggs
Notary Public.

Applications for Enrollment of Creek Newborn
Act of 1905   Volume VI

BIRTH AFFIDAVIT.

DEPARTMENT OF THE INTERIOR.
COMMISSION TO THE FIVE CIVILIZED TRIBES.

IN RE APPLICATION FOR ENROLLMENT, as a citizen of the Creek Nation, of Lela Watson, born on the 2 day of Sept, 1903

| Name of Father: | Sauta[sic] Watson | a citizen of the | Creek | Nation. |
| Name of Mother: | Anna Watson | a citizen of the | Creek | Nation. |

Postoffice   Brush Hill I.T.

AFFIDAVIT OF MOTHER.

UNITED STATES OF AMERICA, Indian Territory,
Western   DISTRICT.

I, Anna Watson, on oath state that I am 22 years of age and a citizen by blood, of the Creek Nation; that I am the lawful wife of Sauta Watson, who is a citizen, by birth of the Creek Nation; that a female child was born to me on 2nd day of Sept, 1903, that said child has been named Lela Watson, and was living March 4, 1905.

Annie Watson

Witnesses To Mark:
{

Subscribed and sworn to before me this 25 day of March, 1905.

My Com Exp Mch 5th 1907

Horace Wilson
Notary Public.

AFFIDAVIT OF ATTENDING PHYSICIAN OR MID-WIFE.

UNITED STATES OF AMERICA, Indian Territory,
Western   DISTRICT.

I, Sarah McFarland, a *(blank)*, on oath state that I attended on Mrs. Anna Watson, wife of Sauta Watson on the 2 day of Sept, 1903; that there was born to her on said date a female child; that said child was living March 4, 1905, and is said to have been named Lela Watson

Sarah McFarland

Witnesses To Mark:
{

Subscribed and sworn to before me this 25 day of March, 1905.

Applications for Enrollment of Creek Newborn
Act of 1905 Volume VI

My Com Exp Mch 5th 1907

Horace Wilson
Notary Public.

BIRTH AFFIDAVIT.

DEPARTMENT OF THE INTERIOR.
COMMISSION TO THE FIVE CIVILIZED TRIBES.

IN RE APPLICATION FOR ENROLLMENT, as a citizen of the Creek Nation, of Dave Watson, born on the 26 day of September, 1904

Name of Father:	Sandy Watson	a citizen of the	Creek	Nation.
Name of Mother:	Annie Watson	a citizen of the	Creek	Nation.

Postoffice Dustin, Ind. Ter.

AFFIDAVIT OF MOTHER.

UNITED STATES OF AMERICA, Indian Territory, Western DISTRICT.

I, Annie Watson, on oath state that I am 22 years of age and a citizen by blood, of the Creek Nation; that I am the lawful wife of Sandy Watson, who is a citizen, by blood of the Creek Nation; that a male child was born to me on 26 day of September, 1904, that said child has been named Dave Watson, and was living March 4, 1905.

Annie Watson

Witnesses To Mark:

Subscribed and sworn to before me this 24 day of March, 1905.

Drennan C Skaggs
Notary Public.

AFFIDAVIT OF ATTENDING PHYSICIAN OR MID-WIFE.

UNITED STATES OF AMERICA, Indian Territory, Western DISTRICT.

I, Sarah McFarland, a midwife, on oath state that I attended on Mrs. Annie Watson, wife of Sandy Watson on the 26 day of September, 1904; that there was born to her on said date a *(blank)* child; that said child was living March 4, 1905, and is said to have been named Dave Watson

her
Yanah x Watson
mark

Applications for Enrollment of Creek Newborn
Act of 1905 Volume VI

Witnesses To Mark:
 { Alex Posey
 { DC Skaggs

   Subscribed and sworn to before me this 24 day of March, 1905.

Drennan C Skaggs
Notary Public.

NC-475.

Muskogee, Indian Territory, August 4, 1905.

Cora Wiley,
   c/o Andrew Wiley,
      Wagoner, Indian Territory.

Dear Madam:

   In the matter of the application for the enrollment of your minor son Haley Wiley as a citizen by blood of the Creek Nation it will be necessary, before the rights of said child as such citizen can be finally determined, for you to furnish this office with the original or a certified copy of the marriage license and certificate showing the marriage between your and Andrew Wiley, the father of said child.

Respectfully,

Commissioner.

Estelle Simpson,
Stenographer and Notary Public.
Wagoner, Ind. Ter.

August 14, 1905.

Commission to the Five Civilized Tribes,
   Muskogee, Indian Territory.

Gentlemen:

   Replying to yours of August 4th, your number NC-475, I beg to advise when my husband Andy Wiley and myself, came down to Muskogee about two years ago to enroll our child Lizzie Wiley, we brought our marriage certificate. You stated that you would

Applications for Enrollment of Creek Newborn
Act of 1905   Volume VI

send same to us, since which time we have neither seen nor heard of of[sic] same. It is therefore in your office.

In case you fail to find it, kindly notify me and I will have a certified copy of same made by the Clerk of the Court here.

Your early advice will be greatly oblige[sic].

Yours respectfully,

(Signed) Cora Wiley.

BIRTH AFFIDAVIT.

DEPARTMENT OF THE INTERIOR.
COMMISSION TO THE FIVE CIVILIZED TRIBES.

IN RE APPLICATION FOR ENROLLMENT, as a citizen of the Creek Nation, of Haley Wiley, born on the 19th day of December, 1903

Name of Father:	Andy Wiley	a citizen of the	Creek	Nation.
Name of Mother:	Cora Wiley	a citizen of the	Nil	Nation.

Postoffice   Wagoner, Ind. Ter.

AFFIDAVIT OF MOTHER.

UNITED STATES OF AMERICA, Indian Territory,
Western   DISTRICT.

I, Cora Wiley, on oath state that I am 25 years of age and a citizen by *(blank)*, of the United States Nation; that I am the lawful wife of Andy Wiley, who is a citizen, by blood of the Creek Nation; that a male child was born to me on 19th day of December, 1903, that said child has been named Haley Wiley, and was living March 4, 1905.

Cora Wiley

Witnesses To Mark:
 { N V Watts
   R S Danielson

Subscribed and sworn to before me this 23d day of March, 1905.

Estelle Simpson
Notary Public.

Applications for Enrollment of Creek Newborn
Act of 1905 Volume VI

AFFIDAVIT OF ATTENDING PHYSICIAN OR MID-WIFE.

UNITED STATES OF AMERICA, Indian Territory, }
Western DISTRICT.

    I, Chaney Trent, a midwife, on oath state that I attended on Mrs. Cora Wiley, wife of Andy Wiley on the 19th day of December, 1903; that there was born to her on said date a male child; that said child was living March 4, 1905, and is said to have been named Haley Wiley

                                        her
                              Chaney x Trent
                                  mark

Witnesses To Mark:
{ R S Danielson
  Mary Jane *(Illegible)*

    Subscribed and sworn to before me this 23d day of March, 1905.

                                  Estelle Simpson
                                  Notary Public.

                                        B. A. 1277

                        Muskogee, Indian Territory, April 21, 1905.

Lonie Foster,
       Fentress, Indian Territory.

Dear Madam:

    The Commission is in receipt of your letter of April 15, 1905, in which you ask if a letter has been received from you in regard to the enrollment of your daughter, Lula B. Foster.

    In reply you are advised that your affidavit, relative to the birth of your minor child, Lula B. Foster, was filed with the Commission March 28, 1905.

    You are further advised that the Commission has been unable to identify you on the approved roll of citizens by blood of the Creek Nation, under the name of Lonie Foster, and that it will be necessary for you to inform the Commission as to the name and roll number appearing on your deed or allotment certificate, if you have received same.

                                  Respectfully,

                                         Chairman.

Applications for Enrollment of Creek Newborn
Act of 1905 Volume VI

                                        Okemah, I.T. 4/15/05
Commission to the Five Civilized Tribes
                Muskogee, I.T.

Gentlemen,

        You will find Lonie Foster on Creek Indian Roll No. 3175.
Commission No. 7122 Homestead Deed
        "   " 7123 Allotment Deed
Filed for record on the 25 day of February 1903 at 2 o'clock P.M. and recorded in Book 6 Page 468.
Deed Delivered July 27-1904 by P. Porter, Principal Chief Muskogee Nation
I think this will enable you to locate her.

                                          Your Respt.
                                          Lonie Foster

BIRTH AFFIDAVIT.
DEPARTMENT OF THE INTERIOR.
COMMISSION TO THE FIVE CIVILIZED TRIBES.

        IN RE APPLICATION FOR ENROLLMENT, as a citizen of the Creek Nation, of Lula B. Foster, born on the 1st day of August, 1903.

Name of Father:	G.C. Foster	NONE	~~a~~ citizen ~~of the~~ (blank)	~~Nation.~~
Name of Mother:	Lonie Foster		a citizen of the Creek	Nation.

                                  Postoffice   Fentress, I.T.

AFFIDAVIT OF MOTHER.

UNITED STATES OF AMERICA, Indian Territory, }
    Western Judicial   **DISTRICT.**

        I, Lonie Foster, on oath state that I am 28 years of age and a citizen by Blood, of the Muskokee[sic] or Creek Nation; that I am the lawful wife of G.C. Foster NONE Citizen, ~~who is a citizen, by of the Creek Nation~~; that a Female child was born to me on 1st day of August, 1903, that said child has been named Lula B Foster, and is now living.

                                          Lonie Foster
Witnesses To Mark:

Applications for Enrollment of Creek Newborn
Act of 1905   Volume VI

Subscribed and sworn to before me this 25th day of March, 1905.

My Commission Expires Sept. 6th 1906.

John H. Phillips
Notary Public.

AFFIDAVIT OF ATTENDING PHYSICIAN OR MID-WIFE.

UNITED STATES OF AMERICA, Indian Territory,
Western Judicial   DISTRICT.

I, Mrs. E.A. Clay, a Mid-Wife, on oath state that I attended on Mrs. Lonie Foster, wife of G.C. Foster on the 1st day of August, 1903; that there was born to her on said date a Female child; that said child is now living and is said to have been named Lula B. Foster

E A Clay

Witnesses To Mark:
{

Subscribed and sworn to before me this 25th day of March, 1905.

My Commission Expires Sept. 6th 1906.

John H. Phillips
Notary Public.

NC-477

DEPARTMENT OF THE INTERIOR,
COMMISSIONER TO THE FIVE CIVILIZED TRIBES.

Muskogee, Indian Territory, December 14, 1905.

In the matter of the application for the enrollment of Andy Simmer as a citizen by blood of the Creek Nation.

Charley Simmer, being duly sworn, testified as follows through Jesse McDermott, Official Interpreter:

EXAMINATION BY THE COMMISSIONER:
Q What is your name? A Charley Simmer.
Q How old are you? A I stated in my affidavit that I was a little over thirty years of age.
Q Ask him if he is Simmer's son [sic] (No answer)
Q Ask him the name of his mother. A I think it was Cinda.
Q Have you a child named Andy Simmer? A Yes sir.

Applications for Enrollment of Creek Newborn
Act of 1905   Volume VI

Q What is the name of the mother of Cinda? A Kizzie.
Q In order to identify Kizzie, we want to know the name of Kizzie's father. A Upna Hill.

Said Charley and Kizzie Simmer are identified on the roll of Creek citizens by blood, opposite Nos. 9170 and 9171, respectively.
Q Is your child, Andy Simmer, living? A When I left home yesterday he was building a fire.

Q Witness is advised that in lieu of the affidavit of the midwife, it being stated in the mother's affidavit that there was no midwife present, this office requires the affidavit of two disinterested witnesses. A letter has been written to said Kizzie Simmer stating that that would be necessary.

The witness--We stated in our affidavit that the child was living March 4, 1905 and she stated in that affidavit also that she attended on herself, and I am unable to furnish any further proof.

The Commissioner--It has been explained to the witness that it is not required that the two disinterested witnesses required should have been present at the birth of the child, but as explained very fully, if they know the child is living and is about the age spoken is what is desired.

The witness refuses to say any more, insisting that he has complied with the law.

INDIAN TERRITORY, Western District.
    I, J. Y. Miller, a stenographer to the Commission to the Five Civilized Tribes, do hereby certify that the above and foregoing is a true and complete translation of my notes as same appear in my stenographic report of this case.

                        JY Miller

Subscribed and sworn to before me
   this the 19th day of December, 1905.   J McDermott
                                Notary Public.

N.C. 447

              DEPARTMENT OF THE INTERIOR,
      COMMISSIONER TO THE FIVE CIVILIZED TRIBES.
         Okemah, Indian Territory, September 24, 1906.

    In the matter of the application for the enrollment of Andy Simmer as a citizen by blood of the Creek Nation.
               KIZZIE SIMMER, being duly sworn, testified as follows (through Jesse McDermott official interpreter):

Applications for Enrollment of Creek Newborn
Act of 1905   Volume VI

BY COMMISSIONER:

Q What is your name? A Kizzie Simmer.
Q What is your age? A About thirty one.
Q What is your postoffice address? A Okemah.
Q Are you a Creek citizen? A Yes.
Q To which Creek Indian Town do you belong? A Fish Pond.
Q Have you filed on your land? A Yes.
Q Have you your deeds? A No, they are at Muskogee.
Q Have you a child named Andy? A Yes.
Q When was Andy Born? A I am unable to state the exact year and month in which he was born but it was in the same month and year that Victor Wesley was killed at the Greenleaf church.

The interpreter states that he was present at the killing of Victor Wesley and that it was on December 25th 1902.

Q Are you positive that Andy was born then? A Yes, Andy was only a little over a week old when that killing took place.
Q [sic]
There is an affidavit on file at the office of the Commissioner to the Five Civilized Tribes signed by you before Tupper Dunn on March 23, 1905, stating that Andy was born December 15, 1903, which makes the child three years old the coming December, but from what you say now, the child will be four years old next December.

Q How do you explain that? A Tupper is responsible for the error because we told him that Andy was born just a few days before Victor was killed and after reckoning the dates he made out the papers and had me to sign it.
Q Did Tupper know when Victor was killed? A I can't say that he did.
Q So the date of Andy's birth as given in your affidavit before Tupper Dunn is incorrect is it? A Yes.
Q Is he living? A There he is. (pointing at a boy)

CHARLEY SIMMER, being duly sworn, testified as follows (through Jesse McDermott official interpreter):

BY COMMISSIONER:

Q What is your name? A Charley Simmer is what they call me.
Q What is your age? A I am over thirty years old.
Q What is your postoffice address? A Okemah.
Q Are you a Creek citizen? A I am a fullblood Creek.
Q To which Creek Indian Town do you belong? A Fish Pond.
Q Have you a child named Andy? A Yes, there he stands.
Q When was Andy born? A I can't tell you just when he was born, the names of his parents and whether or not he was living on March 4, 1905 because I don't know a thing

Applications for Enrollment of Creek Newborn
Act of 1905   Volume VI

about dates but here is a little [sic] of paper that was given me just about a week or little over before he was born.

The witness presents a receipt for $2.00 given him by Richards, Boyle Mercantile Co., of Okemah, Indian Territory dated December 8; 1902.

Q Are you positive that Andy was born a short time after you was given this receipt?
A Yes.
Q For what did the merchants give you that receipt? A It was for $2.00 that I had paid them on the purchase of a saddle. I remember that I was riding 'round in my brand new saddle when Andy was born.

F.S. REESE, being duly sworn, testified as follows:

Q State your name, age and postoffice address? A F.S. Reese; 29; Okemah.
Q Are you a Creek citizen? A No sir.
Q Do you know Charley and Kizzie Simmer? A I do.
Q Do you know a child of theirs named Andy.[sic] A I do.
Q Do you know about when he was born, the names of his parents and whether or not he was living on March 4, 1905? A Andy was born just two months before my child Mertie May was born.
Q When was Mertie May born.[sic] A Here is the record of her birth.

The witness presents a record entitled " Scripture Memoranda " and on page 49 or said record appears the following entry: " Mertie May Reece was born Feb 15, 1903 "

Q You are positive that your child Mertie is two months younger than Andy are you? A Yes, I know it.

---oooOOOooo---

I, Jesse McDermott, on oath state that the above and foregoing is a full and true transcript of my notes as taken in said cause on said date.

Jesse McDermott

Subscribed and sworn to before me this 7th day of November, 1906.

Frank J Smith
Notary Public.

Applications for Enrollment of Creek Newborn
Act of 1905   Volume VI

AFFIDAVIT OF DISINTERESTED WITNESS.

UNITED STATES OF AMERICA,
    Western   DISTRICT,   SS
INDIAN TERRITORY.

    We, the undersigned, on oath state that we are personally acquainted with Kizzie Simmer wife of Charley Simmer; that there was born to her a male child on or about the 15 day of December 1902, that said child has been named Andy Simmer and was living March 4, 1905 and now living.

Witnesses:

_____

_____

                                R C Reece

                                Fleta Reece

Subscribed and sworn to before me this 24 day of Sept 1906.

My Commission   J McDermott
Ex July 25' 1907   Notary Public.

_____

BIRTH AFFIDAVIT.
DEPARTMENT OF THE INTERIOR.
COMMISSION TO THE FIVE CIVILIZED TRIBES.

_____

    IN RE APPLICATION FOR ENROLLMENT, as a citizen of the Creek Nation, of Andy Simmer, born on the 15" day of Dec , 1902

Name of Father:	Charley Simmer	a citizen of the Creek	Nation.
Name of Mother:	Kissie[sic] Simmer	a citizen of the Creek	Nation.

                          Postoffice   Okemah I.T.

_____

AFFIDAVIT OF MOTHER.

UNITED STATES OF AMERICA, Indian Territory,
    Western   DISTRICT.

    I, Kissie[sic] Simmer , on oath state that I am 31 years of age and a citizen by blood, of the Creek Nation; that I am the lawful wife of Charley Simmer , who is a citizen, by blood of the Creek Nation; that a male child was born to me on 15" day

Applications for Enrollment of Creek Newborn
Act of 1905 Volume VI

of December , 1902 , that said child has been named Andy Simmer , and was living March 4, 1905. and is now living.

Witnesses To Mark:
{ Jesse McDermott
{ J E Guy

                      her
Kissie x Simmer
       mark

Subscribed and sworn to before me this 24" day of Sept 1906.

My Commission   J McDermott
Expires July 25" 1907   Notary Public.

BIRTH AFFIDAVIT.

DEPARTMENT OF THE INTERIOR.
COMMISSION TO THE FIVE CIVILIZED TRIBES.

IN RE APPLICATION FOR ENROLLMENT, as a citizen of the Creek Nation, of Andy Simmer, born on the 15 day of December , 1903

Name of Father: Charley Simmer   a citizen of the   Creek   Nation.
Name of Mother: Kizzie Simmer   a citizen of the   Creek   Nation.

                      Postoffice   Okemah I.T.

AFFIDAVIT OF MOTHER.

UNITED STATES OF AMERICA, Indian Territory, }
    Western   DISTRICT. }

I, Kizzie Simmer , on oath state that I am 30 years of age and a citizen by blood , of the Creek Nation; that I am the lawful wife of Charley Simmer , who is a citizen, by blood of the Creek Nation; that a male child was born to me on 15 day of December , 1903 , that said child has been named Andy Simmer , and was living March 4, 1905.

                            her
                   Kizzie x Simmer

Witnesses To Mark: mark
{ Lemsey Deer   attending to myself when Andy Simmer borned to me
{ Tupper Dunn

Subscribed and sworn to before me this 23 day of March , 1905.

My Com. Exp Aug 19-1908   Tupper Dunn
                                     Notary Public.

Applications for Enrollment of Creek Newborn
Act of 1905 Volume VI

(The above Birth Affidavit given again.)

NC 477.

Muskogee, Indian Territory, August 4, 1905.

Kizzie Simmer,
    c/o Charley Simmer,
    Okemah, Indian Territory.

Dear Madam:

    On March 28, 1905, you filed with the Commission to the Five Civilized Tribes an application for the enrollment of your minor son Andy Simmer, born December 15, 1903, as a citizen by blood of the Creek Nation. It is stated in said application that there was no attending physician or midwife when said child was born.

    It will therefore be necessary for you to furnish this office, in the matter of the enrollment of said child, in lieu of the affidavit of the attending physician or midwife, the affidavits of two disinterested persons, relative to the birth of said child; said affidavits to set forth the name of the child, the date of his birth, the names of his parents and whether or not he was living March 4, 1905.

    This matter should have your prompt attention.

    Respectfully,

    Commissioner.

NC 477.

Muskogee, Indian Territory, December 13, 1905.

Kizzie Simmer,
    Care of Charley Simmor[sic],
    Okemah, Indian Territory.

Dear Madam:

    March 28, 1905, you filed with the Commission to the Five Civilized Tribes the application for the enrollment of your minor child, Andy Simmer, born December 15, 1903, as a citizen by blood of the Creek Nation. You stated in said application that there was no attending physician or midwife when said child was born.

Applications for Enrollment of Creek Newborn
Act of 1905 Volume VI

It will be necessary for you to furnish this office in the matter of the enrollment of said child as a citizen of the Creek Nation, in lieu of the affidavit of an attending physician or midwife, the affidavits of two disinterested persons relative to said child's birth, and a blank for that purpose is herewith enclosed.
This matter should receive your prompt attention.

Respectfully,

Dis.

Commissioner.

N C 477

JWH

Muskogee, Indian Territory, March 1, 1907.

Kizzie Simmer,
 c/o Charley Simmer,
  Okemah, Indian Territory.

Dear Madam :--

You are hereby advised that on February 15, 1907, the Secretary of the Interior approved the enrollment of your minor child, Andy Simmer, as a citizen by blood of the Creek Nation, and that the name of said child appears upon the roll of New Born citizens by blood of the Creek Nation, enrolled under the Act of Congress approved March 3, 1905, as number 1152.

This child is now entitled to allotment and application therefor should be made without delay at the Creek Land Office, Muskogee, Indian Territory.

Respectfully,

Commissioner.

BIRTH AFFIDAVIT.

DEPARTMENT OF THE INTERIOR.
COMMISSION TO THE FIVE CIVILIZED TRIBES.

IN RE APPLICATION FOR ENROLLMENT, as a citizen of the Creek Nation, of Charlie Wiley, illegitimate, born on the 19th day of December, 1903

Name of Father: *(blank)*   a citizen of the *(blank)* Nation.
Name of Mother: Susie Wiley   a citizen of the Creek Nation.

Applications for Enrollment of Creek Newborn
Act of 1905 Volume VI

Postoffice   Wagoner, Ind. Ter.

AFFIDAVIT OF MOTHER.

UNITED STATES OF AMERICA, Indian Territory,
Western   DISTRICT.

I, Susie Wiley , on oath state that I am 21 years of age and a citizen by blood, of the Creek Nation; ~~that I am the lawful wife of~~ *(blank)* , ~~who is a citizen, by~~ *(blank)* ~~of the~~ *(blank)* ~~Nation;~~ that a male child was born to me on 19th day of December , 1903 , that said child has been named Charlie Wiley , and was living March 4, 1905.

Susie Wiley

Witnesses To Mark:
{

Subscribed and sworn to before me this 23d day of March , 1905.

Estelle Simpson
Notary Public.

AFFIDAVIT OF ATTENDING PHYSICIAN OR MID-WIFE.

UNITED STATES OF AMERICA, Indian Territory,
Western   DISTRICT.

I, Chaney Trent , a midwife , on oath state that I attended on Mrs. Susie Wiley, wife of *(blank)* on the 19th day of December , 1903 ; that there was born to her on said date a male child; that said child was living March 4, 1905, and is said to have been named Charlie Wiley

her
Chaney x Trent
mark

Witnesses To Mark:
{ R S Danielson
  Mary Jane Kanard

Subscribed and sworn to before me this 23d day of March , 1905.

Estelle Simpson
Notary Public.

Applications for Enrollment of Creek Newborn
Act of 1905   Volume VI

NC-479.

Muskogee, Indian Territory, August 4, 1905.

Washington Proctor,
    Fentress, Indian Territory.

Dear Sir:

    In the matter of the application for the enrollment of your minor children Stella Proctor and Sam Proctor as citizens by blood of the Creek Nation it will be necessary for you to furnish this office with new and properly verified affidavits as to the birth of said children. For that purpose there are inclosed herewith two blanks, which have been filled out, and you are requested to have the same sworn to and return to this office in the inclosed envelope.

    Be careful to see that the notary public, before whom the affidavits are sworn to, attaches his name and seal to each affidavit and also to see that signatures by mark are attested by two <u>disinterested</u> witnesses.

    It is noted in the affidavits now on file as to the birth of said children that you witnesses[sic] signatures by mark. You are an interested party in the matter of the enrollment of these children and are not the proper person to witness signatures to affidavits which are offered in support of the application for the enrollment of your children.

    It is also noted that in the affidavits on file the name of your former wife is given as Leah Robison, nee proctor[sic], and of your present wife as Katie Micco, nee Proctor. This is evidently incorrect and their names should have appeared in said affidavits as Leah Proctor, nee Robison, and Katie Proctor, nee Micco, respectively.

    It is believed that the affidavits inclosed herewith will, when properly executed, cure the defects of the affidavits now on file.

    It will also be necessary for you to furnish, in the matter of the enrollment of your daughter Stella Proctor as a citizen by blood of the Creek Nation, the affidavits of two disinterested persons relative to the birth of said child; said affidavits to set forth the name of said child, the date of her birth, the names of her parents and whether or not she was living on March 4, 1905.

    Please give the matters herein referred to your prompt attention.

                   Respectfully,

                                       Commissioner.

CTD-26
Env.

Applications for Enrollment of Creek Newborn
Act of 1905   Volume VI

*Real Estate Agents
and
Notary Public*

Wetumka, Ind. Ter.,   190

UNITED STATES OF AMERICA.
INDIAN TERRITORY   SS:
WESTERN JUDICIAL DISTRICT

I Chapley Yaholar do hereby certify that I am a citizen of the Creek Nation I am acquainted with Washington Proctor and Leah Proctor (Deceased) and know that they were husband and Wife, and that a female child was born to me on day of , 190, that said child has been named , and was living March 4, 1905. was born to them on the 19th day of December 1901, the said Child was named Stella Proctor, and was liveing[sic] on the 4th day of March 1905.

Chapley Yaholar

Subscribed and sworn to before me this the 14th day of Aug 1905.

B. H. Mills
My Commission expires Aug 15th 1906.   Notary Public.

B. H. MILLS

*Real Estate Agents
and
Notary Public*

Wetumka, Ind. Ter.,   190

UNITED STATES OF AMERICA.
INDIAN TERRITORY   SS:
WESTERN JUDICIAL DISTRICT

I,   John Harjo,   do hereby certify that I am a Citizen of the Creek Nation, and that i[sic] am acquainted with Washington Proctor and Leah Proctor (Deceased) and know that they were husband and wife, and that a female child was born to me on day of , 190, that said child has been named , and was living March 4, 1905. was born to them on the 19th day of December 1901, the said child was named Stella Proctor and was liveing[sic] on the 4th day of March 1905.

John Harjo

Applications for Enrollment of Creek Newborn
Act of 1905 Volume VI

Subscribed and sworn to before me this the 14th day of Aug 1905.

My Commission expires Aug 15th 1906.

B. H. Mills
Notary Public.

BIRTH AFFIDAVIT.

DEPARTMENT OF THE INTERIOR.
COMMISSION TO THE FIVE CIVILIZED TRIBES.

IN RE APPLICATION FOR ENROLLMENT, as a citizen of the Creek Nation, of Stella Proctor, born on the 19 day of December, 1901

Name of Father: Wash Proctor   a citizen of the   Creek   Nation.
Name of Mother: Leah Robison (nee) Proctor   a citizen of the   Creek   Nation.

Postoffice   Fentress Ind. Ter.

Father
AFFIDAVIT OF MOTHER.

UNITED STATES OF AMERICA, Indian Territory,
Western   DISTRICT.

I, Wash Proctor, on oath state that I am 35 years of age and a citizen by blood, of the Creek Nation; that I am the lawful ~~wife~~ husband of Leah Robison(nee) Proctor (deceased), who is a citizen, by blood of the Creek Nation; that a female child was born to ~~me~~ her on 19 day of December, 1901, that said child has been named Stella Proctor, and was living March 4, 1905.

Wash Proctor

Witnesses To Mark:
{

Subscribed and sworn to before me this 23 day of March, 1905.

My Com Exp. Aug 19-1908

Tupper Dunn
Notary Public.

AFFIDAVIT OF ATTENDING PHYSICIAN OR MID-WIFE.

UNITED STATES OF AMERICA, Indian Territory,
Western   DISTRICT.

I, Maggie Harjo, a midwife, on oath state that I attended on Mrs. Leah Robison (nee) Proctor (deceased), wife of Wash Proctor on the 19 day of December,

Applications for Enrollment of Creek Newborn
Act of 1905   Volume VI

1901 ; that there was born to her on said date a female child; that said child was living March 4, 1905, and is said to have been named Stella Proctor

                                        her
Witnesses To Mark: Maggie x Harjo
   { Wash Proctor   mark
     Louisa *(Illegible)*

Subscribed and sworn to before me this 23 day of March, 1905.

My Com Exp. Aug 19-1908   Tupper Dunn
                                                Notary Public.

BIRTH AFFIDAVIT.
DEPARTMENT OF THE INTERIOR.
COMMISSION TO THE FIVE CIVILIZED TRIBES.

IN RE APPLICATION FOR ENROLLMENT, as a citizen of the Creek Nation, of Stella Proctor, born on the 19th day of December , 1901

Name of Father: Washington Proctor   a citizen of the   Creek   Nation.
Name of Mother: Leah Proctor (nee Robison)   a citizen of the   Creek   Nation.

                              Postoffice   Fentress, I.T.

AFFIDAVIT OF MOTHER.

UNITED STATES OF AMERICA, Indian Territory, }
    Western   DISTRICT.

I, Washington Proctor, on oath state that I am 35 years of age and a citizen by blood , of the Creek Nation; that I ~~am~~ was the lawful ~~wife~~ husband of Leah Proctor (deceased) , who ~~is~~ was a citizen, by blood of the Creek   Nation; that a female child was born to ~~me~~ her on 19th day of December , 1901 , that said child has been named Stella Proctor , and was living March 4, 1905.
                                                        Washington Proctor
Witnesses To Mark:
   { D.V. Worsham
     Nat Williams

Subscribed and sworn to before me this 14 day of Aug, 1905.

My Commission Exp. Aug 15-1906   B H Mills
                                                      Notary Public.

Applications for Enrollment of Creek Newborn
Act of 1905 Volume VI

AFFIDAVIT OF ATTENDING PHYSICIAN OR MID-WIFE.

UNITED STATES OF AMERICA, Indian Territory,
Western DISTRICT.

I, Maggie Harjo , a midwife , on oath state that I attended on Mrs. Leah Proctor, wife of Washington Proctor on the 19th day of December, 1901 ; that there was born to her on said date a female child; that said child was living March 4, 1905, and is said to have been named Stella Proctor

                                                her
                                    Maggie Harjo x
Witnesses To Mark: mark
  { DV Worsham
    Nat Williams

Subscribed and sworn to before me this 14 day of Aug, 1905.

My Commission Exp. Aug 15-1906   B. H. Mills
                                                   Notary Public.

BIRTH AFFIDAVIT.

DEPARTMENT OF THE INTERIOR.
COMMISSION TO THE FIVE CIVILIZED TRIBES.

IN RE APPLICATION FOR ENROLLMENT, as a citizen of the Creek Nation, of Sam Proctor, born on the 16 day of May , 1903

Name of Father: Wash Proctor   a citizen of the   Creek   Nation.
Name of Mother: Katie Micco (nee) Proctor   a citizen of the   Creek   Nation.

                            Postoffice   Fentress Ind. Ter.

AFFIDAVIT OF MOTHER.

UNITED STATES OF AMERICA, Indian Territory,
Western DISTRICT.

I, Katie Micco (nee) Proctor , on oath state that I am 25 years of age and a citizen by blood , of the Creek Nation; that I am the lawful wife of Wash Proctor , who is a citizen, by blood of the Creek Nation; that a male child was born to me on 16 day of May , 1903 , that said child has been named Sam Proctor , and was living March 4, 1905.

                                           her
                                 Katie x Micco (nee) Proctor
                                         mark

Applications for Enrollment of Creek Newborn
Act of 1905 Volume VI

Witnesses To Mark:
{ Wash Proctor
{ Tupper Dunn

Subscribed and sworn to before me this 23 day of March, 1905.

My Com Exp. Aug 19-1908   Tupper Dunn
                                        Notary Public.

AFFIDAVIT OF ATTENDING PHYSICIAN OR MID-WIFE.

UNITED STATES OF AMERICA, Indian Territory, }
     Western   DISTRICT. }

I, Maggie Harjo, a midwife, on oath state that I attended on Mrs. Katie Micco (nee) Proctor, wife of Wash Proctor on the 16 day of May, 1903 ; that there was born to her on said date a male child; that said child was living March 4, 1905, and is said to have been named Sam Proctor
                                     her
                              Maggie x Harjo
Witnesses To Mark: mark
{ Wash Proctor
{ Tupper Dunn

Subscribed and sworn to before me this 23 day of March, 1905.

My Com Exp. Aug 19-1905   Tupper Dunn
                                        Notary Public.

BIRTH AFFIDAVIT.
DEPARTMENT OF THE INTERIOR.
COMMISSION TO THE FIVE CIVILIZED TRIBES.

IN RE APPLICATION FOR ENROLLMENT, as a citizen of the Creek Nation, of Sam Proctor, born on the 16th day of May, 1903

Name of Father: Washington Proctor   a citizen of the   Creek   Nation.
Name of Mother: Katie Proctor (nee Micco)   a citizen of the   Creek   Nation.

                          Postoffice   Fentress, I.T.

Applications for Enrollment of Creek Newborn
Act of 1905   Volume VI

AFFIDAVIT OF MOTHER.

UNITED STATES OF AMERICA, Indian Territory, ⎫
  Western   DISTRICT.   ⎭

I, Katie Proctor, on oath state that I am 25 years of age and a citizen by blood, of the Creek Nation; that I am the lawful wife of Washington Proctor, who is a citizen, by blood of the Creek Nation; that a male child was born to me on 16th day of May, 1903, that said child has been named Sam Proctor, and was living March 4, 1905.

                              her
                Katie Proctor x
                            mark

Witnesses To Mark:
  { D.V. Worsham
  { Nat Williams

Subscribed and sworn to before me this 14 day of Aug, 1905.

My Commission Expires Aug 15, 1906   B H Mills
                                                Notary Public.

AFFIDAVIT OF ATTENDING PHYSICIAN OR MID-WIFE.

UNITED STATES OF AMERICA, Indian Territory, ⎫
  Western   DISTRICT.   ⎭

I, Maggie Harjo, a midwife, on oath state that I attended on Mrs. Katie Proctor, wife of Washington Proctor on the 16th day of May, 1903; that there was born to her on said date a male child; that said child was living March 4, 1905, and is said to have been named Sam Proctor

                          Maggie Harjo x

Witnesses To Mark:
  { DV Worsham
  { Nat Williams

Subscribed and sworn to before me this 14 day of Aug, 1905.

My Commission Expires Aug 15, 1906   B. H. Mills
                                                Notary Public.

Applications for Enrollment of Creek Newborn
Act of 1905   Volume VI

BIRTH AFFIDAVIT.

DEPARTMENT OF THE INTERIOR.
COMMISSION TO THE FIVE CIVILIZED TRIBES.

IN RE APPLICATION FOR ENROLLMENT, as a citizen of the Creek Nation, of Lola Colesta Posey, born on the 27th day of April, 1904

| Name of Father: | William A. Posey | a citizen of the | Creek | Nation. |
| Name of Mother: | Nellie H. Posey | a citizen of the | *(blank)* | Nation. |

Postoffice   Tehuacana, Texas

AFFIDAVIT OF MOTHER.

State of Texas
~~UNITED STATES OF AMERICA, Indian Territory,~~
County of Limestone   ~~DISTRICT.~~

I, Nellie A. Posey, on oath state that I am nineteen years of age and a citizen by birth, of the United States Nation; that I am the lawful wife of William A Posey, who is a citizen, by birth of the Creek Nation; that a female child was born to me on 27th day of April, 1904, that said child has been named Lola Colesta Posey, and was living March 4, 1905.

Nellie H. Posey

Witnesses To Mark:

Subscribed and sworn to before me this 21st day of April, 1905.

J.W. Pearson
Notary Public.
in & for Limestone Co. Tex

AFFIDAVIT OF ATTENDING PHYSICIAN OR MID-WIFE.

State of Texas
~~UNITED STATES OF AMERICA, Indian Territory,~~
County of Limestone   ~~DISTRICT.~~

I, Agnes J. Laird, a midwife, on oath state that I attended on Mrs. Nellie H. Posey, wife of William A. Posey on the 27th day of April, 1904; that there was born to her on said date a female child; that said child was living March 4, 1905, and is said to have been named Lola Colesta Posey

her
Agnes J. x Laird
mark

Applications for Enrollment of Creek Newborn
Act of 1905   Volume VI

Witnesses To Mark:
{ Ida B. Stone
  V. S. Nelson

Subscribed and sworn to before me this 21ˢᵗ day of April, 1905.

J.W. Pearson
Notary Public.
in & for Limestone Co. Tex

CERTIFICATE OF RECORD.

United States of America,
INDIAN TERRITORY, } ss.
Western District.

I, ROBERT P. HARRISON, Clerk of the United States Court in the Western District, Indian Territory, do hereby certify that the instrument hereto attached was filed for record in my office the   19   day of   Mch   1903 at   M., and duly recorded in Book   O , Marriage Record, Page   219

WITNESS my hand and seal of said Court at Muskogee, in said Territory, this   19   day of   Mch   A. D. 1903

R P Harrison   Clerk.
By J Harlan   Deputy.

MARRIAGE LICENSE.
••••••••

United States of America,
Indian Territory, } ss.   No. **146**
Western District.

To Any Person Authorized by Law to Solemnize Marriage---Greeting:

You are Hereby Commanded to Solemnize the Rite and publish the Banns of Matrimony between Mr.   W A Posey   of   Wagoner , in the Indian Territory, aged 23   years and Miss Nellie H. Pounds   of   Wagoner   in the Indian Territory aged   18   years according to law, and do you officially sign and return this License to the parties therein named.

WITNESS my hand and official seal at Wagoner, Indian Territory this   16   day of   March   A.D. 1903

Applications for Enrollment of Creek Newborn
Act of 1905 Volume VI

R. P. Harrison
Clerk of the U.S. Court

By A. G. Byons *Deputy*

CERTIFICATE OF MARRIAGE.

🌿🌿

𝔘𝔫𝔦𝔱𝔢𝔡 𝔖𝔱𝔞𝔱𝔢𝔰 𝔬𝔣 𝔄𝔪𝔢𝔯𝔦𝔠𝔞,
INDIAN TERRITORY,   } *ss.*
Western District.

I, G. R. Naylor , a Minister of the Gospel, DO HEREBY CERTIFY that on the 16 day of March A. D. 1903, I did duly and according to law as commanded in the foregoing License, solemnize the Rite and publish the Banns of Matrimony between the parties therein named.

WITNESS my hand this 16 day of March A. D. 1903

My credentials are recorded in the office of the Clerk of the United States Court, Indian Territory, Northern ~~Western~~ District, Book C , Page 90 .

G. R. Naylor
A Minister of the Gospel

Note—This License and Certificate of Marriage must be returned to the Office of the Clerk of the United States Court in the Northern District, Indian Territory, from whence it was issued, within sixty days from the date thereof, or the party to whom the license was issued will be liable in the amount of the One Hundred Dollars ($100.00)

BA-194
BA-1173-B

DEPARTMENT OF THE INTERIOR,
COMMISSION TO THE FIVE CIVILIZED TRIBES.

Muskogee, Indian Territory, March 7, 1905.

In the matter of the application for the enrollment of Otis Buel Crowell as a citizen by blood of the Creek Nation.

Robert Gosset Crowell, being duly sworn, testified as follows:

Applications for Enrollment of Creek Newborn
Act of 1905   Volume VI

EXAMINATION BY THE COMMISSION:
Q What is your name? A Robert Gosset Crowell.
Q Are you a brother of Benjamin F. Crowell? A Yes sir.
Q What is the name of his youngest child? A Otis Crowell.
Q What is the name of the child's mother? A Neta Crowell.
Q Is the mother a citizen of the Creek Nation? A No sir.
Q Is Benjamin F. Crowell a citizen of the Creek Nation? A Yes sir.

Benjamin F. Crowell, the father of the child, is identified on Creek Indian card field No. 15, and his name is contained in partial list of Creek citizens approved by the Secretary of the Interior March 13, 1902, Roll No. 47

Q Where is Benjamin F. Crowell now? A He is now in Hot Springs on account of his health.
Q When was Otis Buel Crowell born? A I don't know the exact date.
Q Do you know the year? A I think it was in 1904; I have application here. I don't know exactly.

The birth affidavit heretofore filed states that said Otis Buel Crowell was born the 9th day of January, 1904.

Q Is Otis Buel Crowell living now? A Yes sir.
Q When did you see or hear from him last? A Heard from my brother last week.
Q Was the child living at that time? A It was living March 4, 1905 and in good health.

The witness is advised that it will be necessary for the parents of the child to submit evidence that the child was living March 4, 1905 on the 4th of March, 1905.

INDIAN TERRITORY, Western District.
   I, J. Y. Miller, a stenographer to the Commission to the Five Civilized Tribes, do hereby certify that the above and foregoing is a true and complete translation of my notes as same appear in my stenographic report of this case.

                                JY Miller
Sworn to and subscribed
   before me this the
   6 day of April, 1905.   Edw C Griesel
                                   Notary Public.

Applications for Enrollment of Creek Newborn
Act of 1905 Volume VI

NC-481.

Muskogee, Indian Territory, August 4, 1905.

Neta E. Crowell,
 #421 3rd. Street,
  Hot Springs, Arkansas.

Dear Madam:

In the matter of the application for the enrollment of your minor son Otis Buel Crowell as a citizen by blood of the Creek Nation it will be necessary, before the rights of said child as a citizen by blood of the Creek Nation can be finally determined the rights of said child as such citizen can be finally determined, for you to file with this office either the original or a certified copy of the marriage license and certificate showing the marriage between you and Ben. F. Crowell, the father of said child.

Respectfully,

Commissioner.

MARRIAGE CERTIFICATE

I S.M. Neel a Minister of the Gospel *hereby certify that on the* Sixth *day of* December *in the year of our Lord one thousand nine hundred* and three *Mr* Benj. F Crowell *of* Kansas City *in the County of* Jackson *and State of* Missouri *and Miss* Neta E Sparks *of* Kansas City *in the County of* Jackson *and State of* Missouri *were by me united in marriage at* Kansas City *in the County of* Jackson *and State of Missouri, according to the laws of said state.*

I further certify that the marriage license was issued in the County of Jackson, State of Missouri on the 30th *day of* Nov *AD* 1903

S. M. Neel Pastor
Central Park Church

Applications for Enrollment of Creek Newborn
Act of 1905   Volume VI

BIRTH AFFIDAVIT

DEPARTMENT OF THE INTERIOR,
COMMISSION TO THE FIVE CIVILIZED TRIBES.

IN RE Application for Enrollment, as a citizen of the Creek Nation, of Otis Buel Crowell, born on the 9th day of January, 1904

Name of Father: Benj. F. Crowell   a citizen of the   Creek   Nation.
Name of Mother: Neta E. Crowell   a citizen of the County of Garland Nation.
State of Arkansas
Post-office: No 421 *(illegible)* St Hot Springs Ark

AFFIDAVIT OF MOTHER.

UNITED STATES OF AMERICA,
~~INDIAN TERRITORY.~~
Garland County Ark ~~District~~.

I, Neta E. Crowell, on oath state that I am eighteen years of age and a citizen by Birth, of the State of Arkansas ~~Nation~~; that I am the lawful wife of Benj. F. Crowell, who is a citizen, by Blood of the Creek Nation; that a Boy child was born to me on 9th day of January, 1904, that said child has been named Otis Buel Crowell, and is now living.

x Neta E. Crowell

WITNESSES TO MARK:
  John Gosler
  Rose S. Gosler

Subscribed and sworn to before me this 18th day of July, 1904.

My Commission expires Aug. 23, 1905.   H.C. Smith
NOTARY PUBLIC.

AFFIDAVIT OF ATTENDING PHYSICIAN OR MID-WIFE.

UNITED STATES OF AMERICA,
~~INDIAN TERRITORY.~~
Garland County Ark ~~District~~.

I, S. H. Cardwell, a practicing physician, on oath state that I attended on Mrs. Neta E. Crowell, wife of Benj. F. Crowell on the 9th day of January, 1904; that there was born to her on said date a Boy child; that said child is now living and is said to have been named Otis Buel Crowell

S. H. Cardwell M.D.

Applications for Enrollment of Creek Newborn
Act of 1905   Volume VI

WITNESSES TO MARK:
{ W. B. Kimery
  O.H. Carpenter

Subscribed and sworn to before me this 18 day of   July , 1904.

My Commission expires Aug. 23, 1905.   H.C. Smith
                                                     NOTARY PUBLIC.

BIRTH AFFIDAVIT.

DEPARTMENT OF THE INTERIOR.
COMMISSION TO THE FIVE CIVILIZED TRIBES.

IN RE APPLICATION FOR ENROLLMENT, as a citizen of the Creek Nation, of   Otis Buel Crowell , born on the 9 day of Jan. , 1904

Name of Father:	Benj. F. Crowell	a citizen of the Creek	Nation.
Name of Mother:	Neta E. Crowell	a citizen of the Non citz.	Nation.

Postoffice   Hot Springs, Ark.

AFFIDAVIT OF ~~MOTHER~~. Father

UNITED STATES OF AMERICA, Indian Territory, ⎫
       Western   DISTRICT.   ⎭

I, Benj. F. Crowell , on oath state that I am 29 years of age and a citizen by blood, of the Creek Nation; that I am the lawful ~~wife~~ Husband of Neta E. Crowell, who is a citizen, by ----- of the ----- Nation; that a male   child was born to me on 9 day of Jan.   , 1904 , that said child has been named Otis Buel Crowell   , and is now living.

                                    Benjamin F. Crowell
Witnesses To Mark:
{

Subscribed and sworn to before me this 17 day of October, 1905.

                                    Edw C Griesel
                                    Notary Public.

Applications for Enrollment of Creek Newborn
Act of 1905 Volume VI

BIRTH AFFIDAVIT.

DEPARTMENT OF THE INTERIOR.
COMMISSION TO THE FIVE CIVILIZED TRIBES.

IN RE APPLICATION FOR ENROLLMENT, as a citizen of the CREEK Nation, of Otis Buel Crowell, born on the 9th day of January, 1904

Name of Father:	B. H. Crowell	a citizen of the Creek	Nation.
Name of Mother:	Neta E. Crowell	State of a citizen of the Arkansas	~~Nation~~.

Postoffice   HOT SPRINGS, ARK.

AFFIDAVIT OF MOTHER.

UNITED STATES OF AMERICA, Indian Territory,
   WESTERN   DISTRICT.

I, Neta E. Crowell, on oath state that I am 18 years of age and a citizen by Birth, of the State of Arkansas ~~Nation~~; that I am the lawful wife of Benjamen F. Crowell, who is a citizen, by Birth of the Creek Nation; that a Male child was born to me on 9th day of January, 190, that said child has been named Otis Buel Crowell, and is now living.

Neta E. Crowell

Witnesses To Mark:
  { John H. Reece
    Garland S. Mooney

Subscribed and sworn to before me this 20th day of March, 1905.

My Commission expires April 4, 1908.   John H. Reece
Notary Public.

AFFIDAVIT OF ATTENDING PHYSICIAN OR MID-WIFE.

UNITED STATES OF AMERICA, ~~Indian Territory~~,   Arkansas, Hot Springs
  ~~Western~~   ~~DISTRICT.~~

I, Dr. S. H. Cardwell, a Physician, on oath state that I attended on Mrs. Neta E. Crowell, wife of Benjamen F. Crowell on the 9th day of January, 1904; that there was born to her on said date a male child; that said child is now living and is said to have been named Otis Buel Crowell

S H Cardwell M D

Applications for Enrollment of Creek Newborn
Act of 1905 Volume VI

Witnesses To Mark:
{ A. Meadows
{ S. S. Williamson

Subscribed and sworn to before me this 20th day of March, 1905.

My Commission expires April 4, 1908.   John H. Reece
                                              Notary Public.

DEPARTMENT OF THE INTERIOR,
COMMISSIONER TO THE FIVE CIVILIZED TRIBES.
Wetumka, Indian Territory,
July 18, 1906.

In the matter of the application for the enrollment, as citizens of the Creek Nation, of minor children born to duly enrolled citizens of the so called Snake faction.

D.W. Fields, being duly sworn, testified as follows:
Through Official Interpreter, Alex Posey.

Q What is your name? A DW. Fields.
Q What is your age? A Twenty-seven.
Q What is your post office address? A Henryetta.
Q Are you a citizen of the Creek Nation? A Yes sir.
Q To what Creek Indian town do you belong? A Hutchechuppa.
Q Do you know of any minor children in your town or neighborhood for whose enrollment application has not been made? A Billy West and Louisa his wife, have a child, a girl but I don't know its name.
Q Is the child living? A Yes sir.
Q To what Creek Indian town do the parents belong? A Billy West belongs to Kialigee and Louisa to Thlopthlocco.
Q What is the post office address of the parents? A Weleetka.
(Note: Notation on the page indicates the number 434 for this party)

Sun Thloppa an old ~~man~~ woman living at Hutchechuppa has an illegitimate child of Joe Brown and Betsey Barnett; the child is two years old and is a girl. I don't know its name.
Q What is the post office address of the parents? A Dustin.
Q To what Creek Indian towns do they belong? A Joe Brown belongs to Okchiye and Betsey Barnett belongs to Hutchechuppa.

Little Tommy Johnson of Nuyaka and his wife Arlie Johnson, also of Nuyaka, have a girl about two years old but I don't know its name.

Applications for Enrollment of Creek Newborn
Act of 1905   Volume VI

Q What is the post office address of the parents? A Henryetta.
Q Is little Tommy Johnson known by any other name? A That is the only name by which I know him.
    Little Tommy Johnson is identified opposite Creek Indian Roll No. 5372 as Little Tom Johnson and Arlie Johnson is identified opposite No. 5373 as Ellie Johnson.
Q Is the child living? A Yes sir.
(Note: Notation on the page indicates the number 435 for this party)

    Nannie Scott of Artussee has a child, a boy, about a year and a half old; I don't know its name. The father is said to be Sandy Watson of Okchiye. The child is living.
Q What is the post office address of the parents? A Weleetka.

    McDaniels Watson of Hutchechuppa and Louisa Watson his wife have a boy child about a year and a half old. I don't know the child's name or the town of its mother. The post office address of the parents is Dustin. The mother's maiden name was Louisa Bird.
Q Is the child living? A Yes sir.
(Note: Notation on the page for this party: See N.B. Mar. 3, 1905 Card # 482.)

    Sandy Wildcat and Losanna Wildcat, both of Thlewarthle town, have a child between two and three years old. It is a boy. I don't know its name. The post office address of the parents is Bryant.

    Sandy and Losanna Wildcat are identified opposite Creek Indian roll Nos. 5072 and 5073.

    Cotchoche and his wife Lucinda have four children. I don't think any of them are enrolled as the father is a strong snake sympathizer and much opposed to the work of the Dawes Commission among the Indians. I don't know the names of any of the children or what their ages are. I three[sic] three[sic] girls and one a boy. Cotchoche belongs to Thlewathle town but I don't know to what town his wife belongs. Lucinda is probably enrolled as Lucinda Mitchell as that was her maiden name. The post office of the parents is Henryetta.
Q Are all these children living? A Yes sir.

    Lumsey West of Kialigee town and Emma West of the same town have three children; one boy and two girls that are probably not enrolled but I don't know the children's names or ages. The post office address of the parents is Bryant. The children are all living.
    Lumsey West is identified opposite Creek Indian roll No, 4944.

    Sam Lowe of Cussehta has one child. I think it is a boy. I don't know the name of the mother nor to what town she belongs.
Q What is the post office address of the parents? A Schulter.
Q What is the post office address of the parents? A Schulter.[sic]
Q Is the child living? A Yes sir.
    Sam Lowe is identified opposite No. 8343 as Samuel Lowe.

Applications for Enrollment of Creek Newborn
Act of 1905   Volume VI

Q You don't think that application has been made for the enrollment of any of the above children about whom you have given information? A No sir, because their parents all belong to the Snake faction.

I, Alex Posey, on oath state that the above and foregoing is a true and correct transcript of my notes as taken in said cause on said date.

SEAL   (Signed) Alex Posey
Subscribed and sworn to before me this 1 day of August, 1906.

(Signed) Edward Merrick,
Notary Public.

Lona Merrick, being duly sworn, states that she copied the above and foregoing and that the same is a correct copy of the original testimony.

Lona Merrick

Subscribed and sworn to before me this 6th day of August, 1906.

Edward Merrick
Notary Public.

N. C. 482.
DEPARTMENT OF THE INTERIOR,
COMMISSIONER TO THE FIVE CIVILIZED TRIBES,
Dustin, Indian Territory, November 16, 1906.

In the matter of the application for the enrollment of Johnny Watson, as a citizen by blood of the Creek Nation.
LOUISA WATSON, being duly sworn, testified as follows (through Jesse McDermott official interpreter):

BY COMMISSIONER:

Q What is your name? A Louisa Watson.
Q What is your age? A About 25.
Q What is your postoffice address? A Dustin.
Q Are you a Creek citizen? A Yes.
Q Have you a child named Johnny Watson? A Yes.
Q When was he born? A He was a year old last February 24th.

There is an affidavit on file at the Office of the Commissioner to the Five Civilized Tribes signed by you on March 24, 1905, in which you state that Johnny was

Applications for Enrollment of Creek Newborn
Act of 1905   Volume VI

born February 24, 1904. There is another affidavit on file signed by you on November 13, 1905, stating that he was born February 24, 1905.

Q   Now, which one of these affidavits give the correct date about the birth of Johnny?
A   The last one has the correct date. I made a mistake of year in my first one.
Q   Is this Johnny here? A Yes.

The child is present. He walks but cannot talk.

Q   Who was the midwife in this case?   A   Maley Riley but she is now dead, died sometime after Christmas last year.

I, Jesse McDermott, on oath state that the bove[sic] and foregoing is a full and true transcript of my notes as taken in said cause on said date.

Jesse McDermott

Subscribed and sworn to before me this 17th day of November, 1906.

J H Swafford
Notary Public.
My Com Ex. 2/26/1910

Copy

In the matter of the application for the enrollment as citizens of the Creek Nation, of minor children born to duly enrolled citizens members of the so called Snake faction.

D.W. Fields being duly sworn, testified as follows through official interpreter Alex Posey

McDaniels[sis] Watson of Hutchechuppa and Louisa Watson his wife have a boy child about a year and a half old. I don't know the child's name or the town of its mother. The post office address of the parents is Dustin. The mother's maiden name was Louisa Bird.
Is the child living? A Yes, sir

Applications for Enrollment of Creek Newborn
Act of 1905   Volume VI

DEPARTMENT OF THE INTERIOR,
COMMISSION TO THE FIVE CIVILIZED TRIBES.

IN RE Application for Enrollment, as a citizen of the Creek Nation, of Johnny Watson, born on the 24 day of February, 1904

Name of Father:	McDaniel Watson	a citizen of the	Creek	Nation.
Name of Mother:	Louisa Watson	a citizen of the	Creek	Nation.

Post-office   Dustin Ind. Ter.

AFFIDAVIT OF MOTHER.

UNITED STATES OF AMERICA, Indian Territory,
Western   DISTRICT.

I, Louisa Watson, on oath state that I am about 24 years of age and a citizen by blood, of the Creek Nation; that I am the lawful wife of McDaniel Watson, who is a citizen, by blood of the Creek Nation; that a *(blank)* child was born to me on 24 day of February, 1904, that said child has been named Johnny Watson, and was living March 4, 1905. That no one attended on me as midwife or physician at the birth of the child. me as midwife or physician at the time the child was born.

            her
            Louisa x Watson
Witnesses To Mark: mark
   { Alex Posey
Seal { DC Skaggs

Subscribed and sworn to before me this 24 *day of* March, *19*05.

            Drennan C Skaggs
            Notary Public.

BIRTH AFFIDAVIT.
DEPARTMENT OF THE INTERIOR.
COMMISSION TO THE FIVE CIVILIZED TRIBES.

IN RE APPLICATION FOR ENROLLMENT, as a citizen of the Creek Nation, of Johnnie Watson, born on the 24 day of February, 1905

Name of Father:	Daniel Watson	a citizen of the	Creek	Nation.
Name of Mother:	Louisa Watson	a citizen of the	Creek	Nation.

Applications for Enrollment of Creek Newborn
Act of 1905 Volume VI

Postoffice Weleetka Ind Ter.

AFFIDAVIT OF MOTHER.

UNITED STATES OF AMERICA, Indian Territory, }
Western DISTRICT.

I, Louisa Watson (nee Byrd), on oath state that I am 24 years of age and a citizen by Blood, of the Creek Nation; that I am the lawful wife of Daniel Watson, who is a citizen, by Blood of the Creek Nation; that a male child was born to me on 24" day of February, 1905, that said child has been named Johnnie Watson, and was living March 4, 1905.

                          her
                 Louisa x Watson (nee Byrd)

Witnesses To Mark: mark
  { John W. Freeman
    Lena Freeman

Subscribed and sworn to before me this 13 day of November, 1905.

                  Harry E. *(Illegible)*
                  Notary Public.

AFFIDAVIT OF ATTENDING PHYSICIAN OR MID-WIFE.

UNITED STATES OF AMERICA, Indian Territory, }
Western DISTRICT.

I, Maley Riley, a midwife, on oath state that I attended on Mrs. Louisa Watson (nee Byrd), wife of Daniel Watson on the 24' day of February, 1905; that there was born to her on said date a male child; that said child was living March 4, 1905, and is said to have been named Johnny[sic] Watson

                      her
               Maley x Riley

Witnesses To Mark: mark
  { Mic Emarthla
    John W Freeman

Subscribed and sworn to before me this 22" day of November, 1905.
Seal
                  T. T. Caves
My Commission   Notary Public.
Expires Nov 28" 1906

(First Birth Affidavit given again.)

Applications for Enrollment of Creek Newborn
Act of 1905 Volume VI

(Second Birth Affidavit given again.)

BIRTH AFFIDAVIT.

DEPARTMENT OF THE INTERIOR.
COMMISSION TO THE FIVE CIVILIZED TRIBES.

IN RE APPLICATION FOR ENROLLMENT, as a citizen of the Creek Nation, of Johnny Watson, born on the 24 day of Feb., 1905

Name of Father:	Daniel Watson	a citizen of the	Creek	Nation.
Name of Mother:	Louisa "	a citizen of the	Creek	Nation.

Postoffice   Dustin IT

AFFIDAVIT OF MOTHER.

UNITED STATES OF AMERICA, Indian Territory,
Western DISTRICT.

I, Louisa Watson, on oath state that I am about 25 years of age and a citizen by blood, of the Creek Nation; that I am the lawful wife of Daniel Watson, who is a citizen, by blood of the Creek Nation; that a male child was born to me on 24 day of February, 1905, that said child has been named Johnny Watson, and was living March 4, 1905. and is now living.

                                                her
                                      Louisa x Watson

Witnesses To Mark: mark
  J McDermott
  Ben Moore

Subscribed and sworn to before me this 16" day of Nov., 1906.

My Commission   J McDermott
Expires July 25' 1907.   Notary Public.

                            The midwife is now dead, died
~~AFFIDAVIT OF ATTENDING PHYSICIAN OR MID-WIFE.~~
                            sometime after Christmas 1905

Applications for Enrollment of Creek Newborn
Act of 1905   Volume VI

NC482

Muskogee, I T August 4, 1905

Louisa Watson,
   c/o McDaniel Watson,
      Dustin, I T

Dear Madam:

    In the matter of the application for the enrollment of your minor son Johnny Watson as a citizen by blood of the Creek Nation this office is unable to identify either you or your husband McDaniel Watson upon the final roll of citizens by blood of the Creek Nation.

    You are, therefore requested to immediately inform this office of the names under which you and your said husband are finally enrolled, the names of your parents and other members of your families, the Creek Indian Town to which you belong and your final roll numbers as the same appear upon your allotment certificates and deeds.

    It appears from your affidavit now on file in the matter of the enrollment of your said son that there was no physician or midwife in attendance at the birth of said child.

    It will be necessary for you to furnish this office, relative to the birth of said child, in lieu of the affidavit of the attending physician or midwife, with the affidavits of two disinterested persons; said affidavits to set forth the name of said child, the names of his parents, the date of his birth and whether or not he was living March 4, 1905.

                        Respectfully,

                                  Commissioner.

Muskogee I T Nov 28 1905

John W. Freeman
   Henryetta I T

Dear Sir:

    Receipt is acknowledged of your letter of November 24, 1905, enclosing affidavits in the matter of the application for the enrollment of Johnny Watson as a citizen of the Creek Nation.

    You are advised that said affidavits give the date of his birth as February 24, 1904, while affidavits already on file in this office state that said child was born February 24, 1905. This discrepancy in dates should be explained by the mother and the midwife.

                        Respectfully,

                                  Acting Comr

Applications for Enrollment of Creek Newborn
Act of 1905 Volume VI

Henryetta I T

November 24th 1905

Commission to the Five Civilized Tribes
Muskogee I T

Gentlemen:

Here inclosed please find application for the enrollment of Johnny Watson as a Creek citizen, by you[sic] request of August the 4th 1905, I am sending said application.

You will also find inclosed a letter from Wm O. Beall which will furnish sufficient information for the identification of Johnny Watson being a Creek citizen as he is the child of Daniel and Louisa Watson. The application contains the affidavit of his mother and the midwife.

Yours very truly
John W Freeman

NC 482

Muskogee, I T December 13, 1905

Louisa Watson
    Care Daniel Watson
        Weleetka, I T

Dear Madam:

In the matter of the application for the enrollment of your minor child, Johnny Watson, as a citizen by blood of the Creek Nation, there is on file at this office an affidavit executed by you on March 24, 1905, in which you state that Johnny Watson was born February 24, 1904; you state in said affidavit that no one attended on you as midwife or physician at the time said child was born. There is also on file at this office your affidavit executed November 13, 1905, in which you state that said Johnny Watson was born February 24, 1905. Accompanying said affidavit and on the same form is the affidavit of Maley Riley. She states that she was the midwife in attendance at the child's birth, and that said Johnny Watson was born February 24, 1905.

In order that these discrepancies may be corrected, there is herewith enclosed blank form of birth affidavit, which you are requested to execute before a notary public, giving the correct date of the birth of said child. If said Maley Riley in fact attended on you as midwife at the birth of said child, you will have her execute the affidavit for the attending midwife, returning said affidavit to this office in the enclosed envelope. If there was in fact no midwife or physician present at the birth of said child, as stated in

Applications for Enrollment of Creek Newborn
Act of 1905 Volume VI

your affidavit of March 24, 1905, it will be necessary for you to furnish this office with the affidavits of two disinterested persons relative to said childs[sic] birth. A blank for that purpose is herewith inclosed.

Rest[sic] Commissioner

N C 482

JWH

Muskogee, Indian Territory, March 1, 1907.

Louisa Watson,
 c/o Daniel Watson,
  Dustin, Indian Territory.

Dear Madam :--

You are hereby advised that on February 15, 1907, the Secretary of the Interior approved the enrollment of your minor child, Johnny Watson, as a citizen by blood of the Creek Nation, and that the name of said child appears upon the roll of New Born citizens by blood of the Creek Nation, enrolled under the Act of Congress approved March 3, 1905, as number 1153.

This child is now entitled to allotment and application therefor should be made without delay at the Creek Land Office, Muskogee, Indian Territory.

Respectfully,

Commissioner.

NC-483.

Muskogee, Indian Territory, August 4, 1905.

Clara Winters,
 c/o Ed Winters,
  Wetumka, Indian Territory.

Dear Madam:

In the matter of the application for the enrollment of your minor son Elijah Winters, as a citizen by blood of the Creek Nation, it will be necessary for you to file with this office either the original or a certified copy of the marriage license and certificate showing the marriage between you and Ed Winters, the father of said child.

Applications for Enrollment of Creek Newborn
Act of 1905   Volume VI

It is also advisable that you file with this office the affidavit of the said Ed Winters as to the birth of said child and a blank for that purpose, which has been partially filled out, is inclosed herewith.

Please have said affidavit properly sworn to before a notary public and return the same to this office in the inclosed envelope.

Respectfully,

Commissioner.

CTDe-29.
Env.

JAS. A. LONG.   NOTARY PUBLIC.
ATTORNEY AT LAW.

Wetumka, I.T. Aug. 5th 1905.

Mr. R. P. Harrison,
    Clerk of the United States Court,
        Muskogee, I. T.

Sir:-

    I send herein one dollar for which please make a certified copy of my marriage license and certificate, showing that I was married to Miss Clara Harding, at Wetumka, by G. A. Alexander, and send the certified copy to Hon. Tams Bixby, at Daws[sic] Commission, Muskogee, I.T.

    I send herein one dollar to pay for the same. Please send the copy to the Commission as soon as possible and greatly oblige,

Respectfully yours,

Ed. Winters

CERTIFICATE OF TRUE COPY.

United States of America, ⎫
  Indian Territory,   ⎬ ss.
  Western District.   ⎭   *I, **R. P. HARRISON**, Clerk of the United States Court in the Western District, Indian Territory, do hereby certify that the instrument hereto attached is a full, true and correct copy of* a Marriage License *as the same appears from the records of my office.*

Applications for Enrollment of Creek Newborn
Act of 1905 Volume VI

WITNESS my hand and seal of said Court at Muskogee *in said Territory, this* 8" *day of* Aug. *A. D.* 1905

By John Harlan
    Deputy Clerk

R. P. Harrison
Clerk and Ex-Officio Recorder.

Book I page 223

MARRIAGE LICENSE

UNITED STATES OF AMERICA
  Indian Territory } *ss.*
Northern ~~Western~~ District

No. 2

To Any Person Authorized by Law to Solemnize Marriage---Greeting:

You are Hereby Commanded to Solemnize the Rite and Publish the Banns of Matrimony between Mr. Edward Winters *of* Wewoka *in the Indian Territory, aged* 21 *years and M*iss Clara Harding *of* Wetumka *in the Indian Territory aged* 18 *years according to law, and do you officially sign and return this license to the parties therein named.*

    WITNESS my hand and official seal ~~at Muskogee Indian Territory~~ *this* 9 *day of* Jany. *A.D.* 1900

                  D. A. Davidson
                           Clerk of the U S Court.

By Sam E. Flannigan *Deputy.*

CERTIFICATE OF MARRIAGE

UNITED STATES OF AMERICA
  Indian Territory } *ss.*
Northern ~~Western~~ District

    I, G. A. Alexander *, a Minister of the Gospel, DO HEREBY CERTIFY that on the* 12 *day of* Jany *A. D.* 1900 *did duly and according to law as commanded in the foregoing License, solemnize the Rite and Publish the Banns of Matrimony between the parties therein named.*

    WITNESS my hand this 12 *day of* Jany *A. D.* 1900

    My credentials are recorded in the office of the Clerk of the United States Court, Indian
      Northern
Territory ^ ~~Western~~ District Book A Page 166

Applications for Enrollment of Creek Newborn
Act of 1905 Volume VI

G. A. Alexander
A Minister of the Gospel

Note This license and certificate of marriage must be returned to the office of the Clerk of the United States court in the Western District Indian Territory from whence it was issued within sixty days from the date thereof of the party to whom the license was issued will be liable in the amount of the one hundred dollars ($100.00)

Filed and duly recorded this 14 day of Feby. 1900.
Book I at page 223

C.A. Davidson   Clerk of this
United States Court.

BIRTH AFFIDAVIT.

DEPARTMENT OF THE INTERIOR.
COMMISSION TO THE FIVE CIVILIZED TRIBES.

IN RE APPLICATION FOR ENROLLMENT, as a citizen of the Creek Nation, of Elijah Winters, born on the 21st day of October, 1902.

Name of Father: Ed Winters   a citizen of the   Creek   Nation.
Name of Mother: Clara Winters   a citizen of the United States ~~Nation~~.

Postoffice   Wetumka, Ind. Ter.

AFFIDAVIT OF MOTHER.

UNITED STATES OF AMERICA, Indian Territory,
    Western   DISTRICT.

I, Ed. Winters, on oath state that I am 24 years of age and a citizen by blood, of the Creek Nation; that I am the lawful ~~wife of~~ husband of Clara Winters, who is a citizen, by *(blank)* of the United States Nation; that a male child was born to ~~me~~ us on 21st day of October, 1902, that said child has been named Elijah Winters, and was living March 4, 1905.

Ed. Winters

Witnesses To Mark:
{

Subscribed and sworn to before me this 5 day of August, 1905.

Jas. A. Long
Notary Public.
My Com Ex 9-1-1905

247

Applications for Enrollment of Creek Newborn
Act of 1905 Volume VI

BIRTH AFFIDAVIT.

DEPARTMENT OF THE INTERIOR.
COMMISSION TO THE FIVE CIVILIZED TRIBES.

IN RE APPLICATION FOR ENROLLMENT, as a citizen of the Creek Nation, of Elijah Winters, born on the 21 day of October, 1902

Name of Father: Edward Winters   a citizen of the   Creek   Nation.
Name of Mother: Clara Winters   a citizen of the   United States.

Postoffice   Wetumka, Ind. Ter.

AFFIDAVIT OF MOTHER.

UNITED STATES OF AMERICA, Indian Territory, }
Western DISTRICT.

I, Clara Winters, on oath state that I am 23 years of age and a citizen ~~by~~ (blank), of the United States ~~Nation~~; that I am the lawful wife of Edward Winters, who is a citizen, by blood of the Creek Nation; that a male child was born to me on 21 day of October, 1902, that said child has been named Elijah Winters, and was living March 4, 1905.

                                Clara Winters
Witnesses To Mark:
{

Subscribed and sworn to before me this 22 day of March, 1905.

                                Drennan C Skaggs
                                Notary Public.

AFFIDAVIT OF ATTENDING PHYSICIAN OR MID-WIFE.

UNITED STATES OF AMERICA, Indian Territory, }
Western DISTRICT.

I, Mary Bledsoe, a midwife, on oath state that I attended on Mrs. Clara Winters, wife of Edward Winters ~~on the day of~~ October, 1902; that there was born to her on said date a male child; that said child was living March 4, 1905, and is said to have been named Elijah Winters

                                Mary Bledsoe
Witnesses To Mark:
{

Applications for Enrollment of Creek Newborn
Act of 1905 Volume VI

Subscribed and sworn to before me this 22 day of March , 1905.

Drennan C Skaggs
Notary Public.

BIRTH AFFIDAVIT.

DEPARTMENT OF THE INTERIOR
COMMISSION TO THE FIVE CIVILIZED TRIBES.

In Re Application for Enrollment, as a citizen of the Creek Nation, of Lena Coser, born on the 17th day of March , 1904
(Deceased)

Name of Father:	Nuttetsa Coser	a citizen of the Creek	Nation.
Name of Mother:	Lizzie Coser	a citizen of the Creek	Nation.

Postoffice Sapulpa, I.T.

Affidavit of Mother

UNITED STATES OF AMERICA, INDIAN TERRITORY,
Western DISTRICT.

I, Lizzie Coser , on oath state that I am 35 years of age and a citizen by blood , of the Creek Nation; that I am the lawful wife of Nuttetsa Coser (Dec'd) , who is a citizen, by blood of the Creek Nation; that a Female child was born to me on 17th day of March , 1904 , that said child has been named Lena , and was living March 4, 1905.

Lizzie Cosar[sic]

WITNESSES TO MARK:
{

Subscribed and sworn to before me this 25th day of March , 1905.

My Commission expires 10/20-1906   Joseph Bruner
Notary Public.

Affidavit of Attending Physician or Mid-Wife

UNITED STATES OF AMERICA, INDIAN TERRITORY,
Western DISTRICT.

I, Hilly Bear , a Mid-wife , on oath state that I attended on Mrs. Lizzie Coser , wife of Nuttetsa Coser on the 17th day of March , 1904 ; that there was born to her on said date a Female child; that said child was living March 4, 1905, and is said to have been named Lena

Applications for Enrollment of Creek Newborn
Act of 1905 Volume VI

                                          her
                                     Hilly x Bear

WITNESSES TO MARK: mark
  { John Wisdom   Sapulpa I.T.
    (Name Illegible) Sapulpa I.T.

Subscribed and sworn to before me this 25th day of March, 1905.

My Commission expires 10/20-1906   Joseph Bruner
                                                    Notary Public.

BIRTH AFFIDAVIT.

DEPARTMENT OF THE INTERIOR.
COMMISSION TO THE FIVE CIVILIZED TRIBES.

IN RE APPLICATION FOR ENROLLMENT, as a citizen of the Creek Nation, of Minnie Deer, born on the 11 day of May, 1902

Name of Father: Lemsey Deer   a citizen of the Creek   Nation.
Name of Mother: Nancy Deer   a citizen of the Creek   Nation.

                                Postoffice   Okemah I.T.

AFFIDAVIT OF MOTHER.

UNITED STATES OF AMERICA, Indian Territory, }
    Western   DISTRICT.

I, Nancy Deer, on oath state that I am 18 years of age and a citizen by blood, of the Creek Nation; that I am the lawful wife of Lemsey Deer, who is a citizen, by blood of the Creek Nation; that a female child was born to me on 11 day of May, 1902, that said child has been named Minnie Deer, and was living March 4, 1905.
                                                      her
                                                Nancy x Deer

Witnesses To Mark: mark
  { Lemsey Deer
    Tupper Dunn

Subscribed and sworn to before me this 23 day of March, 1905.

my com exp. Aug 19-1908   Tupper Dunn
                                                  Notary Public.

Applications for Enrollment of Creek Newborn
Act of 1905 Volume VI

AFFIDAVIT OF ATTENDING PHYSICIAN OR MID-WIFE.

UNITED STATES OF AMERICA, Indian Territory,
Western DISTRICT.

    I, Milochee Harjo , a midwife , on oath state that I attended on Mrs. Nancy Deer , wife of Lemsey Deer on the 11 day of May , 1902 ; that there was born to her on said date a female child; that said child was living March 4, 1905, and is said to have been named Minnie Deer

                                                        her
Witnesses To Mark: Milochee x Harjo
    Lemsey Deer   mark
    Tupper Dunn

Subscribed and sworn to before me this 23 day of March , 1905.

my com exp. Aug 19-1908   Tupper Dunn
                                                Notary Public.

COMMISSIONERS:
TAMS BIXBY,
THOMAS B. NEEDLES,   **DEPARTMENT OF THE INTERIOR,**   REFER IN REPLY TO THE FOLLOWING:
C.R. BRECKINRIDGE.   **COMMISSIONER TO THE FIVE CIVILIZED TRIBES.**

WM. O. BEALL   NC-486.
Secretary

ADDRESS ONLY THE
COMMISSION TO THE FIVE CIVILIZED TRIBES.   Muskogee, Indian Territory, May 31, 1905.

Mollie Cowe[sic] Tiger,
    Kellyville, Indian Territory.

Dear Madam:

    In the matter of the application for the enrollment of your minor child, Robert Tiger, as a citizen of the Creek Nation, you are advised that the Commission is unable to identify David Tiger, the father of said child, under the name given.

    You are requested to inform the Commission as to the Euchee name of said David Tiger, and as to both the English and Euchee names of both parents of said David Tiger.

    This matter should receive your prompt attention.

                                       Respectfully,

Dave Tiger (Euchee)   Tams Bixby
                                                          Chairman.

Applications for Enrollment of Creek Newborn
Act of 1905 Volume VI

BIRTH AFFIDAVIT.

DEPARTMENT OF THE INTERIOR.
COMMISSION TO THE FIVE CIVILIZED TRIBES.

IN RE APPLICATION FOR ENROLLMENT, as a citizen of the Creek Nation, of Josie Tiger, born on the 27 day of June, 1904

Name of Father: David Tiger a citizen of the Creek Nation.
Euchee
Name of Mother: Mollie C̶o̶w̶e̶ Tiger a citizen of the " Nation.
Euchee (Crow)
  Postoffice Kellyville

AFFIDAVIT OF MOTHER.

UNITED STATES OF AMERICA, Indian Territory,
Western DISTRICT.
row

I, Mollie (C̶o̶w̶e̶) Tiger, on oath state that I am 22 years of age and a citizen by blood, of the Creek Nation; that I am the lawful wife of David Tiger, who is a citizen, by blood of the Creek Nation; that a male child was born to me on 27 day of June, 1904, that said child has been named Josie Tiger, and was living March 4, 1905.

Mollie Crow Tiger

Witnesses To Mark:
 { David Shelby
 { Jesse McDermott

Subscribed and sworn to before me this 24 day of April, 1905.

(Seal) Edw C Griesel
  Notary Public.

AFFIDAVIT OF ATTENDING PHYSICIAN OR MID-WIFE.

UNITED STATES OF AMERICA, Indian Territory,
Western DISTRICT.

I, For-co-wee Yellowhead, a Mid wife, on oath state that I attended on Mrs. Mollie Tiger, wife of David Tiger on the 27 day of June, 1904; that there was born to her on said date a male child; that said child was living March 4, 1905, and is said to have been named Josie Tiger

Her
For-co-wee x Yellowhead
mark

Applications for Enrollment of Creek Newborn
Act of 1905   Volume VI

Witnesses To Mark:
{ David Shelby
  Jesse McDermott

Subscribed and sworn to before me this 24 day of April, 1905.

(Seal)   Edw C Griesel
                          Notary Public.

BIRTH AFFIDAVIT.

DEPARTMENT OF THE INTERIOR,
COMMISSION TO THE FIVE CIVILIZED TRIBES.

In Re- Application for Enrollment, as a citizen of the Creek Nation, of Jossie Tiger, born on the 27 day of June, 1904

Name of Father:	Dave Tiger	a citizen of the	Creek	Nation.
Name of Mother:	Mollie Crow Tiger	a citizen of the	Creek	Nation.

Post-office   Kellyville Ind Tery

AFFIDAVIT OF MOTHER.

UNITED STATES OF AMERICA,
    INDIAN TERRITORY,
  Western   District.

I, Mollie Crow Tiger, on oath state that I am 22 years of age and a citizen by Birth, of the Creek Nation; that I am the lawful wife of Dave Tiger, who is a citizen, by birth of the Creek Nation; that a Male child was born to me on 27 day of June, 1904, that said child has been named Jossie Tiger, and is now living.

                                  Mollie Crow Tiger

Witnesses To Mark:
{ Albert Skeeter
  (Name Illegible)

Subscribed and sworn to before me this 25 day of March, 1905.

                                 E.W. Sims
                                     Notary Public.

Applications for Enrollment of Creek Newborn
Act of 1905 Volume VI

AFFIDAVIT OF ATTENDING PHYSICIAN OR MID-WIFE.

UNITED STATES OF AMERICA, }
INDIAN TERRITORY, }
Western District. }

I, Susie Yellowhead, a Midwife, on oath state that I attended on Mrs. Mollie Crow Tiger, wife of Dave Tiger on the 27 day of June, 1904; that there was born to her on said date a Male child; that said child is now living and is said to have been named Jossie Tiger

                                          her
                              Susie x Yellowhead

Witnesses To Mark: mark
{ Albert Skeeter
  Hiram Lane

Subscribed and sworn to before me this 25 day of March, 1905.

                              E.W. Sims
                                    Notary Public.

BIRTH AFFIDAVIT.

DEPARTMENT OF THE INTERIOR,
COMMISSION TO THE FIVE CIVILIZED TRIBES.

In Re- Application for Enrollment, as a citizen of the Creek Nation, of Robert Tiger, born on the 17 day of July, 1902.

Name of Father:	Dave Tiger	a citizen of the	Creek	Nation.
Name of Mother:	Mollie Crow Tiger	a citizen of the	Creek	Nation.

                          Post-office   Kellyville Ind Tery

AFFIDAVIT OF MOTHER.

UNITED STATES OF AMERICA, }
INDIAN TERRITORY, }
Western District. }

I, Mollie Crow Tiger, on oath state that I am 29 years of age and a citizen by Birth, of the Creek Nation; that I am the lawful wife of Dave Tiger, who is a citizen, by Birth of the Creek Nation; that a Male child was born to me on 17th day of July, 1902, that said child has been named Robert Tiger, and is now living.

                                        Mollie Crow Tiger

Applications for Enrollment of Creek Newborn
Act of 1905 Volume VI

Witnesses To Mark:
{ Albert Skeeter

Subscribed and sworn to before me this 25 day of March, 1905.

E.W. Sims
Notary Public.

AFFIDAVIT OF ATTENDING PHYSICIAN OR MID-WIFE.

UNITED STATES OF AMERICA,
INDIAN TERRITORY,
Western   District.

I, Susie Yellowhead , a Midwife , on oath state that I attended on Mrs. Mollie Crow Tiger , wife of Dave Tiger on the 17 day of July , 1902; that there was born to her on said date a Male child; that said child is now living and is said to have been named Robert Tiger

                   her
           Susie x Yellowhead
Witnesses To Mark: mark
{ Albert Skeeter
  Emily Johnson

Subscribed and sworn to before me this 25 day of March, 1905.

E.W. Sims
Notary Public.

BIRTH AFFIDAVIT.

DEPARTMENT OF THE INTERIOR.
COMMISSION TO THE FIVE CIVILIZED TRIBES.

IN RE APPLICATION FOR ENROLLMENT, as a citizen of the Creek Nation, of Robert Tiger, born on the 17 day of July , 1902

Name of Father: David Tiger   a citizen of the Creek   Nation.
(Euchee)
Name of Mother: Mollie (Cowe) Tiger   a citizen of the Creek   Nation.
(Euchee)   (Crow)
                          Postoffice   Kellyville

Applications for Enrollment of Creek Newborn
Act of 1905   Volume VI

AFFIDAVIT OF MOTHER.

Child Present

UNITED STATES OF AMERICA, Indian Territory, }
Western   DISTRICT.   }
row

I, Mollie C~~owe~~ Tiger , on oath state that I am 22 years of age and a citizen by blood , of the Creek Nation; that I am the lawful wife of David Tiger , who is a citizen, by blood of the Creek Nation; that a male child was born to me on 17 day of July , 1902 , that said child has been named Robert Tiger , and was living March 4, 1905.

Mollie Crow Tiger

Witnesses To Mark:
{ David Shelby
{ Jesse McDermott

Subscribed and sworn to before me this 24 day of April , 1905.

(Seal)   Edw C Griesel
                              Notary Public.

AFFIDAVIT OF ATTENDING PHYSICIAN OR MID-WIFE.

UNITED STATES OF AMERICA, Indian Territory, }
Western   DISTRICT.   }

I, For-co-wee Yellowhead , a Midwife , on oath state that I attended on Mrs. Mollie Tiger , wife of David Tiger on the 17 day of July , 1902 ; that there was born to her on said date a male child; that said child was living March 4, 1905, and is said to have been named Robert Tiger

                              Her
                        For-co-wee x Yellowhead
Witnesses To Mark: mark
{ David Shelby
{ Jesse McDermott

Subscribed and sworn to before me this 24 day of April , 1905.

(Seal)   Edw C Griesel
                              Notary Public.

Note:
  Mr. Reed, Creek Atty's office reports, original identification of parents in error, and that the recent proof of heirship and the Probate Attorney's report correct. That he (Reed) made a personal investigation
                              OCH
                              5/7/19__

Applications for Enrollment of Creek Newborn
Act of 1905 Volume VI

BIRTH AFFIDAVIT.

DEPARTMENT OF THE INTERIOR.
COMMISSION TO THE FIVE CIVILIZED TRIBES.

IN RE APPLICATION FOR ENROLLMENT, as a citizen of the Creek Nation, of Roley Gray, born on the 12 day of June, 1904

Name of Father: Unknown ~~a citizen of the~~ ~~Nation.~~
Name of Mother: Annie Gray a citizen of the Creek Nation.

Postoffice Wetumka, Ind. Ter.

AFFIDAVIT OF MOTHER.

UNITED STATES OF AMERICA, Indian Territory,
  Western   DISTRICT.

I, Annie Gray, on oath state that I am about 28 years of age and a citizen by blood, of the Creek Nation; ~~that I am the lawful wife of , who is a citizen, by of the Creek Nation~~; that a male child was born to me on 12 day of June, 1904, that said child has been named Roley Gray, and was living March 4, 1905.

Annie Gray

Witnesses To Mark:
{

Subscribed and sworn to before me this 22 day of March, 1905.

Drennan C Skaggs
Notary Public.

AFFIDAVIT OF ATTENDING PHYSICIAN OR MID-WIFE.

UNITED STATES OF AMERICA, Indian Territory,
  Western   DISTRICT.

I, Louisa Gray, a midwife, on oath state that I attended on Mrs. Annie Gray, ~~wife of~~ on the 12 day of June, 1904; that there was born to her on said date a male child; that said child was living March 4, 1905, and is said to have been named Roley Gray

her
Louisa x Gray
mark

Witnesses To Mark:
 { Alex Posey
   DC Skaggs

Applications for Enrollment of Creek Newborn
Act of 1905   Volume VI

Subscribed and sworn to before me this 22 day of March, 1905.

Drennan C Skaggs
Notary Public.

NC-488.

Muskogee, Indian Territory, August 5, 1905.

Sallie Bruner,
    c/o John Bruner,
        Carson, Indian Territory.

Dear Madam:

    In the matter of the application for the enrollment of your minor children Bunnie Bruner, born June 8, 1902, and Thomas Bruner, born February 8, 1905, as citizens by blood of the Creek Nation there are on file your affidavits only relative to the birth of said children, from which it appears that there was no physician or midwife in attendance when said children were born.

    You are advised that it will be necessary, before the rights of said children as citizens by blood of the Creek Nation can be finally determined, for you to file with this office the affidavits of two disinterested persons relative to the birth of said children; said affidavits to set forth the names of said children, the dates of their birth, the names of their parents and whether or not they were living on March 5, 1905.

Respectfully,

Commissioner

AFFIDAVIT OF DISINTERESTED WITNESSES.

United States of America,
    Indian Territory.
    Western District.

    We, the undersigned, on oath state that we are personally acquainted with Sallie Bruner, wife of John Bruner; and that there was born to her on or about the 8th day of June, 1902, a male child; that said child was living March 4, 1905, and is said to have been named Bunnie Bruner. We further state that we have no interest in this case. that we have no interest in this case.

Applications for Enrollment of Creek Newborn
Act of 1905 Volume VI

                                                her
                                  Minnie x Bruner
                                            mark
                                              his
                                Robison x Bruner
                                            mark

(2) Witnesses to mark:

(Name Illegible)

Subscribed and sworn to before me this 4 day of Dec 1905.

                                          Barney C. Robison
                                              Notary Public.

Department of the Interior,
COMMISSION TO THE FIVE CIVILIZED TRIBES.

    IN RE Application for Enrollment, as a citizen of the Creek Nation, of Bunnie Bruner, born on the 8 day of June, 1902

Name of Father:	John Bruner	a citizen of the	Creek	Nation.
Name of Mother:	Sallie Bruner	a citizen of the	Creek	Nation.

                            Post Office   Carson

AFFIDAVIT OF MOTHER.

UNITED STATES OF AMERICA,
    INDIAN TERRITORY,
    Western   District.

    I, Sallie Bruner, on oath state that I am 25 years of age and a citizen by Blood, of the Creek Nation; that I am the lawful wife of John Bruner, who is a citizen, by Blood of the Creek Nation; that a male child was born to me on 8 day of June, 1902, that said child has been named Bunnie Bruner, and is now living.

                                          Sallie Bruner

Applications for Enrollment of Creek Newborn
Act of 1905 Volume VI

Subscribed and sworn to before me this 19 day of Sept, 1905.

> Barney C. Robison
> Notary Public.

AFFIDAVIT OF ATTENDING PHYSICIAN OR MID-WIFE.

UNITED STATES OF AMERICA,
INDIAN TERRITORY,
Western   District.

I, Robison Bruner, a Witness, on oath state that I attended on Mrs. Sallie Bruner, wife of John Bruner on the 8 day of June, 1904; that there was born to her on said date a male child; that said child is now living and is said to have been named Bunnie Bruner

> Robison Bruner

Subscribed and sworn to before me this 19 day of Sept, 1905.

> Barney C. Robison
> Notary Public.

BIRTH AFFIDAVIT.

DEPARTMENT OF THE INTERIOR.
COMMISSION TO THE FIVE CIVILIZED TRIBES.

IN RE APPLICATION FOR ENROLLMENT, as a citizen of the Creek Nation, of Bunnie Bruner, born on the 8 day of June, 1902

Name of Father:	John Bruner	a citizen of the Creek	Nation.
Name of Mother:	Sally Bruner	a citizen of the Creek	Nation.

Postoffice   Carson, Ind. Ter.

AFFIDAVIT OF MOTHER.

UNITED STATES OF AMERICA, Indian Territory,
Western   DISTRICT.

I, Sally Bruner, on oath state that I am about 25 years of age and a citizen by blood, of the Creek Nation; that I am the lawful wife of John Bruner, who is a citizen, by blood of the Creek Nation; that a male child was born to me on 8 day of June, 1902, that said child has been named Bunnie Bruner, and was living March 4, 1905. That no one attended on me as midwife or physician at the birth of the child.

Applications for Enrollment of Creek Newborn
Act of 1905 Volume VI

her
Sally x Bruner
mark

Witnesses To Mark:
{ Alex Posey
{ DC Skaggs

Subscribed and sworn to before me 22 day of March, 1905.

Drennan C Skaggs
Notary Public.

BIRTH AFFIDAVIT.

DEPARTMENT OF THE INTERIOR.
COMMISSION TO THE FIVE CIVILIZED TRIBES.

IN RE APPLICATION FOR ENROLLMENT, as a citizen of the Creek Nation, of Thomas Bruner, born on the 8 day of February, 1905

Name of Father:	John Bruner	a citizen of the	Creek	Nation.
Name of Mother:	Sally Bruner	a citizen of the	Creek	Nation.

Postoffice   Carson, Ind. Ter.

AFFIDAVIT OF MOTHER.

UNITED STATES OF AMERICA, Indian Territory,
Western DISTRICT.

I, Sally Bruner, on oath state that I am about 25 years of age and a citizen by blood, of the Creek Nation; that I am the lawful wife of John Bruner, who is a citizen, by blood of the Creek Nation; that a male child was born to me on 8 day of February, 1905, that said child has been named Thomas Bruner, and was living March 4, 1905. That no one attended on me as midwife or physician at the birth of the child.

her
Sally x Bruner
mark

Witnesses To Mark:
{ Alex Posey
{ DC Skaggs

Subscribed and sworn to before me 22 day of March, 1905.

Drennan C Skaggs
Notary Public.

Applications for Enrollment of Creek Newborn
Act of 1905   Volume VI

Department of the Interior,
COMMISSION TO THE FIVE CIVILIZED TRIBES.

IN RE Application for Enrollment, as a citizen of the Creek Nation, of Thomas Bruner, born on the 8 day of Feb., 1905

Name of Father:	John Bruner	a citizen of the	Creek	Nation.
Name of Mother:	Sallie Bruner	a citizen of the	Creek	Nation.

Post Office   Carson I.T.

AFFIDAVIT OF MOTHER.

UNITED STATES OF AMERICA,
   INDIAN TERRITORY,
  Western   District.

I, Sallie Bruner, on oath state that I am 25 years of age and a citizen by Blood, of the Creek Nation; that I am the lawful wife of John Bruner, who is a citizen, by Blood of the Creek Nation; that a male child was born to me on 8 day of Feb., 1905, that said child has been named Thomas Bruner, and is now living.

                                  Sallie Bruner

Subscribed and sworn to before me this 19 day of Sept, 1905.

                              Barney C. Robison
                              Notary Public.

AFFIDAVIT OF ATTENDING PHYSICIAN OR MID-WIFE.

UNITED STATES OF AMERICA,
   INDIAN TERRITORY,
  Western   District.

I, Minnie Bruner, a midwife, on oath state that I attended on Mrs. Sallie Bruner, wife of John Bruner on the 8 day of Feb., 1905; that there was born to her on said date a male child; that said child is now living and is said to have been named Thomas Bruner

                                Minnie Bruner

Subscribed and sworn to before me this 19 day of Sept, 1905.

                              Barney C. Robison
                              Notary Public.

Applications for Enrollment of Creek Newborn
Act of 1905 Volume VI

NC-489.

Muskogee, Indian Territory, August 5, 1905.

Millie Washington,
    c/o David Washington,
        Stidham, Indian Territory.

Dear Madam:

    In the matter of the application for the enrollment of your minor son Claud Washington as a citizen by blood of the Creek nation this office is unable to identify you upon the final roll of citizens by blood of the Creek Nation.

    You are therefore requested to state the name under which you were finally enrolled, the names of your parents and other members of your family, the Creek town to which you belong and your final roll number as the same appears upon your allotment certificate and deeds.

        Respectfully,

        Commissioner.

Checotah, Indian Ter.

August 17, 1905.

Hon. Commissioner to the Five Civilized Tribes,
    Muskogee, I.T.

Dear Sir:

    In reply to your favor of the 5th instant addressed to Millie Washington and numbered N.C. 489, I would state that Millie Washington was my wife. She died on the 17th day of October 1904. Prior to her death she had made application for the removal of the restriction upon the alienation of her allotment which application was pending at the time of her death. At the request of Mr. Tisdell at that time in the office of the Indian Agent and in charge of the hearing of the applications for the removal of restrictions, the deeds to her allotment, both homestead and surplus land, were given to him, Mr. Tisdell, who wished to have descriptions of land listed in application for the removal of restrictions compared with the original deed. These deeds have never been returned. The Indian Agent was notified by Mr. McIntosh, her attorney in the matter of the removal of restrictions, of the death of Millie Washington a few days after her death. I have written today to the agent for the deeds and will transmit the same or rather the roll number on the same to you as soon as the same is returned from agents[sic] office. Millie

Applications for Enrollment of Creek Newborn
Act of 1905 Volume VI

Washington, the mother of my minor son, Claude Washington was enrolled as Millie Ireland, her father was Henry Ireland, her mother is living and her name is Susie Ireland. The town she belonged to is Coweta town. I am the husband of Millie Ireland Washington and the father of Claude Washington, am a Creek citizen by blood and belong to the Deep fork Arbeka town. I give herewith description of the lands filed on by Millie Ireland and for which deeds have been issued to her; Homestead SW 1/4 of SW 1/4 of sec. 34-1~~34151~~ allotment[sic] N.W. 1/4 of S.W. 1/4
N.E. 1/4 of N.W. 1/4

30 acres in N W 1/4 of S W 1/4 sec 26-11-15
10 acres being S E 1/4 of S.E. 1/4 of N.E. 1/4 33-11-16

                Very respectfully,
                (Signed) David Washington
                P.O. Brush Hill I.T.

United States of America
Indian Territory
Western District

I, Roley McIntosh state on oath that Millie Washington wife of David Washington a citizen of the Creek nation[sic] by blood died on the forteenth[sic] day of October 1904 and further state that her child Claud Washington borned[sic] on the eleventh day of July 1902 is now living.

                Roley McIntosh

Subscribed and sworn to before me
this 22 day of March 1902

                Preston Janway
My commission   Notary Public
Expires May 19 1908

United States of America
Indian Territory
Western District

I, E.H. Walker state on oath that Millie Washington wife of David Washington a citizen of the Creek Nation by blood died on the 14th day of October 1904 and further state that her child Claud Washington borned[sic] on the 11th day of July 1902 is now living.

                E.H. Walker

Subscribed and sworn to before me
  this 22 day of March 1902

                Preston Janway
My commission   Notary Public
Expires May 19 1908

Applications for Enrollment of Creek Newborn
Act of 1905 Volume VI

United States of America
  Indian Territory
  Western District

I, David Washington state on oath that on the 11th day of July 1902 there was borned to my lawfull[sic] wife Millie Washington a male child and has been named Claud and is now living. I further state that my wife Millie Washington died on the 14th day of October 1904.

David Washington

Subscribed and sworn to before me this 22 day of March 1902

Preston Janway
Notary Public

BIRTH AFFIDAVIT.

Department of the Interior,
COMMISSION TO THE FIVE CIVILIZED TRIBES.

IN RE APPLICATION FOR ENROLLMENT, as a citizen of the Creek Nation, of Claud Washington, born on the Eleventh day of July , 1902

Name of Father: David Washington a citizen of the Creek Nation.
Name of Mother: Millie Washington a citizen of the Creek Nation.

Post-Office: Stidham

AFFIDAVIT OF ATTENDING PHYSICIAN OR MID-WIFE.

UNITED STATES OF AMERICA,
  Indian Territory.
  Western District.

I, F.L. Smith , a Physician , on oath state that I attended on Mrs. Millie Washington , wife of David Washington on the 11 day of July , 1902 ; that there was born to her on said date a male child; that said child was living March 4, 1905, and is said to have been named Claud

F. L. Smith

WITNESSES TO MARK:

Subscribed and sworn to before me this 22 day of March, 1905.

My commission
Expires May 19 1908

Preston Janway
Notary Public

Applications for Enrollment of Creek Newborn
Act of 1905 Volume VI

NC-490.

Muskogee, Indian Territory, August 5, 1905.

Ah-sey Tiger (or Cloud),
    c/o Stephen Cloud,
        Bristow, Indian Territory.

Dear Madam:

    In the matter of the application for the enrollment of your minor daughter Hattie Cloud as a citizen by blood of the Creek Nation this office is unable to identify you upon the final roll of Creek citizens by blood.

    In order that you may be identified you are requested to state the name under which you were finally enrolled, the names of your parents and other members of your family your final roll number as the same appears upon your allotment certificate and deeds.

        Respectfully,

                Commissioner.

                N.C. 490.

Law office of
W.L. Cheatham   Bristow, I.T. Sept. 9, 1905.

Hon. Tams Bixby,
    Muskogee, I.T.

Dear Sir:

    In answer to your letter of the 5th ult[sic] addressed to Ah-sey Tiger or Cloud, will say that she is a full blood Euchee Indian and the best that I can get from her is that she has neither deeds or the certificate, having sent the latter to Chief Porter for the deeds. She does not know her roll number. She says that her certificate read to Ah-sey Tiger; that her mothers[sic] name is Ah-oo-con-ney her fater[sic] being dead and having no allotment and further she does not know his name; she has a brother deceased named John Yargee who has an allotment in section 31, twp 18, rng 8 Creek Nation, and another brother named Co-pah-tanney and another named Dat-cha

    This is the best information I can get from her. Hoping that this will be sufficient information to identify her, I await your answer.

                Yours truly,
                    Wm L. Cheatham.

Applications for Enrollment of Creek Newborn
Act of 1905 Volume VI

BIRTH AFFIDAVIT.

DEPARTMENT OF THE INTERIOR,
COMMISSION TO THE FIVE CIVILIZED TRIBES.

In Re- Application for Enrollment, as a citizen of the Creek Nation, of Hattie Cloud, born on the 10 day of March, 1903

Name of Father:	Steven Cloud	a citizen of the	Creek	Nation.
Name of Mother:	Ah-sey Tiger	a citizen of the	Creek	Nation.

Post-office   Bristow Ind Tey

AFFIDAVIT OF MOTHER.

UNITED STATES OF AMERICA,
   INDIAN TERRITORY,
Western District.

I, Ah-sey Tiger, on oath state that I am 29 years of age and a citizen by birth, of the Creek Nation; that I am the lawful wife of Steven Cloud, who is a citizen, by birth of the Creek Nation; that a Female child was born to me on 10th day of March, 1903, that said child has been named Hattie Cloud, and is now living.

                              her
                        Ah sey x Tiger
Witnesses To Mark: mark
  Albert Skeeter
  Poll Skeeter

Subscribed and sworn to before me this 25 day of March, 1905.

                        E W Sims
                            Notary Public.

AFFIDAVIT OF ATTENDING PHYSICIAN OR MID-WIFE.

UNITED STATES OF AMERICA,
   INDIAN TERRITORY,
Western District.

I, Ah-Con-Ko-ney, a Midwife, on oath state that I attended on Mrs. Ah-sey-Tiger, wife of Steven Cloud on the 10 day of March, 1903; that there was born to her on said date a Female child; that said child is now living and is said to have been named Hattie Cloud

Applications for Enrollment of Creek Newborn
Act of 1905   Volume VI

                                her
                        Ah.com.ko.ney x
Witnesses To Mark: mark
  { Albert Skeeter
    Poll Skeeter

Subscribed and sworn to before me this 25 day of March, 1905.

                        E W Sims
                            Notary Public.

BIRTH AFFIDAVIT.

Department of the Interior,
COMMISSION TO THE FIVE CIVILIZED TRIBES.

IN RE APPLICATION FOR ENROLLMENT, as a citizen of the Creek Nation, of Hattie Cloud, born on the ----- day of March, 1903

Name of Father: Stephen Cloud   a citizen of the   Creek   Nation.
(Tuskegee)
Name of Mother: Ahsey Cloud   a citizen of the   "   Nation.
(Euchee)
                      Post-Office: Bristow

                    AFFIDAVIT OF MOTHER.

UNITED STATES OF AMERICA,
    INDIAN TERRITORY,
  Western   District.

    I, Ahsey Cloud, on oath state that I am 29 years of age and a citizen by blood, of the Creek Nation; that I am the lawful wife of Stephen Cloud, who is a citizen, by blood of the Creek Nation; that a female child was born to me on ----- day of March, 1903, that said child has been named Hattie Cloud, and is now living.

                              Her
                        Ahsey x Cloud
WITNESSES TO MARK: mark
  { David Shelby
    Jesse McDermott

    Subscribed and sworn to before me this 1 *day of* May, 1905.

        (Seal)   Edw C Griesel
                               Notary Public.

Applications for Enrollment of Creek Newborn
Act of 1905 Volume VI

BIRTH AFFIDAVIT.
DEPARTMENT OF THE INTERIOR,
COMMISSIONER TO THE FIVE CIVILIZED TRIBES.

IN RE APPLICATION FOR ENROLLMENT, as a citizen of the Creek Nation, of Hattie Cloud, born ~~on the day of~~, during the year 1903

Name of Father: Stephen Cloud (In Penitentiary) a citizen of the Creek Nation. (Tuskegee)
Name of Mother: Acie Cloud a citizen of the Creek Nation. (Euchee)

Postoffice Bristow

AFFIDAVIT OF ~~MOTHER~~. Acquaintance

UNITED STATES OF AMERICA, Indian Territory,
Western District.

I, Edmond Harry, on oath state that I am 60 years of age and a citizen by blood, of the Creek Nation; that I am ~~the lawful wife of~~ an acquaintance of Stephen Cloud and Acie Cloud, who ~~is a~~ are citizens, by blood of the Creek Nation; that a female child was born to ~~me~~ them ~~on~~ during ~~day of~~ the year, 1903, that said child has been named Hattie Cloud, and was living March 4, 1905.

His
Edmond x Harry
mark

Witness to Mark:
David Shelby
Jesse McDermott

Subscribed and sworn to before me this 27 day of April, 1905.

(Seal)   Edw C Griesel
                      Notary Public.

BIRTH AFFIDAVIT.
DEPARTMENT OF THE INTERIOR,
COMMISSIONER TO THE FIVE CIVILIZED TRIBES.

IN RE APPLICATION FOR ENROLLMENT, as a citizen of the Creek Nation, of Hattie Cloud, born on the 10th day of March, 1903

Name of Father: Stephen Cloud   a citizen of the Creek Nation.
Name of Mother: Ahsey   "   a citizen of the   "   Nation.

Postoffice Bristow

Applications for Enrollment of Creek Newborn
Act of 1905 Volume VI

AFFIDAVIT OF MOTHER.

UNITED STATES OF AMERICA, Indian Territory,
Western District.

I, Ahsey Cloud , on oath state that I am 29 years of age and a citizen by blood , of the Creek Nation; that I am the lawful wife of Stephen Cloud , who is a citizen, by blood of the Creek Nation; that a female child was born to me on 10th day of March , 1903 , that said child has been named Hattie Cloud , and was living March 4, 1905.

                                                    her
                                        Ashey x Cloud

Witness to Mark: mark
  { Jim John
    Thomas J Lillard

Subscribed and sworn to before me this 6th day of March , 1905.

                                        Thomas J Lillard
                                            Notary Public.

AFFIDAVIT OF ATTENDING PHYSICIAN OR MID-WIFE.

UNITED STATES OF AMERICA, Indian Territory,
Western District.

I, Ar-gon-ga-ne , a Midwife , on oath state that I attended on Mrs. Aliscy Cloud, wife of Stephen Cloud on the 10th day of May , 1903 ; that there was born to her on said date a female child; that said child was living March 4, 1905, and is said to have been named Hattie Cloud

                                            her
                                      Ar-gon-ga-ne x
Witness to Mark: mark
  { Jim John
    Thomas J Lillard

Subscribed and sworn to before me this 6th day of March , 1905.

                                        Thomas J Lillard
                                          Notary Public.

Applications for Enrollment of Creek Newborn
Act of 1905 Volume VI

DEPARTMENT OF THE INTERIOR,
COMMISSION TO THE FIVE CIVILIZED TRIBES.
April 19, 1905, Bristow, I.T.

In the matter of the application for the enrollment of David and Viola Williams, as citizens by blood of the Creek Nation.

Sam Williams, being duly sworn, by E.C. Griesel, a Notary Public, testified as follows:

By Commission.
Q What is your name? A Sam Williams.
Q How old are you? A About 29.
Q What is your post office? A Bristow.
Q You have previously made applications for the enrollment of Davis and Viola Williams as citizens by blood of the Creek Nation, have you? A Yes sir.
Q Who is the mother of these children? A Rena Williams.
Q Both of you are citizens of the Creek Nation, are you? A No, sir. I am am[sic] Seminole and she is a Creek by blood.
Q To what town does she belong to? A Tuskogee.
Q What was her name before she married you? A Rena Fish.
Q How does her deed read, Rena Fish or Rena Williams? A Rena Williams.
Q When were these children born? A Davis was born June 17, 1901, and Viola was born March 11, 1904.
Q Both of these children are living are they? A Yes, sir.
Q If it should be found that these children, Davis and Viola Williams are entitled to enrollment in both the Creek and Seminole Nations, in which Nation do you elect to have them enrolled and receive their allotments of land? A In the Creek Nation.
Q You wife agrees to this, does she? A Yes sir.

E. C. Griesel, being duly sworn, on his oath, states that the above and foregoing is a true and complete transcript of his stenographic notes as taken in said cause on said date.

Edw C Griesel

Subscribed and sworn to before me this 5 day of May, 1905.

Zera E Parrish
Notary Public.

Applications for Enrollment of Creek Newborn
Act of 1905 Volume VI

BIRTH AFFIDAVIT.

DEPARTMENT OF THE INTERIOR,
COMMISSIONER TO THE FIVE CIVILIZED TRIBES.

IN RE APPLICATION FOR ENROLLMENT, as a citizen of the Creek Nation, of Viola Williams, born on the 11th day of March, 1904

Name of Father:	Sam Williams	a citizen of the Seminole	Nation.
Name of Mother:	Rena Williams	a citizen of the Creek	Nation.

Postoffice Bristow Ind Ter

AFFIDAVIT OF MOTHER.

UNITED STATES OF AMERICA, Indian Territory,
Western District.

I, Rena Williams, on oath state that I am 26 years of age and a citizen by ~~Creek~~ blood, of the Creek Nation; that I am the lawful wife of Sam Williams, who is a citizen, by blood of the Seminole Nation; that a Female child was born to me on 11th day of March, 1904, that said child has been named Viola Williams, and was living March 4, 1905.

Rena Williams

Witness to Mark:

Subscribed and sworn to before me this 23 day of March, 1905.

My Com Exp Aug 1st 1906   A. H. Purdy
                                                Notary Public.

AFFIDAVIT OF ATTENDING PHYSICIAN OR MID-WIFE.

UNITED STATES OF AMERICA, Indian Territory,
Western District.

I, Lizzie Taylor, a Midwife, on oath state that I attended on Mrs. Rena Williams, wife of Sam Williams on the 11th day of March, 1905; that there was born to her on said date a female child; that said child was living March 4, 1905, and is said to have been named Viola Williams

her
Lizzie x Taylor
mark

Witness to Mark:
 A H Purdy
 R B Budlong

Applications for Enrollment of Creek Newborn
Act of 1905 Volume VI

Subscribed and sworn to before me this 23 day of March , 1905.

My Com Exp Aug 1st   A. H. Purdy
         1906   Notary Public.

BIRTH AFFIDAVIT.

Department of the Interior,
COMMISSION TO THE FIVE CIVILIZED TRIBES.

IN RE Application for Enrollment, as a citizen of the Creek Nation, of Davis Williams , born on the 17 day of June , 1901

Name of Father:	Sam Williams	a citizen of the Seminole	Nation.
Name of Father:	Rena Williams	a citizen of the Creek	Nation.

Post-office   Bristow I.T.

AFFIDAVIT OF MOTHER.

UNITED STATES OF AMERICA,
    INDIAN TERRITORY,
Northern   District.

     I, Rena Williams , on oath state that I am 22 years of age and a citizen by birth , of the Creek Nation; that I am the lawful wife of Sam Williams , who is a citizen, by Birth of the Seminole Nation; that a Male child was born to me on 17 day of June , 1901 , that said child has been named Davis Williams , and is now living.

                                       Rena Williams

WITNESSES TO MARK:
     J L Murray

Subscribed and sworn to before me this 19th day of August , 1901.

                             E. W. Sims
                             NOTARY PUBLIC.
                 My Com Ex Dec 7th 1901

Applications for Enrollment of Creek Newborn
Act of 1905 Volume VI

AFFIDAVIT OF ATTENDING PHYSICIAN OR MID-WIFE.

UNITED STATES OF AMERICA,
INDIAN TERRITORY,
Northern   District.

I, Sam Williams , a Midwife , on oath state that I attended on Mrs. Rena Williams , wife of Sam Williams on the 17 day of June , 1901 ; that there was born to her on said date a Male child; that said child is now living and is said to have been named Davis Williams

Sam Williams

WITNESSES TO MARK:
J L Murray

Subscribed and sworn to before me this 19th day of August , 1901.

E. W. Sims
NOTARY PUBLIC.

My Com Ex Dec 7th 1901

BIRTH AFFIDAVIT.

DEPARTMENT OF THE INTERIOR,
COMMISSIONER TO THE FIVE CIVILIZED TRIBES.

IN RE APPLICATION FOR ENROLLMENT, as a citizen of the Creek Nation, of Davis Williams , born on the 17 day of June , 1901

Name of Father:	Sam Williams	a citizen of the Seminole	Nation.
Name of Mother:	Rena Williams	a citizen of the Creek	Nation.

Postoffice   Bristow Ind Teritory[sic]

AFFIDAVIT OF MOTHER.

UNITED STATES OF AMERICA, Indian Territory,
Western   District.

I, Rena Williams , on oath state that I am Twenty[sic] 24 years of age and a citizen by blood, of the Creek Nation; that I am the lawful wife of Sam Williams , who is a citizen, by blood of the Seminole Nation; that a Male child was born to me on 17 day of June , 1901 , that said child has been named Davis Williams , and was living March 4, 1905.

Rena Williams

Witness to Mark:

Applications for Enrollment of Creek Newborn
Act of 1905 Volume VI

Subscribed and sworn to before me this 23 day of March , 1905.

My Com Exp Aug 1st 1906   A. H. Purdy
                                                         Notary Public.

AFFIDAVIT OF ATTENDING PHYSICIAN OR MID-WIFE.

UNITED STATES OF AMERICA, **Indian Territory,**
Western   **District.**

       I, Lizzie Taylor , a Midwife , on oath state that I attended on Mrs. Rena Williams , wife of Sam Williams on the 17th day of June , 1901 ; that there was born to her on said date a male child; that said child was living March 4, 1905, and is said to have been named Davis Williams
                                                         her
                                                         Lizzie x Taylor
Witness to Mark: mark
     A H Purdy
     R B Budlong

Subscribed and sworn to before me this 23 day of March , 1905.

My Com Exp Aug 1st 1906   A. H. Purdy
                                                         Notary Public.

                                                         Ba-Nc-98.

                             Muskogee, Indian Territory, March 22, 1905.

Sam B. Williams,
       Bristow, Indian Territory.

Dear Sir:

       The Commission is in receipt of your letter of March 16, in which you ask if an affidavit relative to the birth of your child, Davis Williams, filed with the commission June 17, 1901, is sufficient.

       In reply you are advised that the Commission requires the affidavit of the mother of the child and the midwife in attendance at the birth.

       There is herewith enclosed a blank form of birth affidavit, together with printed circular, giving information relative to enrollment of children born since May 25, 1901.

                                       Respectfully,

                                                       Chairman.

Applications for Enrollment of Creek Newborn
Act of 1905 Volume VI

1 B A
Circular

NC. 491.

Muskogee, Indian Territory, July 14, 1905.

Commissioner to the Five Civilized Tribes,
    Seminole Enrollment Division,
        Muskogee, Indian Territory.

Gentlemen:

    March 25, 1905, application was made to the Commission to the Five Civilized Tribes for the enrollment of Davis Williams, born June 17, 1901, and Viola Williams, born March 11, 1904, as citizens by blood of the Creek Nation. It is stated in said application that the father of said children is Sam Williams, a citizen of the Seminole nation, and that the mother is Rena Williams a citizen of the Creek Nation.

    You are requested to inform the Creek Enrollment Division as to whether application has been made for the enrollment of said children as citizens of the Seminole Nation, and if so, what disposition has been made of the same.

Respectfully,

Commissioner.

DEPARTMENT OF THE INTERIOR.
COMMISSION TO THE FIVE CIVILIZED TRIBES.

Muskogee, Indian Territory, July 19, 1905.

Chief Clerk,
    Creek Enrollment Division.

Dear Sir:

    Receipt is acknowledged of your letter of July 14, 1905 (NC-491) stating that application was made to the Commission to the Five Civilized Tribes for the enrollment of Davis Williams, born June 17, 1901, and Viola Williams, born March 11, 1904, children of Sam Williams, a citizen of the Seminole Nation, and Rena Williams, a citizen of the Creek Nation, as citizens by blood of the Creek Nation and requesting to be informed as to whether application has been made for the enrollment of said children as citizens of the Seminole Nation.

Applications for Enrollment of Creek Newborn
Act of 1905 Volume VI

In reply to your letter you are advised that it does not appear from an examination of the records of this office that any application was made to the Commission to the Five Civilized Tribes for the enrollment of Davis Williams and Viola Williams as citizens of the Seminole Nation.

Respectfully,

Tams Bixby Commissioner.

NC 491

Muskogee, Indian Territory, November 12, 1906.

Chief Clerk,
  Seminole Enrollment Division,
    General Office.

Dear Sir:

You are hereby advised that the names of Davis and Viola Williams, children of Sam Williams, an alleged citizen of the Seminole Nation, and Rena Williams, a citizen by blood of the Creek Nation, are contained in a schedule of New Born citizens of the Creek Nation, approved by the Secretary of the Interior November 27, 1905, opposite Roll Nos. 491 and 492.

Respectfully,

Commissioner.

BIRTH AFFIDAVIT.

Department of the Interior,
COMMISSION TO THE FIVE CIVILIZED TRIBES.

IN RE Application for Enrollment, as a citizen of the Creek Nation, of Peyton Simon , born on the 24 day of February , 1902

Name of Father: Joe Simon   a citizen of the Creek   Nation.
Name of Father: Emma Simon   a citizen of the United States Nation.

Post-office   Bearden I.T.

Applications for Enrollment of Creek Newborn
Act of 1905   Volume VI

AFFIDAVIT OF MOTHER.

UNITED STATES OF AMERICA,
   INDIAN TERRITORY,
  Western   District.

I, Emma Simon , on oath state that I am 27 years of age and a citizen by *(blank)* , of the United States Nation; that I am the lawful wife of Joe Simon , who is a citizen, by Blood of the Creek Nation; that a *(blank)* child was born to me on 24 day of February , 1902 , that said child has been named Peyton Simon , and is now living.

                                    her
                            Emma x Simon
WITNESSES TO MARK: mark
  Chaney Wallas
  John R McBeth

Subscribed and sworn to before me this 21 *day of* March , 1905.

                                  J C Johnson
                                      NOTARY PUBLIC.

AFFIDAVIT OF ATTENDING PHYSICIAN OR MID-WIFE.

UNITED STATES OF AMERICA,
   INDIAN TERRITORY,
  Western   District.

I, Chaney Wallas , a midwife , on oath state that I attended on Mrs. Emma Simon , wife of Joe Simon on the 24th day of February , 1902 ; that there was born to her on said date a male child; that said child is now living and is said to have been named Peyton Simon

                                  Cheney Wallas
WITNESSES TO MARK:

Subscribed and sworn to before me this 21 *day of* March , 1905.

                                  J C Johnson
                                      NOTARY PUBLIC.

Applications for Enrollment of Creek Newborn
Act of 1905 Volume VI

BIRTH AFFIDAVIT.

Department of the Interior,
COMMISSION TO THE FIVE CIVILIZED TRIBES.

IN RE Application for Enrollment, as a citizen of the Creek Nation, of Levada Simon, born on the 15 day of March, 1904

Name of Father: Joe Simon   a citizen of the Creek   Nation.
Name of Father: Emma Simon   a citizen of the United StatesNation.

Post-office   Bearden I.T.

AFFIDAVIT OF MOTHER.

UNITED STATES OF AMERICA,
　INDIAN TERRITORY,
　　Western   District.

I, Emma Simon, on oath state that I am 27 years of age and a citizen by *(blank)*, of the United States Nation; that I am the lawful wife of Joe Simon, who is a citizen, by Blood of the Creek Nation; that a Female child was born to me on 15th day of March, 1904, that said child has been named Levada Simon, and is now living.

　　Chaney Wallas　　　　　　　　　　　　her
WITNESSES TO MARK:　　　　　　　　　Emma x Simon
　　　　　　　　　　　　　　　　　　　　　mark
　John R McBeth

Subscribed and sworn to before me this 21 day of March, 1905.

　　　　　　　　　　　　　　　J C Johnson
　　　　　　　　　　　　　　　　　NOTARY PUBLIC.

AFFIDAVIT OF ATTENDING PHYSICIAN OR MID-WIFE.

UNITED STATES OF AMERICA,
　INDIAN TERRITORY,
　　Western   District.

I, Chaney Wallas, a midwife, on oath state that I attended on Mrs. Emma Simon, wife of Joe Simon on the 15 day of March, 1904 ; that there was born to her on said date a Female child; that said child is now living and is said to have been named Levada Simon

　　　　　　　　　　　　　　　Cheney Wallas

Applications for Enrollment of Creek Newborn
Act of 1905 Volume VI

WITNESSES TO MARK:

{

Subscribed and sworn to before me this 21 *day of* March , *1905*.

J C Johnson
NOTARY PUBLIC.

BIRTH AFFIDAVIT.

Department of the Interior,
COMMISSION TO THE FIVE CIVILIZED TRIBES.

IN RE *Application for Enrollment,* as a citizen of the Creek Nation, of Thomas J Brown, born on the 1st day of March, 1905

Name of Father:	Thomas J Brown	a citizen of the United States Nation.
Name of Father:	Julia Brown	a citizen of the Creek Nation.

Post-office   Wewoka I.T.

AFFIDAVIT OF MOTHER.

UNITED STATES OF AMERICA,
INDIAN TERRITORY,
Western   District.

I, Julia Brown, on oath state that I am about 32 years of age and a citizen by Blood , of the Creek Nation; that I am the lawful wife of Thomas J Brown , who is a citizen, by *(blank)* of the United States Nation; that a male child was born to me on First day of March , 1905 , that said child has been named Thomas Jefferson Brown , and is now living.

Julia Brown

WITNESSES TO MARK:

{

Subscribed and sworn to before me this 21 *day of* March , *1905*.

J C Johnson
NOTARY PUBLIC.

Applications for Enrollment of Creek Newborn
Act of 1905 Volume VI

AFFIDAVIT OF ATTENDING PHYSICIAN OR MID-WIFE.

UNITED STATES OF AMERICA,
    INDIAN TERRITORY,
Western   District.

I, Matilda Smith , a midwife , on oath state that I attended on Mrs. Julia Brown , wife of Thomas Brown on the first day of March , 1905 ; that there was born to her on said date a male child; that said child is now living and is said to have been named Thomas Jefferson Brown

                                              Matilda Smith

WITNESSES TO MARK:

Subscribed and sworn to before me this 21 day of March , 1905.

                                               J C Johnson
                                               NOTARY PUBLIC.

NC 494.

                                      Muskogee, Indian Territory, November 12, 1906.

Chief Clerk,
    Seminole Enrollment Division,
        General Office.

Dear Sir:

    You are hereby advised that the name of Martha Riley, born November 8, 1904, to William Riley, a citizen by blood of the Seminole Nation, and Annie Riley, a citizen by blood of the Creek nation, is contained in a schedule of New Born citizens of the Creek Nation, approved by the Secretary of the Interior September 27, 1905, opposite Roll No. 496.

                                Respectfully,

                                                Commissioner.

Applications for Enrollment of Creek Newborn
Act of 1905 Volume VI

BIRTH AFFIDAVIT.

DEPARTMENT OF THE INTERIOR.
COMMISSION TO THE FIVE CIVILIZED TRIBES.

IN RE APPLICATION FOR ENROLLMENT, as a citizen of the Muskogee or Creek Nation, of Nathan & Lynn, born on the 14 day of June, 1902

Name of Father:	M A Hallford	a citizen of the U.S.	Nation.
Name of Mother:	Emaline Hallford	a citizen of the Creek	Nation.

Postoffice   Yeager Ind. Ter.

AFFIDAVIT OF MOTHER.

UNITED STATES OF AMERICA, Indian Territory,
Western   DISTRICT.

I, Emaline Hallford, on oath state that I am twenty nine years of age and a citizen by blood, of the Creek Nation; that I am the lawful wife of M A Hallford, who is a citizen, by Marriage of the Creek Nation; that a two male children was born to me on 14 day of June, 1902, that said child has been named Nathan & Lynn, and was living March 4, 1905.

              her
          Emaline x Hallford
Witnesses To Mark: mark
{ Mary Nasley
{ J W Grissom

Subscribed and sworn to before me this 25 day of March, 1905.

My Commission Expires June 13th, 1908.   W R Clawson
              Notary Public.

AFFIDAVIT OF ATTENDING PHYSICIAN OR MID-WIFE.

UNITED STATES OF AMERICA, Indian Territory,
Western   DISTRICT.

I, J W Grissom, a physician, on oath state that I attended on Mrs. Emaline Hallford, wife of M A Hallford on the 14 day of June, 1902; that there was born to her on said date a two male children; that said children was living March 4, 1905, and is said to have been named Nathan & Lynn

            Dr. J W Grissom

Witnesses To Mark:
{ Mary Nasley

Applications for Enrollment of Creek Newborn
Act of 1905   Volume VI

Subscribed and sworn to before me this 25 day of March, 1905.

<small>My Commission Expires June 13th, 1908.</small>   W R Clawson
Notary Public.

DEPARTMENT OF THE INTERIOR,
COMMISSIONER TO THE FIVE CIVILIZED TRIBES.
WETUMKA, INDIAN TERRITORY.
JULY 18, 1906.

In the matter of the application for the enrollment ~~of~~ as citizens of the Creek Nation of children born to duly enrolled citizens members of the so called "Snake" Faction.

J.R. Dunzy, being duly sworn, testified as follows, through Official Interpreter, Alex Posey.

By Commissioner:
Q What is your name? A J.R. Dunzy.
Q What is your age? A 40.
Q What is your post office address? A Wetumka.
Q Are you a citizen of the Creek Nation? A Yes sir.
Q To what town do you belong? A Tuckabatchee[sic], I am town king.
Q Do you know of any minor children in your town or neighborhood for whose enrollment application has not been made? A I wrote to the Commission about two children in the Seminole Nation, but didn't make application for them, because I did not know what their names were or ages--one is a child of a Tuckabatchee[sic] woman named Mullie. Her husband is a Seminole, named Echo Ela---the other child belongs to Millie's daughter. I wrote to them and got a reply the other day--I will get the dates and names which I have at home.

Witness presents a piece of paper giving certain dates and names, which is made a part of the record herein.

I, Alex Posey, being duly sworn, states that the above and foregoing is a true and correct transcript of his notes as taken on said date in said cause.

Alex Posey

Subscribed and sworn to before me this 31st day of July, 1906.

Edward Merrick
Notary Public.

Applications for Enrollment of Creek Newborn
Act of 1905 Volume VI

DEPARTMENT OF THE INTERIOR,
COMMISSIONER TO THE FIVE CIVILIZED TRIBES,
HAZEL, I. T., September 18, 1906.

MULLIE being duly sworn, testified as follows
Through Alex Posey, Official Interpreter.

BY THE COMMISSIONER:

Q What is your name? A Mullie.
Q How old are you? A I do not know my age. (Witness appears to be about 45 years old).
Q What is your postoffice address? A Hazel, I. T.
Q Are you a citizen of the Creek Nation? A Yes sir.
Q To what Creek town do you belong? A Tuckbatche.
Q On July 18, 1906, J. R. Dunzy appeared before the Commissioner to the Five Civilized Tribes at Wetumka and made application for the enrollment of an unnamed minor child of yours. Have you such child? A Yes sir.
Q What is the child's name? A Tingka.
Q Who is the child's father? A Echoille Chupco.
Q Is he a citizen of the Creek Nation? A No sir, he is a Seminole.
Q Is he your lawful husband? A Yes sir, we have been living together many years.
Q Is he living? A Yes sir, but he is absent from home today.
Q When was your child Tingka born? A I do not know; all I know about the child birth of the child is that it was born in blackberry time, probably in June.
Q How many years old is the child? A The child is five years old. It was born while we were living down there in the bottom, and just before we moved to this place; we have been living here five years.
Q The child's full name is Tingka Chupco, is it? A Yes sir.
Q Who attended on you at the birth of this child? A No one.
Q Does the father know when the child was born? A No sir, he knows less about dates than I do. Since thinking the matter over I can now state positively that the child was born in June and was five years old last June.
Q You are enrolled and have your allotment in the Creek Nation, have you? A Yes sir.
Q Do you know under what name you are enrolled in the Creek Nation? A Simply as Mullie.
Q If it should be found that your child is entitled to enrollment in either the Creek or Seminole Nations in which Nation do you elect to have the child enroll? A In the Creek nation.
Q You are advised that it will be necessary for you to furnish this office with a joint affidavit of two disinterested witnesses as to the birth of your minor child Tingka Chupco? A I will be unable to do that as I had no near neighbors at the time the child was born.
Q The child is living, is it? A Yes sir, this is the child here. (Indicating a child present).

Applications for Enrollment of Creek Newborn
Act of 1905 Volume VI

Q Is Tingka a boy or a girl A A boy.

James B. Myers, being first duly sworn, states, that as stenographer to the Commissioner to the Five Civilized Tribes, he recorded the testimony in the foregoing proceedings, and that the above is a true, and correct transcript of his stenographic notes thereof.

James B Myers

Subscribed and sworn to before me,
this, the 3 day of October, 1905.

Alex Posey
Notary Public.

JBM.

N.C. 496.

DEPARTMENT OF THE INTERIOR,
COMMISSIONER TO THE FIVE CIVILIZED TRIBES,
HAZEL, I. T., OCTOBER 25, 1906.

In the matter of the application for the enrollment of Tinka Chupco as a citizen by blood of the Creek Nation.

MULLIE, being first duly sworn by, and examined through Alex Posey, a Notary Public, and Official Interpreter, testified as follows:

BY THE COMMISSIONER:

Q What is your name? A Mullie.
Q How old are you? A I don't know. (Witness appears to be about 45 years old).
Q What is your postoffice address? A Hazel.
Q Are you a citizen of the Creek Nation? A Yes sir.
Q To what Creek town do you belong? A Tuckabatche[sic].
Q You have heretofore testified in the matter of the application for the enrollment of your minor child, Tinka Chupco, have you not? A Yes sir.
Q You were advised that it would be necessary for you to furnish the joint affidavit of two disinterested witnesses as to the birth of this child. Can you furnish such affidavit now? A I told you that I would be unable to secure an affidavit of two disinterested witnesses as no one living near me knows when my child was born.
Q Was there no one present at the birth of your child? A There was no one present except my daughter Sallie.
Q Did she act as mid-wife? A No sir, but she was present and waited on me during my sickness.
Q The child is still living, is he? A Yes sir.

Applications for Enrollment of Creek Newborn
Act of 1905   Volume VI

James B. Myers, being first duly sworn, states, that as stenographer to the Commissioner to the Five Civilized Tribes, he recorded the testimony in the foregoing proceedings, and that the above is a true, and correct transcript of his stenographic notes thereof.

James B Myers

Subscribed and sworn to before me,
this 16 day of Nov, 1906.

Alex Posey
Notary Public.

BIRTH AFFIDAVIT.
DEPARTMENT OF THE INTERIOR,
COMMISSIONER TO THE FIVE CIVILIZED TRIBES.

ENROLLMENT OF MINORS. ACT OF CONGRESS, APPROVED APRIL 26, 1906.

IN RE APPLICATION FOR ENROLLMENT, as a citizen of the Creek Nation, of Tingka Chupco, born on the ----- day of June, 1901

Name of Father:	Echoilla Chupco	a citizen of the	Seminole	Nation.
Name of Mother:	Mullie	a citizen of the	Creek	Nation.

Tribal enrollment of father   -----   Tribal enrollment of mother Tuckabatche[sic]

Postoffice   Hazel   Indian Territory

AFFIDAVIT OF ATTENDING PHYSICIAN OR MID-WIFE.

UNITED STATES OF AMERICA, Indian Territory, }
  Western   District.

I, Sallie Mullie, a -----, on oath state that I attended on Mullie, wife of Echoilla Chupco on the ----- day of June, 1901 ; that there was born to her on said date a male child; that said child was living March 4, 1906, and is now living and is said to have been named Tingka Chupco   her

Sallie x Mullie

WITNESSES TO MARK: mark
{ Alex Posey
{ JB Myers

Subscribed and sworn to before me this 25 day of October, 1906.

Alex Posey
Notary Public.

Applications for Enrollment of Creek Newborn
Act of 1905 Volume VI

BIRTH AFFIDAVIT.
DEPARTMENT OF THE INTERIOR.
COMMISSION TO THE FIVE CIVILIZED TRIBES.

IN RE APPLICATION FOR ENROLLMENT, as a citizen of the Creek or Muskogee Nation, of Ohland Morton, born on the 14 day of May, 1902.

Name of Father:	J C Morton	a citizen of the U. S.	Nation.
Name of Mother:	Mattie Morton	a citizen of the Creek	Nation.

Postoffice   Hitchita I T.

AFFIDAVIT OF MOTHER.

UNITED STATES OF AMERICA, Indian Territory,
  Western   DISTRICT.

I, Mattie Morton, on oath state that I am 28 years of age and a citizen by Blood, of the Creek Nation; that I am the lawful wife of J C Morton, who is a citizen, by *(blank)* of the United Stated ~~Nation~~; that a Male child was born to me on 14 day of May, 1902, that said child has been named Ohland Morton, and was living March 4, 1905.

Mattie Morton

Witnesses To Mark:
{

Subscribed and sworn to before me this 25 day of March, 1905.

Joseph C Morton
Notary Public.

My Commission Expires Feb 29-1908

AFFIDAVIT OF ATTENDING PHYSICIAN OR MID-WIFE.

UNITED STATES OF AMERICA, Indian Territory,
  Western   DISTRICT.

I, S. H. Hamilton, a Physician, on oath state that I attended on Mrs. Mattie Morton, wife of J C Morton on the 14 day of May, 1902; that there was born to her on said date a male child; that said child was living March 4, 1905, and is said to have been named Ohland Morton

S. H. Hamilton M.D.

Applications for Enrollment of Creek Newborn
Act of 1905   Volume VI

Witnesses To Mark:
{

Subscribed and sworn to before me this 25 day of March , 1905.

Joseph C Morton
Notary Public.

My Commission Expires Feb 29-1908

NC-497

Muskogee, Indian Territory, August 5, 1905.

Lillian Foshee,
    c/o William R. Foshee,
        Hitchita, Indian Territory.

Dear Madam:

In the matter of the application for the enrollment of your minor son Henry C. Foshee as a citizen by blood of the Creek Nation you are advised that it will be necessary for you to file with this office either the original or a certified copy of the marriage license and certificate showing the marriage between you and William R. Foshee, the father of said child.

Respectfully,

Commissioner.

NC-497

Muskogee, Indian Territory, December 13, 1905.

Lillian Foshee,
    Care of William R. Foshee,
        Hitchita, Indian Territory.

Dear Madam:

In the matter of the application for the enrollment of your minor son, Henry C. Foshee, as a citizen by blood of the Creek Nation, you are again advised that it will be necessary for you to file with this office either the original or a certified copy of the marriage license and certificate, showing [sic] marriage between you and William R. Foshee, the father of said child.

Applications for Enrollment of Creek Newborn
Act of 1905   Volume VI

Respectfully,

Commissioner.

BIRTH AFFIDAVIT.

DEPARTMENT OF THE INTERIOR.
COMMISSION TO THE FIVE CIVILIZED TRIBES.

IN RE APPLICATION FOR ENROLLMENT, as a citizen of the Creek or Muskogee Nation, of Henry C. Foshee, born on the 27 day of Dec , 1902

Name of Father:	William R Foshee	a citizen of the	Creek	Nation.
Name of Mother:	Lillian Foshee	a citizen of the	U. S.	Nation.

Postoffice   Hitchita I.T.

AFFIDAVIT OF MOTHER.

UNITED STATES OF AMERICA, Indian Territory,
Western   DISTRICT.

I, Lillian Foshee , on oath state that I am 25 years of age and a citizen by *(blank)* , of the   United States   ~~Nation~~; that I am the lawful wife of Wm. R. Foshee , who is a citizen, by Blood of the Creek   Nation; that a Male child was born to me on 27 day of December , 1902 , that said child has been named Henry C. Foshee , and was living March 4, 1905.

Lillian Foshee

Witnesses To Mark:

Subscribed and sworn to before me this 25 day of March , 1905.

Joseph C Morton
Notary Public.

My Commission Expires Feb 29-1908

AFFIDAVIT OF ATTENDING PHYSICIAN OR MID-WIFE.

UNITED STATES OF AMERICA, Indian Territory,
Western   DISTRICT.

I, S. H. Hamilton , a Physician , on oath state that I attended on Mrs. Lillian Foshee , wife of William Foshee on the 27 day of December , 1902 ; that there was

Applications for Enrollment of Creek Newborn
Act of 1905 Volume VI

born to her on said date a male child; that said child was living March 4, 1905, and is said to have been named Henry C Foshee

S H Hamilton, M.D.

Witnesses To Mark:
{

Subscribed and sworn to before me this 25 day of March, 1905.

Joseph C Morton
Notary Public.

My Commission Expires Feb 29-1908

NC-498.

Muskogee, Indian Territory, August 5, 1905.

Lucy Barnett,
   c/o Scipio Barnett
      Weleetka, Indian Territory.

Dear Madam:

In the matter of the application for the enrollment of your minor daughter Leola Barnett as a citizen by blood of the Creek Nation it will be necessary, before the rights of said child as a citizen by blood of the Creek Nation can be finally determined, for you to file with this office either the original or a certified copy of the marriage license and certificate showing the marriage between you and Scipio Barnett, the father of said child.

Respectfully,

Commissioner.

Department of the Interior,

Commission to the Five Civilized Tribes.

-----oOo-----

IN RE APPLICATION FOR ENROLLMENT, as a citizen of the Creek Nation of Leola Barnett, born on the 10 day of March, 1904

Name of Father   Scipio Barnett   a citizen of the Creek Nation
                                                                            U.S.
Name of Mother   Lucy Barnett   a citizen of the Creek Nation.

Applications for Enrollment of Creek Newborn
Act of 1905 Volume VI

Post office Weleetka, Ind. Ter.

Affidavit of Mother.

United States of America,)
Western District of the Indian Territory,) SS.

    I, Lucy Barnett, on my oath state that I am 24 years of age and a citizen by birth of the U. S. Nation; that I am the lawful wife of Scipio Barnett, who is a citizen by birth of the Creek Nation; that a Female child was born to me on 10th day of March, 1904; that said child has been named Leola Barnett, and was living on the 4" day of March, 1905.

                                                                 Lucy Barnett

Witness to Mark:

Subscribed and sworn to before me this 25" day of March, 1905.

MY COMMISSION EXPIRES FEBY. 29, 1906.   John B Patterson
                                                                 Notary Public.

Affidavit of attending Physician or Midwife.

United States of America,)
Western District of the Indian Territory,) SS.

    I, Jencey Barnett a Midwife on my oath state that I attended on Mrs. Lucy Barnett on the 10" day of March 1904, that there was born to her on said date a Female child; that said child was living on the 4" day of March 1905, and is said to have been named Leola Barnett

                                                             her
Witness Mark   Jencey x Barnett
    Robert Jefferson   mark
    Mary Barnett

Subscribed and sworn to before me this 25" day of March, 1905.

MY COMMISSION EXPIRES FEBY. 29, 1906.   John B Patterson
                                                                 Notary Public.

Applications for Enrollment of Creek Newborn
Act of 1905   Volume VI

CERTIFICATE OF RECORD.

United States of America, ⎱
   INDIAN TERRITORY,   ⎰ ss.
   Northern District.

I, *CHARLES A. DAVIDSON*, Clerk of the United States Court in the Northern District, Indian Territory, do hereby certify that the instrument hereto attached was filed for record in my office the   21   day of   Sept   1902 at   M., and duly recorded in Book   J , Marriage Record, Page   287

    WITNESS my hand and seal of said Court at Muscogee, in said Territory, this   12   day of   Dec   A. D. 1902

                      Chas A Davidson   Clerk.
              By   (blank)   Deputy.

MARRIAGE LICENSE

✤ ✤ ✤

United States of America, ⎱
   INDIAN TERRITORY,   ⎰ ss.   No. **930**
   Northern District.

To Any Person Authorized by Law to Solemnize Marriage---Greeting:

    You are Hereby Commanded to Solemnize the Rite and publish the Banns of Matrimony between Mr.   Scipio Barnett   of   McDermott , in the Indian Territory, aged   25   years and Miss Lucy Roberson   of   McDermott   in the Indian Territory aged   21   years according to law, and do you officially sign and return this License to the parties therein named.

    WITNESS my hand and official seal at Muscogee Indian Territory this   12   day of   Sept   A.D. 1900

                            Chas. A. Davidson
                            Clerk of the U.S. Court

By   ? M Ford   Deputy

Applications for Enrollment of Creek Newborn
Act of 1905 Volume VI

CERTIFICATE OF MARRIAGE.

United States of America, } ss.
INDIAN TERRITORY,
Northern District.

I, Rev. Wm Burns , *a Minister of the Gospel, DO HEREBY CERTIFY that on the* 16 *day of* Sept *A. D.* 1900, *I did duly and according to law as commanded in the foregoing License, solemnize the Rite and publish the Banns of Matrimony between the parties therein named.*

WITNESS my hand this 16 *day of* Sept *A. D.* 1900

My credentials are recorded in the office of the Clerk of the United States Court, Indian Territory, Northern District, Book B *, Page* 105 *.*

Rev. Wm Burns
A Minister of the Gospel

Note—This License and Certificate of Marriage must be returned to the Office of the Clerk of the United States Court in the Northern District, Indian Territory, from whence it was issued, within sixty days from the date thereof, or the party to whom the license was issued will be liable in the amount of the One Hundred Dollars ($100.00)

BIRTH AFFIDAVIT.
DEPARTMENT OF THE INTERIOR,
COMMISSIONER TO THE FIVE CIVILIZED TRIBES.

IN RE APPLICATION FOR ENROLLMENT, as a citizen of the Creek Nation, of Fannie Ann Ditzler , born on the 15 day of December , 1*(blank)*
and is 2 years and 3 months old.
Name of Father: Will Ditzler a citizen of the United States Nation.
Name of Mother: Melvina Ditzler a citizen of the Creek Nation.

Postoffice Weleetka, Ind. Terr.

AFFIDAVIT OF MOTHER.

UNITED STATES OF AMERICA, Indian Territory, }
Western District.

I, Melvina Ditzler , on oath state that I am 21 years of age and a citizen by blood, of the Creek Nation; that I am the lawful wife of Will Ditzler , who is a citizen, by *(blank)* of the United States Nation; that a female child was born to me on 15

Applications for Enrollment of Creek Newborn
Act of 1905   Volume VI

day of December   and is 2 years and 3 months old, that said child has been named Fannie Ann Ditzler , and was living March 4, 1905.

                                 her
                         Melvina   x   Ditzler

Witness to Mark: mark
{ DC Skaggs
  Alex Posey

Subscribed and sworn to before me this   21   day of March   , 1905.

                              Drennan C Skaggs
                                    Notary Public.

AFFIDAVIT OF ATTENDING PHYSICIAN OR MID-WIFE.

UNITED STATES OF AMERICA, Indian Territory, ⎫
  Western   District. ⎭

I, Sally M Ditzler   , a mid-wife   , on oath state that I attended on Mrs. Melvina Ditzler , wife of Will Ditzler on the 15 day of December , 1902 ; that there was born to her on said date a   female   child; that said child was living March 4, 1905, and is said to have been named Fannie Ann Ditzler

                               her
                       Sally M. x   Ditzler

Witness to Mark: mark
{ Alex Posey

Subscribed and sworn to before me this   22   day of March   , 1905.

                              Drennan C Skaggs
                                   Notary Public.

NC 500

                     Muskogee, Indian Territory, January 8, 1907.

Joseph Yadeke,
    Dustin, Indian Territory.

Dear Sir:

    This office is advised that your son John Yadeke died October 25, 1902, and desires information as to the date of his birth. For that purpose there is herewith inclosed

Applications for Enrollment of Creek Newborn
Act of 1905   Volume VI

a blank form of birth affidavit which you should have properly executed and return to this office in the inclosed envelope within ten days.

                Respectfully,

                              Commissioner.

1 BA

BIRTH AFFIDAVIT.

DEPARTMENT OF THE INTERIOR,
COMMISSIONER TO THE FIVE CIVILIZED TRIBES.

IN RE APPLICATION FOR ENROLLMENT, as a citizen of the Creek Nation[sic] Nation, of Indian Territory[sic], born on the 21 day of September, 1903

Name of Father: Robert D. Atkins   a citizen of the Creek Nation Nation.
Name of Mother: Alice Atkins   a citizen of the Creek Nation Nation.

                Postoffice   Red Ford, Ind Ter.

AFFIDAVIT OF MOTHER.

UNITED STATES OF AMERICA, Indian Territory,
    Western District   District.

    I, Alice Atkins, on oath state that I am 27 years of age and a citizen by blood, of the Creek Nation Nation; that I am the lawful wife of Robert D. Atkins, who is a citizen, by blood of the Creek Nation Nation; that a female child was born to me on 21st day of September, 1903, that said child has been named Mildred Atkins, and was living March 4, 1905.

                              Alice Atkins

Witness to Mark:

    Subscribed and sworn to before me this 25th day of March, 1905.

                              W.S. McCluskey
                                  Notary Public.

Applications for Enrollment of Creek Newborn
Act of 1905 Volume VI

AFFIDAVIT OF ATTENDING PHYSICIAN OR MID-WIFE.

UNITED STATES OF AMERICA, Indian Territory,
Western District   District.

I, Fred S. Clinton, M. D. , a Physician , on oath state that I attended on Mrs. Alice Atkins , wife of Robert D. Atkins on the 21st day of September , 1903 ; that there was born to her on said date a female child; that said child was living March 4, 1905, and is said to have been named Mildred Atkins

Fred S Clinton M.D.

Witness to Mark:

Subscribed and sworn to before me this 25th day of March , 1905.

W.S. McCluskey
Notary Public.

N.C. 502

DEPARTMENT OF THE INTERIOR, COMMISSIONER TO THE FIVE CIVILIZED TRIBES.

Muskogee, Indian Territory, September 21, 1905

In the matter of the application for the enrollment of Louls Bigpond as a citizen of the Creek Nation.

James Bigpond, being duly sworn, testified as follows:

EXAMINATION BY THE COMMISSION:
Q What is your name? A James Bigpond.
Q What is the name of your father? A Billy Bigpond.
Q What is the name of your mother? A Kizzie.
Q How old are you? A About 28 or 29.
Q What is your postoffice address? A Bristow.
Q Are you a full-blood Euchee? A Yes sir.
Q You have a child Louis Bigpond? A Yes sir.
Q Is he living? A Yes sir.
Q What is the name of the mother of the child? A Sela.
Q You are married to her? A Yes sir.
Q How about Sarah Bigpond, the first wife? A She is dead; died along about three years ago.
Q After Sarah died you married Sela? A Yes sir.
Q You know the name of the father of Sela? A Com-pe-the-le-nay.
Q The mother, Lucy? A Yes sir.

Applications for Enrollment of Creek Newborn
Act of 1905 Volume VI

Q When was this child, Louis, born? A March 3.
Q Was he born in the day time or night time? A Night time.
Q In the night? A Yes sir.
Q Sela made affidavit here and said the child was born March 2. A March 2?
Q Yes. Joe__her father, said he was born March 2, on one time, and another time he said March 3. We want to know just what time he was born. You think it was March? A Yes sir.
Q What time of the night was it? A About 10 o'clock.
Q Ten o'clock in the morning? A In the night.
Q March 3? A Yes sir.
Q You know the day of the week? A No sir.
Q How do you know it was ten o'clock at night, did you look at the clock? A Yes sir. I looked at the clock.
Q What kind of a clock did you have? A I had a big clock.
Q A Wooden clock? A Yes sir; wooden clock.
Q Don't you know the day of the week? was it Monday, Tuesday, Wednesday, Thursday, Friday or Saturday? A Thursday.
Q The night of Thursday? A Yes sir.
Q That was March 2; and Friday was March 3, Saturday March 4. You are sure it was Thursday? A Yes sir.
Q Did you put it down anywhere, on a piece of paper? A On paper, but I left it at home.
Q When did you put it down? A On the same day--next day.
Q What does it say on the piece of paper, do you know? A No.
Q You wrote that yourself? A Yes sir.
Q Did you write in Euchee or English? A English. I can write in Euchee.
Q You wrote that down in English? A Yes sir.
Q Just put it down on a piece of paper, not in a book? A Yes sir.
Q Any white people there when the child was born? A No sir.
Q Who was present when the child was born--who was in the house? A Joe.
Q Your father in law? A Yes sir.
Q Was he the only one there? A Another boy, Cooper Tiger.
Q He was there? A Yes sir.
Q Did you have a doctor? A No sir.

The witness is advised to bring in the paper on which is entered the date of the birth of the child. Also to have the witness who was present at the birth make out an affidavit as to the time of the night it was and bring it in here.

John Bigpond, being duly sworn, testified as follows:

EXAMINATION BY THE COMMISSION:
Q What is your name? A John Bigpond.
Q Are you any relation (or kin) to him? A Yes, sir; that's my brother.
Q How old are you? A 31.
Q What is your postoffice address? A Bristow.
Q Do you know when this child, Louis, was born? A Yes, I know. March 3, I believe. I've been there. Stayed there several days.

Applications for Enrollment of Creek Newborn
Act of 1905   Volume VI

Q Do you know what day of the week it was born? A No, I don't know that.
Q You don't know whether it was Monday, Tuesday, Wednesday, Thursday, Friday or Saturday? A About Thursday, I guess.
Q What time was it, day or night? A Night.
Q What hour, do you know? A About ten o'clock.
Q You are sure it was before midnight? A Yes sir. About ten o'clock at night.
Q You think it was 10 o'clock Thursday? A Thursday night.
Q 10 o'clock? A Yes sir.
Q I will tell you now--you don't understand English very well--that Thursday about that time was March 2 and not March 3. So you may be mistaken in the day. A I believe it is, I am mistaken. I had other business. I am mistaken.
Q You don't know the days very well? A No sir.
Q You think it was Thursday at 10 o'clock? A (after counting up the days of the week) I believe it was Thursday.
Q You think it was March 2--the night of March 2nd? A No sir, not March 2nd, March 3rd.
Q March 3rd was Friday. A Friday?
Q Yes. You are sure it was before Saturday? A Yes sir.
Q You are sure that it was before 12 o'clock that the child was born? A No sir; it was Thursday night at 10 o'clock.

This witness and witness James Bigpond talk and understand English with difficulty, but agree on the fact that the child was born Thursday night at 10 o'clock.

INDIAN TERRITORY, Western District.
I, J. Y. Miller, a stenographer to the Commission to the Five Civilized Tribes, do hereby certify that the above and foregoing is a true and complete translation of my notes as same appear in my stenographic report of this case.

J Y Miller

Sworn to and subscribed before me
this the 21st day of September,
1905.

Edw C Griesel
Notary Public.

BIRTH AFFIDAVIT.

DEPARTMENT OF THE INTERIOR.
COMMISSION TO THE FIVE CIVILIZED TRIBES.

IN RE APPLICATION FOR ENROLLMENT, as a citizen of the Creek Nation, of Louis Bigpond, born on the 2nd day of March, 1905

Name of Father: James Bigpond   a citizen of the Creek (Euchie)Nation.
Name of Mother: Selah Bigpond   a citizen of the   Creek   Nation.

Applications for Enrollment of Creek Newborn
Act of 1905   Volume VI

Postoffice   Bristow, Ind Terr.

AFFIDAVIT OF MOTHER.

UNITED STATES OF AMERICA, Indian Territory,
Western   DISTRICT.

I, Selah Bigpond , on oath state that I am 25 years of age and a citizen by blood , of the Creek Nation; that I am the lawful wife of James Bigpond , who is a citizen, by blood of the Creek Nation; that a male child was born to me on Second day of March , 1905 , that said child has been named Louis Bigpond , and was living March 4, 1905.

                          her
             Selah Bigpond x
Witnesses To Mark: mark
 { Tom Bigpond
  Wesley Moore

Subscribed and sworn to before me this 25th day of March , 1905.

              T. W. Flynn
              Notary Public.

AFFIDAVIT OF ATTENDING PHYSICIAN OR MID-WIFE.

UNITED STATES OF AMERICA, Indian Territory,
Western   DISTRICT.

I, Joe Bigpond , a *(blank)* , on oath state that I attended on Mrs. Selah Bigpond, (am her father) , wife of James Bigpond on the 2nd day of March , 1905 ; that there was born to her on said date a male child; that said child was living March 4, 1905, and is said to have been named Louis Bigpond

                          his
             Joe Bigpond x
Witnesses To Mark: mark
 { Tom Bigpond
  Wesley Moore

Subscribed and sworn to before me this 25th day of March , 1905.

              T. W. Flynn
              Notary Public.

Applications for Enrollment of Creek Newborn
Act of 1905 Volume VI

In the Interior Department--Creek Enrolling Division.

In the Matter of the Application
for Enrollment of Louis Bigpond.

Affidavit.

Indian Territory,

ss

Western District,

John Tiger of lawful age being duly sworn on his oath says, that he is acquainted with Louis Bigpond, who is a Citizen by blood of the Creek Nation; that Louis Bigpond was born March 3rd 1905 and was living March 4, 1905 on the 4th day of March 1905 and is living to day; that Louis Bigpond is [sic] child of James Bigpond and Selah Bigpond, Citizens of the Creek Nation. That this affiant makes this affidavit from personal knowledge, having been present at the birth of said child and being intimately acquainted with the family of James and Selah Bigpond. Affiant states that he has no interest in this case.

John Tiger

Subscribed and sworn to before me this the 12th day of August 1905.

William L. Cheatham
Notary Public.

Witnesses
William L. Cheatham
W. J. McIntosh   } Bristow I.T.

In the Interior Department--Creek Enrolling Division.

In the Matter of the Application
for enrollment of Louis Bigpond.

Affidavit

Indian Territory,

ss.

Western District,

Joe Bigpond of lawful age being duly sworn on his oath says, that he is acquainted with Louis Bigpond, who is a Citizen by blood of the Creek Nation; that Louis Bigpond was born on the 3rd day of March 1905 and was living on the 4th day of March 1905 and is now living; that Louis Bigpond is the child of James Bigpond and Selah Bigpond, Citizens of the Creek Nation, that Selah Bigpond is my daughter; that the said Louis Bigpond was born to the said Selah Bigpond in my house south west of Bristow, I. T. This statement is made from my own personal knowledge. I have no interest in this claim other than as the Father of Selah Bigpond.

Applications for Enrollment of Creek Newborn
Act of 1905   Volume VI

Joe ^{his} + _{mark} Bigpond

Subscribed and sworn to before me this the 2nd day of August 1905.

William L. Cheatham
Notary Public.

My commission expires Jany 3, 1907

Witnesses:
    William L. Cheatham
                     Bristow Ind. Ter.
    James Bigpond

NC-502.

Muskogee, Indian Territory, August 5, 1905.

Selah Bigpond,
    c/o James Bigpond,
        Bristow, Indian Territory.

Dear Madam:

    In the matter of the application for the enrollment of Louis Bigpond as a citizen by blood of the Creek Nation you are advised that it will be necessary for you to furnish this office with the affidavits of two disinterested persons relative to the birth of said child; said affidavits to set forth the name of said child, the date of his birth, the names of his parents and whether or not he was living on March 4, 1905. The affidavits should also set forth the source of the knowledge of the affiants.

    You are also requested to inform this office as to the name under which you were finally enrolled, the names of your parents and other members of your family and to state your roll number as the same appears upon your allotment certificate and deeds.

Respectfully,

Commissioner.

Applications for Enrollment of Creek Newborn
Act of 1905 Volume VI

(Copy)

Bristow, I. T., Sept. 2, 1905

Hon. Tams Bixby
  Muskogee, I.T.

Dear Sir:

Inclosed find affidavits relative to birth of Louis Bigpond as requested in letter of Aug. 5th.

I am enrolled under name "Pelah." My fathers[sic] name is "Conpethloney." Other members of Family "Wattie" "Cotetan" "Hethahconeney." Allottment[sic] certificate shows Creek Roll Card Field No. 2115-Selection 10447.

Let me know if this is sufficient proof and when I can file.

Yours Truly, "Pelah"

Selah Bigpond.

NC-502

Muskogee, Indian Territory, September 7, 1905.

Selah Bigpond,
  Bristow, Indian Territory.

Dear Madam:

Receipt is acknowledged of your letter of September 2, 1905, enclosing affidavit in the matter of the application for the enrollment of your minor child, Louis Bigpond.

You are hereby advised that you will be allowed fifteen days from date hereof within which to appear at this Office with two witnesses who know the date of the birth of said child, for the purpose of being examined under oath.

Respectfully,

Acting Commissioner.

Applications for Enrollment of Creek Newborn
Act of 1905 Volume VI

DEPARTMENT OF THE INTERIOR,
COMMISSION TO THE FIVE CIVILIZED TRIBES.
Holdenville, I. T., March 29, 1905.

In the matter of the application for the enrollment of Bettie Alexander as a citizen by blood of the Creek Nation.

MARTHA ALEXANDER, being duly sworn, testified as follows:

BY COMMISSION:
Q What is your name? A Martha Alexander.
Q How old are you? A Twenty-four.
Q What is your post office address? A Wetumka.
Q Are you a citizen of the Creek Nation? A No, sir, I am a Seminoe[sic].
Q Do you make application for the enrollment of your minor child, Bettie Alexander, as a citizen of the Creek Nation? A Yes, sir.
Q What is the name of the father of this child? A Robert L. Alexander.
Q Is he a citizen of the Creek Nation? A Yes, sir.
Q To what town does he belong? A Hickory Ground.
Q Is he your lawful husband? A Yes, sir.

Q If it should be found that your child, Bettie Alexander, is entitled to enrollment in either the Creek or Seminole Nations[sic] in which nation do you desire to have her enrolled? A In the Creek Nation.

---oooOOOooo---

I, D. C. Skaggs, on oath state that the above and foregoing is a full and true transcript of my stenographic notes as taken in said cause on said date.

DC Skaggs

Subscribed and sworn to before me this 20" day of July, 1905.

Edw C Griesel
Notary Public.

BIRTH AFFIDAVIT.

DEPARTMENT OF THE INTERIOR.
COMMISSION TO THE FIVE CIVILIZED TRIBES.

IN RE APPLICATION FOR ENROLLMENT, as a citizen of the Creek Nation, of Bettie Alexander, born on the 27th day of July, 1903

Name of Father: Robert L. Alexander   a citizen of the Creek Nation.
Name of Mother: Martha Alexander   a citizen of the Seminole Nation.

Applications for Enrollment of Creek Newborn
Act of 1905 Volume VI

Postoffice   Wetumka, Ind. Ter.

AFFIDAVIT OF ~~MOTHER~~. Father

UNITED STATES OF AMERICA, Indian Territory, }
Western   DISTRICT.

I, Robert L. Alexander, on oath state that I am 31 years of age and a citizen by blood, of the Creek Nation; that I am the lawful ~~wife of~~ husband of Martha Alexander, who is a citizen, by blood of the Seminole Nation; that a female child was born to me on 27th day of July, 1903, that said child has been named Bettie Alexander, and is now living.

Robert L. Alexander

Witnesses To Mark:
{

Subscribed and sworn to before me this 10th day of Aug 1905.

B. H. Mills
Notary Public.

My Commission Exp Aug 15. 1906.

BIRTH AFFIDAVIT.

DEPARTMENT OF THE INTERIOR.
COMMISSION TO THE FIVE CIVILIZED TRIBES.

IN RE APPLICATION FOR ENROLLMENT, as a citizen of the Creek Nation, of Bettie Alexander, born on the 27 day of July, 1903

Name of Father: Robert L. Alexander   a citizen of the   Creek   Nation.
Hickory Ground Town
Name of Mother: Martha Alexander   a citizen of the Seminole Nation.

Postoffice   Wetumka, Ind. Ter.

AFFIDAVIT OF MOTHER.

UNITED STATES OF AMERICA, Indian Territory, }
Western   DISTRICT.

I, Martha Alexander, on oath state that I am 24 years of age and a citizen by blood, of the Seminole Nation; that I am the lawful wife of Robert L. Alexander, who is a citizen, by blood of the Creek Nation; that a female child was born to me

Applications for Enrollment of Creek Newborn
Act of 1905   Volume VI

on 27 day of July, 1903, that said child has been named Bettie Alexander, and was living March 4, 1905.

Martha Alexander

Witnesses To Mark:
{

Subscribed and sworn to before me this 29 day of March, 1905.

Drennan C Skaggs
Notary Public.

AFFIDAVIT OF ATTENDING PHYSICIAN OR MID-WIFE.

UNITED STATES OF AMERICA, Indian Territory,
Western   DISTRICT.

I, Nancy Alexander, a mid-wife, on oath state that I attended on Mrs. Martha Alexander, wife of Robert L. Alexander on the 27 day of July, 1903; that there was born to her on said date a female child; that said child was living March 4, 1905, and is said to have been named Bettie Alexander

her
Nancy x Alexander
mark

Witnesses To Mark:
{ DC Skaggs
  Alex Posey

Subscribed and sworn to before me this 29 day of March, 1905.

Drennan C Skaggs
Notary Public.

NC-503.

Muskogee, Indian Territory, July 14, 1905.

Commissioner to the Five Civilized Tribes,
    Seminole Enrollment Division,
        Muskogee, Indian Territory.

Gentlemen:

March 31, 1905, application was made to the Commission to the Five Civilized Tribes for the enrollment of Bettie Alexander, born July 17, 1903, as a citizen by blood of the Creek Nation. It is stated in said application that the father of said child is Robert L. Alexander, a citizen of the Creek Nation, and that the mother is Martha Alexander, a citizen of the Seminole Nation.

Applications for Enrollment of Creek Newborn
Act of 1905   Volume VI

You are requested to inform the Creek Enrollment Division as to whether application has been made for the enrollment of said Bettie Alexander, as a citizen of the Seminole Nation, and if so, what disposition has been made of the same.

Respectfully,

Commissioner.

(NC-503)
DEPARTMENT OF THE INTERIOR.
COMMISSION TO THE FIVE CIVILIZED TRIBES.

Muskogee, Indian Territory, July 19, 1905.

Chief Clerk,
    Creek Enrollment Division.

Dear Sir:

Receipt is acknowledged of your letter of July 14, 1905 stating that application was made to the Commission to the Five Civilized Tribes for the enrollment of Bettie Alexander, born July 27, 1903, child of Robert L. Alexander, a citizen of the Creek Nation, and Martha Alexander, a citizen of the Seminole Nation, as a citizen by blood of the Creek Nation and requesting to be informed as to whether an application was ever made for the enrollment of said child as a citizen of the Seminole Nation.

In reply to your letter you are advised that it does not appear from an examination of the records of this office that any application was ever made to the Commission to the Five Civilized Tribes for the enrollment of said Bettie Alexander as a citizen of the Seminole Nation.

Respectfully,

Tams Bixby   Commissioner.

NC-503.

Muskogee, Indian Territory, August 5, 1905.

Martha Alexander,
    c/o Robert L. Alexander,
        Wetumka, Indian Territory.

Dear Madam:

In the matter of the application for the enrollment of your minor daughter Bettie Alexander as a citizen by blood of the Creek Nation you are advised that it will be necessary for you to furnish this office with the affidavit of the father of said child

Applications for Enrollment of Creek Newborn
Act of 1905 Volume VI

relative to her birth; for that purpose there is inclosed herewith a blank for proof of birth, which has been partially filled out.

You are requested to have the same sworn to before a notary public and when executed return the same of this office in the inclosed envelope.

Respectfully,

Commissioner.

CTD-30.
Env.

NC 503.

Muskogee, Indian Territory, November 12, 1906.

Chief Clerk,
    Seminole Enrollment Division,
        General Office.

Dear Sir:

You are hereby advised that the name of Bettie Alexander, born July 27, 1903, to Robert Alexander, a citizen by blood of the Creek Nation, and Martha Alexander, an alleged citizen of the Seminole Nation, is contained in a schedule of New Born citizens of the Creek Nation approved by the Secretary of the Interior September 27, 1905, opposite Roll No. 503.

Respectfully,

Commissioner.

BIRTH AFFIDAVIT.
DEPARTMENT OF THE INTERIOR.
COMMISSION TO THE FIVE CIVILIZED TRIBES.

IN RE APPLICATION FOR ENROLLMENT, as a citizen of the Creek Nation, of Jacob Alexander, born on the 26 day of April, 1902

Name of Father: John L. Alexander   a citizen of the   Creek   Nation.
    Hickory Ground Town
Name of Mother: Hettie Alexander   a citizen of the   Creek   Nation.
    Tuckahatche Town
                      Postoffice   Wetumka, I.T.

Applications for Enrollment of Creek Newborn
Act of 1905   Volume VI

AFFIDAVIT OF MOTHER.   Child present

UNITED STATES OF AMERICA, Indian Territory,
Western   DISTRICT.

I, Hettie Alexander, on oath state that I am about 29 years of age and a citizen by blood, of the Creek Nation; that I am the lawful wife of John L. Alexander, who is a citizen, by blood of the Creek Nation; that a male child was born to me on 26 day of April, 1902, that said child has been named Jacob Alexander, and was living March 4, 1905.

Hettie Alexander

Witnesses To Mark:

Subscribed and sworn to before me this 29 day of March, 1905.

Drennan C Skaggs
Notary Public.

AFFIDAVIT OF ATTENDING PHYSICIAN OR MID-WIFE.

UNITED STATES OF AMERICA, Indian Territory,
Western   DISTRICT.

I, Nancy Alexander, a mid-wife, on oath state that I attended on Mrs. Hettie Alexander, wife of John L. Alexander on the 26 day of April nearly 3 years ago.; that there was born to her on said date a male child; that said child was living March 4, 1905, and is said to have been named Jacob Alexander

her
Nancy x Alexander
mark

Witnesses To Mark:
  DC Skaggs
  Alex Posey

Subscribed and sworn to before me this 29 day of March, 1905.

Drennan C Skaggs
Notary Public.

Applications for Enrollment of Creek Newborn
Act of 1905 Volume VI

BIRTH AFFIDAVIT.

DEPARTMENT OF THE INTERIOR.
COMMISSION TO THE FIVE CIVILIZED TRIBES.

IN RE APPLICATION FOR ENROLLMENT, as a citizen of the Creek Nation, of Christie Alexander, born on the 16 day of August, 1904

Name of Father: John L. Alexander a citizen of the Creek Nation. Hickory Ground Town
Name of Mother: Hettie Alexander a citizen of the Creek Nation. Tuckahatche Town

Postoffice Wetumka, I.T.

AFFIDAVIT OF MOTHER.

UNITED STATES OF AMERICA, Indian Territory,
Western DISTRICT.

I, Hettie Alexander, on oath state that I am about 29 years of age and a citizen by blood, of the Creek Nation; that I am the lawful wife of John L. Alexander, who is a citizen, by blood of the Creek Nation; that a female child was born to me on 16 day of August, 1904, that said child has been named Christie Alexander, and was living March 4, 1905.

Hettie Alexander

Witnesses To Mark:
{

Subscribed and sworn to before me this 29 day of March, 1905.

Drennan C Skaggs
Notary Public.

AFFIDAVIT OF ATTENDING PHYSICIAN OR MID-WIFE.

UNITED STATES OF AMERICA, Indian Territory,
Western DISTRICT.

I, Nancy Alexander, a mid-wife, on oath state that I attended on Mrs. Hettie Alexander, wife of John L. Alexander on the 16 day of August last year; that there was born to her on said date a female child; that said child was living March 4, 1905, and is said to have been named Christie Alexander

her
Nancy x Alexander
mark

Applications for Enrollment of Creek Newborn
Act of 1905 Volume VI

Witnesses To Mark:
{ DC Skaggs
{ Alex Posey

Subscribed and sworn to before me this 29 day of March, 1905.

Drennan C Skaggs
Notary Public.

DEPARTMENT OF THE INTERIOR,
COMMISSION TO THE FIVE CIVILIZED TRIBES.
Holdenville, I. T., March 29, 1905.

In the matter of the application for the enrollment of London Coker as a citizen by blood of the Creek Nation.

HETTIE COKER, being duly sworn, testified as follows:
Through Alex Posey Official Interpreter:

BY COMMISSION:
Q What is your name? A Hettie Coker.
Q How old are you? A About thirty-five.
Q What is your post office address? A Mekasukey.
Q Are you a citizen of the Creek Nation? A No, sir, I am a Seminole.
Q Do you make application for the enrollment of your minor child, London Coker, as a citizen of the Creek Nation? A Yes, sir.
Q What is the name of the child's father? A Dave Coker.
Q Is he a citizen of the Creek Nation? A Yes, sir.
Q To what town does he belong? A Eufaula Canadian.
Q If it should be found that your child, London Coker, is entitled to enrollment in either the Creek or Seminole Nations[sic] in which nation do you desire to have him enrolled? A In the Creek Nation.

---oooOOOooo---

I, D. C. Skaggs, on oath state that the above and foregoing is a full and true transcript of my stenographic notes as taken in said cause on said date.

DC Skaggs

Subscribed and sworn to before me this 20th day of July, 1905.

Edw C Griesel
Notary Public.

Applications for Enrollment of Creek Newborn
Act of 1905   Volume VI

BIRTH AFFIDAVIT.

DEPARTMENT OF THE INTERIOR.
COMMISSION TO THE FIVE CIVILIZED TRIBES.

IN RE APPLICATION FOR ENROLLMENT, as a citizen of the Creek Nation, of London Coker, born on the 20 day of November, 1904

Name of Father: Dave Coker   a citizen of the   Creek   Nation.
Eufaula Canadian Town
Name of Mother: Hettie Coker   a citizen of the   Seminole   Nation.

Postoffice   Mekusukey, Ind Ter.

AFFIDAVIT OF MOTHER.

UNITED STATES OF AMERICA, Indian Territory,
Western   DISTRICT.   Child is present

I, Hettie Coker, on oath state that I am about 35 years of age and a citizen by blood, of the Seminole Nation; that I am the lawful wife of Dave Coker, who is a citizen, by blood of the Creek Nation; that a male child was born to me on 20 day of November, 1904, that said child has been named London Coker, and was living March 4, 1905.

                                                  her
                                    Hettie x Coker
Witnesses To Mark: mark
  { Alex Posey
    DC Skaggs

Subscribed and sworn to before me this 29 day of March, 1905.

                                       Drennan C Skaggs
                                       Notary Public.

AFFIDAVIT OF ATTENDING PHYSICIAN OR MID-WIFE.

UNITED STATES OF AMERICA, Indian Territory,
Western   DISTRICT.

                                                          my wife
I, Dave Coker, a *(blank)*, on oath state that I attended on ^ Mrs. Hettie Coker, wife of *(blank)* on the 20 day of November, 1904 ; that there was born to her on said date a male child; that said child was living March 4, 1905, and is said to have been named London Coker   his
                                       Dave x Coker
                                       mark

Applications for Enrollment of Creek Newborn
Act of 1905   Volume VI

Witnesses To Mark:
{ Alex Posey
{ DC Skaggs

Subscribed and sworn to before me this 29 day of March, 1905.

Drennan C Skaggs
Notary Public.

United States of America)
Western District)
Indian Territory)

Personally appeared before me Frank Jacobs a citizen of the Creek nation[sic], Indian Territory by birth, and state upon oath that he is personally acquainted with David Coker the father of the said London Coker who was born on the 20th day of November 1904, and the said London Coker died on the 6th day of April 1905, the mother of the said London Coke[sic] is named Hettie Coker, I have no interst[sic] in this claim and make this statement anly[sic] as a disinterested party.

Frank Jacobs

Subscribed and sworn to before me this the 18th day of August, 1905

Chas Rider
Notary Public.

My Commission expires July 11th, 1906

United States of America)
Western District)
Indian Territory)

Personally appeared before me Thomas West a citizen of the Creek nation[sic], Indian Territory by birth, and state upon oath that he is personally acquainted with David Coker the father of the said London Coker who was born on the 20th day of November 1904, and the said London Coker died on the 6th day of April 1905, the mother of the said London Coke[sic] is named Hettie Coker, I have no interst[sic] in this claim and make this statement anly[sic] as a disinterested party.

Thomas West

Applications for Enrollment of Creek Newborn
Act of 1905   Volume VI

Subscribed and sworn to before me this the 18th day of August, 1905

Chas Rider
Notary Public.

My Commission expires July 11th, 1906

NC. 505.

Muskogee, Indian Territory, July 14, 1905.

Commissioner to the Five Civilized Tribes,
    Seminole Enrollment Division,
        Muskogee, Indian Territory.

Gentlemen:

    March 31, 1905, application was made to the Commission to the Five Civilized Tribes for the enrollment of London Coker, born November 20, 1904, as a citizen by blood of the Creek. It is stated in said application that the father of said child is Dave Coker, an alleged citizen of the Creek Nation, and that the mother is Hattie[sic] Coker, a citizen of the Seminole Nation.

    You are requested to inform the Creek Enrollment Division as to whether application has been made for the enrollment of London Coker, as a citizen of the Seminole Nation, and if so, what disposition has been made of the same.

Respectfully,

Commissioner.

DEPARTMENT OF THE INTERIOR.
COMMISSION TO THE FIVE CIVILIZED TRIBES.

Muskogee, Indian Territory, July 19, 1905.

Chief Clerk,
    Creek Enrollment Division.

Dear Sir:

    Receipt is acknowledged of your letter of July 14, 1905 (NC-505) stating that application was made to the Commission to the Five Civilized Tribes for the enrollment of London Coker, born November 20, 1904, child of Dave Coker, an alleged citizen of the Creek Nation, and Hattie[sic] Coker, a citizen of the Seminole Nation, as a citizen by blood of the Creek Nation and requesting to be informed as to whether an application was ever made for the enrollment of said child as a citizen of the Seminole Nation.

Applications for Enrollment of Creek Newborn
Act of 1905 Volume VI

In reply to your letter you are informed that it does not appear from an examination of the records of this office that any application was made to the Commission to the Five Civilized Tribes for the enrollment of said London Coker as a citizen of the Seminole Nation.

Respectfully,

Tams Bixby   Commissioner.

REFER IN REPLY TO THE FOLLOWING:
NC-505.

**DEPARTMENT OF THE INTERIOR,
COMMISSIONER TO THE FIVE CIVILIZED TRIBES.**

Muskogee, Indian Territory, August 5, 1905.

David Coker,
    Mekusukey, Indian Territory.

Dear Sir:

    In the matter of the application for the enrollment of your child London Coker, born November 20, 1904, as a citizen by blood of the Creek Nation, You are advised that it will be necessary for you to furnish this office with the affidavits of two disinterested persons, relative to the birth of said child; said affidavits should set forth the name of said child, the date of his birth, the names of his parents and whether or not he was living on March 4, 1905.

Respectfully,

Tams Bixby
Commissioner.

Muskogee, Indian Territory, November 12, 1906.

Chief Clerk,
    Seminole Enrollment Division,
        General Office,

Dear Sir:

    You are hereby advised that the name of London Coker, born November 20, 1904, to Dave Coker, a citizen by blood of the Creek Nation, and Hettie Coker, an alleged citizen of the Seminole nation, is contained in a

Applications for Enrollment of Creek Newborn
Act of 1905   Volume VI

schedule of New Born citizens of the Creek Nation, approved by the Secretary of the Interior September 27, 1905, opposite Roll No. 506.

Respectfully,

Commissioner.

C506

DEPARTMENT OF THE INTERIOR,
COMMISSION TO THE FIVE CIVILIZED TRIBES.
Holdenville, I. T., March 29, 1905.

In the matter of the application for the enrollment of Jesse and Wylie Moses as citizens by blood of the Creek Nation.

MOSES BEAR, being duly sworn, testified as follows:

Through Alex Posey Official Interpreter:

BY COMMISSION:
Q What is your name? A Moses Bear.
Q How old are you? A About thirty-five.
Q What is your post office address? A Keokuk Falls, Oklahoma.
Q Are you a citizen of the Creek Nation? A No, sir, I am a Seminole.
Q Are you the father of Wylie and Jesse Moses? A Yes, sir.
Q Are they both living? A Wylie is living but Jesse is dead.
Q When did Jesse die? A March 18, 1905.
Q How old was he at the time of his death? A About two years old.
Q Did you make a record of his death? A No, sir.
Q When was he born? A I have a record.

Witness presents a piece of paper on which appears a record of the births of his children, Wylie and Jesse Moses, as follows:
"Jesse Moses was born in June 5th 1903."
"Wylie Moses was born in September 18, 1901."

Q Who made this record? A Willie Yamie.
Q When did Willie Yamie make the record? A The record was made yesterday, at my request.
Q Does Willie Yamie know when your children were born? A No, sir, but he made the record at my request and we figured out the dates together.
Q Are you positive that these dates, given in the record which you have presented, are correct? A Yes, sir.

Applications for Enrollment of Creek Newborn
Act of 1905   Volume VI

NANCY BEAR, being duly sworn, testified as follows:

THROUGH ALEX POSEY OFFICIAL INTERPRETER:

BY COMMISSION:
Q What is your name? A Nancy Bear.
Q How old are you? A About 35.
Q What is your post office address? A Keokuk Falls, O. T.
Q Are you a citizen of the Creek Nation? A Yes, sir.
Q To what town do you belong? A Thlewathle.
Q Do you make application for the enrollment of your minor children, Jesse and Wylie Moses, as citizens of the Creek Nation? A Yes, sir.
Q Do you know when Jesse died? A The child has not been dead quite two weeks.
Q Did he die in this month? A Yes, sir.
Q On what day did he die? A On Saturday.
Q How old was the child at the time he died? A He was about two yes[sic] years old but was not able to walk on account of cronic[sic] illness.
Q What is the name of the father of these children? A Moses Bear.
Q Is he a citizen of the Creek Nation? He is a Seminole.
Q Is he your lawful husband? A Yes, sir.
Q Have you any other children besides Jesse and Wylie? A Yes, sir, Jennie, Hannah and Maude. Jennie and Maude are dead.
Q When did Jennie die? A She has been dead a long time. I do not know when she died.
Q How old was she at the time of her death? A She would be over nine were she living.
Q How old is Hannah?

Witness presents a piece of paper on which appears the following:
"Hannah Moses born in March 2, 1894."
"Maud Moses was born in February 1st, 1898."

Q Have you made selection of land for Hannah? A No, sir.
Q Do you know whether or not she has been arbitrarily filed by the Commission? A I have tries to find out but I have been unable to do so.
Q If it should be found that your children, Wylie and Jesse Moses, are entitled to be enrolled in either the Creek or Seminole Nations in which nation do you desire to have them enrolled? A In the Creek Nation.

---oooOOOooo---

I, D. C. Skaggs, on oath state that the above and foregoing is a full and true transcript of my stenographic notes as taken in said cause on said date.

DC Skaggs

Applications for Enrollment of Creek Newborn
Act of 1905 Volume VI

Subscribed and sworn to before me this 20" day of July, 1905.

Edw C Griesel
Notary Public.

N.C.-506.

OCH
JCL

DEPARTMENT OF THE INTERIOR,
COMMISSIONER TO THE FIVE CIVILIZED TRIBES.

In the matter of the application for the enrollment of Wylie Bearhead, and Jesse Bearhead, deceased, as citizens by blood of the Creek Nation.

DECISION.

The record in this office shows that on March 29, 1905, application was made, in affidavit form, for the enrollment of Wylie Moses, and Jesse Moses, deceased, as citizens by blood of the Creek Nation, under the provisions of the Act of Congress approved March 3, 1905 (33 Stats., 1048), and testimony was offered in support thereof on said date. Affidavits duly executed by the parents of said children, electing to have them enrolled as citizens of the Creek Nation were filed January 9, 1907.

It appears from the records of this office that the parents of these children are known under several names including Moses (or Moser), Bear (or Bearhead) and Nancy Bear (or Bearhead). Said parents have two children other than the applicants who have been scheduled for enrollment in the Creek Nation, under the Act of March 3, 1905, under the surname of Bearhead, and for the sake of uniformity reference will hereafter be made to the applicants under the names, Wylie Bearhead and Jesse Bearhead.

The evidence and the records in possession of this office show that said Wylie Bearhead, and Jesse Bearhead, deceased, are the children of Nancy Bearhead, whose name appears as Nancy King upon a schedule of citizens by blood of the Creek Nation approved by the Secretary of the Interior, March 13, 1902, opposite number 499, and Moses Bearhead, a citizen of the Seminole Nation.

The evidence further shows that said Wylie Bearhead was born September 18, 1902, and was living March 4, 1905 March 4, 1905. That sad Jesse Bearhead was born June 5, 1903 and died March 18, 1905.

The evidence further shows that no application has ever been made for the enrollment of said Wylie Bearhead, and said Jesse Bearhead, deceased, as citizens of the Seminole Nation, and that the parents of said children elected to have the, enrolled as citizens of the Creek Nation.

It is, therefore, ordered and adjudged that said Rena Johnson is entitled to be enrolled as a citizen by blood of the Creek Nation under the provisions of the Act of Congress approved March 3, 1905 (33 Stat. L., 1048), and the application for their enrollment as such is accordingly granted.

Tams Bixby Commissioner.

Muskogee, Indian Territory.
FEB 18 1907

Applications for Enrollment of Creek Newborn
Act of 1905   Volume VI

Indian Territory, I
I SS:
Western District.I

We, the undersigned, do hereby elect to have our child, Wylie Moses, born on the 18 day of Sept , 1901, enrolled as a citizen of the Creek Nation, and to have said child receive his allotment of land and distribution of moneys in said nation.

	his
	Moses x Bear
Witnesses to mark:	mark
Jesse McDermott	his
G.W. *(Illegible)*	Nancy x Bear
Jesse McDermott	mark
G.W. *(Illegible)*	

Subscribed and sworn to before me this 9 day of Jan, 1907

My Commission   J McDermott
Expires Jan 25" 1907   Notary Public.

Indian Territory, I
I SS:
Western District,I

We, the undersigned, do hereby elect to have our child, Jesse Moses, born on the 5th day of June , 1903, enrolled as a citizen of the Creek Nation, and to have said child receive his allotment of land and distribution of moneys in said nation.

	his
	Moses x Bear
Witnesses to mark:	mark
Jesse McDermott	his
G.W. *(Illegible)*	Nancy x Bear
Jesse McDermott	mark
G.W. *(Illegible)*	

Subscribed and sworn to before me this 9 day of Jan, 1907

My Commission   J McDermott
Expires Jan 25" 1907   Notary Public.

Applications for Enrollment of Creek Newborn
Act of 1905 Volume VI

BIRTH AFFIDAVIT.

Supplemental testimony taken

DEPARTMENT OF THE INTERIOR.
COMMISSION TO THE FIVE CIVILIZED TRIBES.

IN RE APPLICATION FOR ENROLLMENT, as a citizen of the Creek Nation, of Wylie Moses, born on the 18 day of September, 1901

Name of Father: Moses Bear   a citizen of the Seminole   Nation.
Name of Mother: Nancy Bear (or Moses)   a citizen of the Creek   Nation.
Thlewathle[sic] Town
                            Postoffice   Keokuk Falls, Okla.

AFFIDAVIT OF MOTHER.

UNITED STATES OF AMERICA, Indian Territory, }   Child is present
         Western   DISTRICT.

I, Nancy Bear, on oath state that I am about 35 years of age and a citizen by blood, of the Creek Nation; that I am the lawful wife of Moses Bear, who is a citizen, by blood of the Seminole Nation; that a male child was born to me on 18 day of September, 1901, that said child has been named Wylie Moses, and was living March 4, 1905.

                                  her
                         Nancy x Bear
Witnesses To Mark: mark
 { Alex Posey
 { DC Skaggs

Subscribed and sworn to before me this 29 day of March, 1905.

                         Drennan C Skaggs
                              Notary Public.

AFFIDAVIT OF ATTENDING PHYSICIAN OR MID-WIFE.

UNITED STATES OF AMERICA, Indian Territory, }
         Western   DISTRICT.

                                               my wife
I, Moses Bear, a *(blank)*, on oath state that I attended on ^ Mrs. Nancy Bear, wife of *(blank)* on the 18 day of September, 1901; that there was born to her on said date a male child; that said child was living March 4, 1905, and is said to have been named Wylie Moses
                                   his
                          Moses x Bear
                              mark

Applications for Enrollment of Creek Newborn
Act of 1905 Volume VI

Witnesses To Mark:
- Alex Posey
- DC Skaggs

Subscribed and sworn to before me this 29 day of March, 1905.

        Drennan C Skaggs
        Notary Public.

(The above Birth Affidavit given again)

BIRTH AFFIDAVIT.

Supplemental testimony taken

DEPARTMENT OF THE INTERIOR.
COMMISSION TO THE FIVE CIVILIZED TRIBES.

IN RE APPLICATION FOR ENROLLMENT, as a citizen of the Creek Nation, of Jesse Moses, born on the 5" day of June, 1903

Name of Father: Moses Bear   a citizen of the Seminole Nation.
Name of Mother. Nancy Bear (or Moses)   a citizen of the Creek Nation.
Thlewathle[sic] Town
      Postoffice   Keokuk Falls, Okla.

AFFIDAVIT OF MOTHER.

UNITED STATES OF AMERICA, Indian Territory, }   Child is present
  Western   DISTRICT.

I, Nancy Bear, on oath state that I am about 35 years of age and a citizen by blood, of the Creek Nation; that I am the lawful wife of Moses Bear, who is a citizen, by blood of the Seminole Nation; that a male child was born to me on 5" day of June, 1903, that said child has been named Jesse Moses, and is now was living March 4, 1905.

        her
      Nancy x Bear
        mark

Witnesses To Mark:
- Alex Posey
- DC Skaggs

Subscribed and sworn to before me this 29" day of March, 1905.

        Drennan C Skaggs
        Notary Public.

Applications for Enrollment of Creek Newborn
Act of 1905 Volume VI

AFFIDAVIT OF ATTENDING PHYSICIAN OR MID-WIFE.

UNITED STATES OF AMERICA, Indian Territory,
Western DISTRICT.

I, Moses Bear, a ~~(blank)~~, on oath state that I attended on ^ Mrs. *(blank)*, ~~wife of~~ *(blank)* on the 5 day of June, 1903; that there was born to her on said date a male child; that said child ~~is now~~ was living March 4, 1905 and is said to have been named Jesse Moses

                              his
                            Moses x Bear

Witnesses To Mark: mark
{ Alex Posey
{ DC Skaggs

Subscribed and sworn to before me this 29" day of March, 1905.

                            Drennan C Skaggs
                            Notary Public.

(The above Birth Affidavit given again.)

DEPARTMENT OF THE INTERIOR.
COMMISSION TO THE FIVE CIVILIZED TRIBES.

In the matter of the death of Jesse Moses a citizen of the Creek Nation, who formerly resided at or near Keokuk Falls, Okla, ~~Ind. Ter.~~, and died on the 18 day of March, 1905

AFFIDAVIT OF RELATIVE.

UNITED STATES OF AMERICA, Indian Territory,
Western DISTRICT.

I, Moses Bear, on oath state that I am about 35 years of age and a citizen by blood, of the Creek Nation; that my postoffice address is Keokuk Falls, Okla, ~~Ind. Ter.~~; that I am father of Jesse Moses who was a citizen, by blood, of the Creek Nation and that said Jesse Moses died on the 18 day of March, 1905

                            his
                          Moses x Bear

Witnesses To Mark: mark
{ Alex Posey
{ D.C. Skaggs

Applications for Enrollment of Creek Newborn
Act of 1905 Volume VI

Subscribed and sworn to before me this 2" day of March, 1905.

Drennan C Skaggs
Notary Public.

(Jesse Moses' Birth Affidavit given again.)

(Jesse Moses' Death Affidavit given again.)

NC 506.

Muskogee, Indian Territory, July 14, 1905.

Commissioner to the Five Civilized Tribes,
    Seminole Enrollment Division,
        Muskogee, Indian Territory.

Gentlemen:

    March 31, 1905, application was made to the Commission to the Five Civilized Tribes for the enrollment of Jesse Moses, born June 5, 1903, and Wylie Moses, born September 18, 1901, as citizens by blood of the Creek Nation. It is stated in said application that the father of said child is Mose[sic] Bear, a citizen of the Seminole Nation, and that the mother is Nancy Bear, an alleged citizen of the Creek Nation.

    You are requested to inform the Creek Enrollment Division as to whether application has been made for the enrollment of said children as citizens of the Seminole Nation, and if so, what disposition has been made of the same.

Respectfully,

Commissioner.

Applications for Enrollment of Creek Newborn
Act of 1905   Volume VI

HGH

DEPARTMENT OF THE INTERIOR.
COMMISSION TO THE FIVE CIVILIZED TRIBES.

NC. 506.

Muskogee, Indian Territory, July 17, 1905.

Nancy Bear (or Moses),
   c/o Moses Bear,
      Keokuk Falls, Oklahoma Territory.

Dear Madam:

    In the matter of the application for the enrollment of your minor children, Jesse and Wylie Moses, as citizens of the Creek Nation, you are advised that this office requires further information in order to identify you on its rolls of citizens of said Nation.

    You are requested to inform this office as to your maiden name, the names of your parents, the Creek Indian Town to which you belong, and, if possible, the numbers which appear on your deeds to land in the Creek Nation, and any other information that will help to identify you as a citizen of the Creek Nation.

                  Respectfully,

                  Tams Bixby

                          Commissioner.

DEPARTMENT OF THE INTERIOR.
COMMISSION TO THE FIVE CIVILIZED TRIBES.

Muskogee, Indian Territory, July 19, 1905.

Chief Clerk
   Creek Enrollment Division.

Dear Sir:

    Receipt is acknowledged of your letter of July 14, 1905 (NC-505) stating that application was made to the Commission to the Five Civilized Tribes for the enrollment of Jesse Moses, born June 5, 1903, and Wylie Moses, born September 18, 1901, children of Mose Bear, a citizen of the Seminole Nation, and Nancy Bear, an alleged citizen of the Creek Nation, as citizens by blood of the Creek Nation and requesting to be informed as to whether application was ever made for the enrollment of said children as citizens of the Seminole Nation.

    In reply to your letter you are advised that it does not appear from an examination of the records of this office that any application was made for the enrollment of Jesse Moses and Wylie Moses as citizens of the Seminole Nation.

Applications for Enrollment of Creek Newborn
Act of 1905 Volume VI

Respectfully,

Tams Bixby Commissioner.

HGH

REFER IN REPLY TO THE FOLLOWING:

N.C. 506.

DEPARTMENT OF THE INTERIOR,
COMMISSIONER TO THE FIVE CIVILIZED TRIBES.

Muskogee, Indian Territory, August 12, 1905.

Nancy Bear (or Moses),
    Care Moses Bear,
        Keokuk Falls, Oklahoma.

Dear Madam:

In the matter of the application for the enrollment of your minor children, Jesse and Wylie Moses, as citizens of the Creek Nation, you are advised that this office requires further information in order to identify you on its rolls of citizens of said Nation.

You are requested to inform this office as to your maiden name, the names of your parents, the Creek Indian Town to which you belong, and, if possible, the numbers which appear on your deeds to land in the Creek Nation, and any other information that will help to identify you as a citizen of the Creek Nation.

Respectfully,

Wm O. Beall
Commissioner.

HGH

REFER IN REPLY TO THE FOLLOWING:

NC 506

DEPARTMENT OF THE INTERIOR,
COMMISSIONER TO THE FIVE CIVILIZED TRIBES.

Muskogee, Indian Territory, January 11, 1907.

Nancy Bear or Moses,
    Care of Moses Bear,
        Keokuk Falls, Oklahoma Territory.

Dear Madam:

You are requested to furnish this office with information that will assist us in identifying you as a citizen by blood of the Creek Nation, within five days from date

Applications for Enrollment of Creek Newborn
Act of 1905   Volume VI

hereof; such as your maiden name, the name of your parents and of other members of your family and your roll number as same appears on your deeds or certificates to land in the Creek Nation.

This matter should receive your immediate attention as the right to enrollment of your minor children Jessie and Wiley Moses, as citizens of the Creek Nation can not be adjudicated until you are identified as a citizen of said Nation.

Respectfully,

Tams Bixby   Commissioner.

JWH

N C 506

Muskogee, Indian Territory, March 9, 1907.

Nancy Bearhead,
    c/o Moses Bearhead,
        Keokuk Falls, Oklahoma.

Dear Madam :--

You are hereby advised that on March 2, 1907, the Secretary of the Interior approved the enrollment of your minor children, Jesse Bearhead, deceased, and Wylie Bearhead, as citizens by blood of the Creek Nation, and that the names of said children appear upon the roll of new born citizens by blood of the Creek Nation, enrolled under the Act of Congress approved March 3, 1905, as numbers 1269 and 1270, respectively.

These children are now entitled to allotment and application therefor should be made without delay for Jesse Bearhead, by the duly appointed administrator, and for Wylie Bearhead, by yourself of the father of said child, at the Creek Land Office, Muskogee, Indian Territory.

Respectfully,

Commissioner.

It appears from the record of this office that the parents of this child are known under several names including Moses (or Moser), Bear (or Bearhead), Nancy Bear (or Bearhead). Said parents ~~already~~ have two children other than the applicants who have been scheduled for enrollment in the Creek Nation under the Act of March 3, 1905 ~~and it~~ under the surname of Bearhead, and for the sake of uniformity reference will hereafter be made to the applicants under the names Wylie Bearhead and Jesse Bearhead.

Applications for Enrollment of Creek Newborn
Act of 1905   Volume VI

N.C. 506.

2/14/07

Seminole Div.

      Has appl. ever been made for the enroll. of

         Wylie Moses   or Bearhead
or   Jesse   " , dec'd or "
as Seminoles?

      Fa: Moses Bear, Seminole
      Mo: Nancy Bear (or King) Cr.

                       OCH

not identified as applicant for enrollment in Seminole Nation under surname of Moses, Bear, or King or Bearhead

                       AB.

2/14/07

Index

AH.COM.KO.NEY 268
AH-CON-KO-NEY 267
AHFONOKE
   Sayochee 153,154,155
   Simmer 144,146,149
AHFORNOKE
   Sayochee 157
AH-OO-CON-NEY 266
ALEXANDER
   Bettie 303,304,305,306,307
   Christie 309
   G A 245,246,247
   Hettie 307,308,309
   Jacob 307,308
   John L 307,308,309
   Martha 303,304,305,306,307
   Nancy 23,305,308,309
   Nancy (Larney) 22
   Nancy Larney 23,24
   Rev G A 29
   Robert 307
   Robert L 303,304,305,306
   Willie 22,23
ANDERSON
   Phoebe 185
AR-GON-GA-NE 270
ATKINS
   Alice 295,296
   Mildred 295,296
   Robert D 295,296
AURD
   F S 198
AUSTIN
   Mary 108,110,112,138,139,141,
   142,150

BAKER
   Lucy 177,178
   W R 132
BARD
   Daniel N 15,178
BARNETT
   Betset 67

Betsey 235
Cookie 149,150,151
Daniel 149,150,151
James 151
Jencey 291
Jesse 149,150
Leola 290,291
Lucy 290,291
Mary 291
Scipio 290,291,292
BARRY
   W N 138,140,141
BEALL
   Wm O 35,114,243,324
BEAR 325,326
   Hilly 249,250
   Mose 322,323
   Moses .. 315,316,318,319,320,321,
   323,324,326
   Nancy .. 316,317,318,319,320,322,
   323,324,325,326
BEARHEAD 325,326
   Jesse 317,325,326
   Moses 317,325
   Nancy 317,325
   Wylie 317,325,326
BEAVER
   B J 3
   Ida 3
   Mary Capitola 49,50
   Ollie 50
   Sam 49
   Samuel 50
   Tiller 3
BEAVERS
   B J 3,4
BENSON
   Edward 198,199
   Katie 199,200
   William 199,200
BIG WILLIAM 73
BIGPOND
   Billy 296

Index

James 296,298,299,300,301
Joe.................299,300,301
John 297
Kizzie 296
Louis..........296,297,298,299,300, 301,302
Sarah 296
Sela 296
Selah..........298,299,300,301,302
Tom 299
BIRD
   Louisa 68,236,238
BIXBY
   Tams...34,46,71,100,120,143,149, 163,191,245,251,266,277,302,306, 314,317,323,324,325
BLEDSOE
   Mary 248
BONNER
   H R 177,196
BOWMAN
   Dollie 25
   H W ,,,,..................... 176
BOYD
   A Lee 6
BRADLEY
   B E 50
   Mrs B E 50
BROWN
   Joe........................ 67,235
   Julia 280,281
   Sally......................... 89
   Thomas 281
   Thomas J 280
   Thomas Jefferson 280,281
BRUNER
   Bunnie 258,259,260
   Freeland 65
   Iva M 65
   John 102,104,258,259,260,261, 262
   Joseph 1,50,51,249,250
   Minnie 259

   Rhoda 65,96,99
   Robison 259,260
   Sallie.................258,259,260,262
   Sally..................89,90,91,260,261
   Thomas 258,261,262
BUCKNER
   Jack......................... 73
   Susie 73
   Wiley 73
BUDLONG
   R B 272,275
BUFORD
   Charles...................13,15,178
BULLET
   Chitto Harjo...............27,30,31,33
   Hannah 73
   Jacob......................73,83
   John 27,28,30,31,33
   Maxey 73
   Zoie 28,29
   Zoye....................27,30,31,33
BULLETT
   Bailey 26
   Chitto Harjo.......25,26,27,32,34,35
   Jemima 26
   John 25,26,32,34,35
   Zoye....................26,32,34,35
BULLETTE
   Chitto Harjo................. 26
   John 26
BURGESS
   Edmund 3
   Ida........................... 3
BURNS
   Rev Wm 293
BURT
   R L......................... 38
BYERS
   M J.........................174
BYONS
   A G........................229
BYRD
   Louisa......................240

Index

CAIN
  Ruth 38
  W A 38
CALMES
  W M 134,135,136
CANTRELL
  Jim 91,92
CARDWELL
  Dr S H 234
  S H 232
  S H, MD 232,234
CARPENTER
  O H 233
CARR
  Bettie 200
CAVES
  T T 240
CHARLES
  N E 4
CHEATHAM
  W L 266
  William L 300,301
  Wm L 266
CHILDERS
  Eliza 4
  Emmet 3,4
  Garfield 3,4
  Hattie 3
  Ida 2,3,4
  James 3
CHISHOLM
  Anderson 21
  Christie Richard 38
  Ida 42,43
  Lizzie 39,40
  Mary 41,42,43
  Minnie 21
  Rosa 21
CHITAGGO 29
CHITWOOD
  B B 201
CHUPCO
  Echoilla 286

Echoille 284
  Tingka 285
  Tinka 285
  Tomgla 286
CHUPSO
  Tingka 284
CINDA 211,212
CLARK
  G F 42,43,44
CLAWSON
  W R 282,283
CLAY
  E A 211
  Mrs E A 211
CLINTON
  Fred S, MD 296
CLOUD
  Acie 269
  Ahsey 268,269,270
  Ah-sey 266
  Hattie 266,267,268,269,270
  Stephen 266,268,269,270
  Steven 267
COKE
  London 312
COKER
  Dave 310,311,313
  David 312,314
  Hattie 313
  Hettie 310,311,312,314
  London 310,311,312,313,314
COLLINS
  Wash 178
COM-PE-THE-LE-NAY 296
CONPETHLONEY 302
COOPER
  Albert 202
  Nancy 201,202
  Nellie 201,202
  Sam 201,202
CO-PAH-TANNEY 266
COSAR
  Lizzie 249

329

COSER
  Lena 249
  Lizzie 249
  Nuttetsa 249
COTCHOCHE 68,236
COTETAN 302
COX
  J P 17,18,21
  J P, MD 17,18,21
CRAVENS
  J O 161,164
CROW
  Annie 101,102,103
CROWELL
  B H 234
  Ben F 231
  Benj F 231,232,233
  Benjamen F 234
  Benjamin F 230
  Neta 230
  Neta E 231,232,233,234
  Oti Buel 231
  Otis 230
  Otis Buel 229,230,232,233,234
  Robert Gosset 229,230
CROWELS
  Annie 102
  Jonah 102
  Katie 102
  Turner 102
CUNNINGHAM
  C N 11,12
  Laura 11,12
  William Leo 11,12
  Wm Leo 11

DANIELSON
  R S 208,209,219
DARLING
  A M 173
DAT-CHA 266
DAVIDSON
  Charles A 5,292
  Chas A 6,123,124,292
  D A 246
DEER
  Amanda 37
  Joe 36,37
  Lemsey 216,250,251
  Minnie 250,251
  Nancy 250,251
  Sealy 36
  Yarner 36,37
DEO
  Amos 74,76,77,84
  Ceboley 78
  Ceboly 74,75,76,78,81,82,83
  Nahsa 74,81,82,83
  Nancy 73,74,75,76,77,78,79,80, 81,82,84
  Nandy 83
  Nasha 78,79,82
  Susie 74,80,81,84
  Thomas .. 73,74,75,76,77,78,79,80, 81,83,84
DITZLER
  Fannie Ann 293,294
  Melvina 293,294
  Sally M 294
  Will 293,294
DOBBS
  M A 174
DONOVAN
  Irwin 12,14,160,166
DUNN
  Tupper 9,213,216,222,223, 225,250,251
DUNSON
  Kizzie 85,86,87,88
DUNZY
  J R 283,284

ELA
  Echo 283
EMARTHLA
  Mic 240

Index

EMERTHLA
  Sandy 83
  Sarty 83
ENGLISH
  A Z 132,175
ESKRIDGE
  C C 127,128,129,130,145,146,
  148,156,157,199,200
EUBANKS
  Minnie 37,38
  William 37,38
  William Albert 37,38
EVANS
  Alva Arizona 58
  Charley 58
  Charlie 58
  Mary J E 58
  Minnie 37
EWESS
  Albert 98

FIELD
  D W 66
  Dick 136
  Foster 136,137,139,141,142
  Henry 137,141,142
  Ida
    106,107,108,109,110,111,112,113,
    114
  Louina .. 107,108,109,110,111,112,
    113,114
  Lula 136,137,139,142
  Mary 137,139,141,142,151
  William 107,108,109,110,111,
    112,113,114
FIELDS
  D W 66,67,235,238
FISH
  Dora 132
  Posey 83
  Rena 271
  Rose 91
FISHER

Aggie 179,180,182
Bettie 83
Hettie 83
Lussee 73
Nancy 3
Willie 73
FIXECO
  Okchun 103
FIXICO
  Dela 9
  Okchun 101
  Robert 8,9
  Salley 8,9
  Tul mo chus 8,9
FLANNIGAN
  Sam E 246
FLOWERS
  Ella 185,188
FLYNN
  T W 65,66,96,97,99,299
FOLEY
  Melinda 73
  Tayloe 73
FORD
  ? M 292
FOSHEE
  Henry C 288,289,290
  Lillian 288,289
  William 289
  William R 288,289
  Wm R 289
FOSTER
  Chotka 136,137,138,141,143
  Chotkey 107
  Cotka 140
  G C 210,211
  Henry 136,140,141,143
  Janie 153,154,155,157
  Lola 107,108
  Lonie 209,210,211
  Lowiney 153,154,155,156,157
  Lula 136,137,138,143
  Lula B 209,210,211

Index

Mary 137,138,140,141,143
FOWLER
   J W 169
FOX
   Elgie 174
   John 174
   Lenie 174
FREEMAN 102
   John W 240,242,243
   Lena 240

GAINES
   Linn D 161,164
GAINS
   Hiawatha 118
GARRIGUES
   Anna 13,48,190
GEMIMA 29
GEORGE
   Nellie 73
   Timonthluppy 73
GIBSON
   Dicey 190
   Wilson 75,80
GIERKE
   Wm F A 104,133
GILLARD
   E C 159
GIPSON
   Dicey 195
GLESHER
   M B 28
GOOCH
   Adella 158,159,160,161,162,
   163,164,165
   Claudie 158,160,161
   Claudy 159,160
   Ed 158,159,160,161,162,163,
   164,165
   James A 162,163
   Maudie 158,163,164
   Maudy 164,165
GOODEN

Carrie 95,96
Dora 95,96,97,98,100,101
Henderson 95,96,97,98
Hendrson 65
Sam 96,98,99,100,101
GOSLER
   John 232
   Rose S 232
GOWN
   Bud 119
   Sarah 118,119
GRAY
   Annie 257
   Louisa 257
   Roley 257
GRAYSON
   Dora 131,133
   Joe 131,132,133
   Mary 184
   Nannie 134,136
   Panzie May 131,132
GREEN
   Bettie 73
   Cumsey 74,76,78,79,81
   Jacob 73
   W W 130
GREY
   J E 110
GRIESEL
   E C 12,48,49,159,162,165,181,
   183,271
   Edw C 2,8,12,25,49,74,75,159,
   165,182,184,188,230,233,252,253,
   256,268,269,271,298,303,310,317
GRISSOM
   Dr J W 282
   J W 282
GROSS
   Annie 121,122,125
   Myrtle 123
GUY
   J E 146,147,155,216

Index

HAINS
- H G 14,25,27,32,137
- Henry G 13,194

HAIRN
- H B 32

HALL
- Alta 93,94
- Hannah E 93,94
- J F 196
- Louisa 94
- Samuel 93,94

HALLFORD
- Emaline 282
- Lynn 282
- M A 282
- Nathan 282

HAMILTON
- S H 287,289
- S H, MD 287,290

HARDING
- Clara 245,246

HARJO
- John 221
- Maggie 222,223,224,225,226
- Milochee 251
- Thomas 172

HARLAN
- J228
- John 123,131,246

HARPER
- Peggie 118,119

HARRAL
- C H 44
- A M 44

HARRIS
- Lulu May 120,121,122
- Luly May 121
- Murtle 124
- Myrtle 120,121,122,125,126
- Theodore Quincy 120,124,125,126
- Walter 120,121,122,123,124, 125,126

HARRISON
- R P 123,131,132,175,229, 245,246
- Robert P 175,228

HARRY
- Edmond 269

HARSLMAN
- D 21,22,23,24

HARVISON
- Geo A 93,94

HAWKINS
- Connie 73
- Nellie 83
- Pink 83
- Sebella 73

HAYMES
- Frank L 21,22,23,24

HAYNES
- James 56,57
- Jim 73
- Joe 73
- Martha 56,57
- Roley 56,57

HAYS
- Thomas 168

HERBERGER
- Joseph 145,148,156

HETHAHCONENEY 302

HICKS
- Janie 152,154,156,157
- Lowiney 157
- Lowiny 152,153
- Sawyer 152,153,156,157
- Seamen 145,147,148
- Siah 153,154
- Simmer 144
- Usey 145,147,148
- Wallace 145,146,147,148
- Yusie 144

HILL
- Earnest 29
- John 73
- Millie 73
- Upna 212

333

Index

HOLDER
 W W 17,18,19,20,21
HOLT
 Z I J 22,23,24
HOOKS
 Alice 197,198
 Lem P 197,198
 Richard Roy 197,198
HOPE
 Melinda 57
 Willie 57
HOWELL
 Annie 203,204

IRELAND
 Henry 264
 Millie 264
 Susie 264
ISAAC
 Ella 48
ISLAND
 Callie 178,179,180,181,182, 183,184
 George 178,179,180,181,182, 183,184
 Louisa 179,180,181,182
 Louvinna 182,183
 Luvena 183,184

JACOB
 Nellie 70
JACOBS
 Frank 312
JANWAY
 Preston 264,265
JEFFERSON
 Robert 291
JOBE
 G W 177
 G W, MD 177
JOE 297
JOHN
 Jim 270

JOHNSON
 Arlie 67,235,236
 Ellie 67,236
 Emily 255
 J C 278,279,280,281
 Little Tom 67,236
 Little Tommy 67,235,236
 Rena 317
KANARD
 Mary Jane 219
KAY
 Bessie 65,96,99
 Sina 65,96,97
KENNEDY
 J A 199
 J A, MD 199
KEPLEY
 James K 133
KEY
 Palissa 127
KILLINGSWORTH
 M Y 174,175
KIMERY
 W B 233
KING 326
 Luila 167
 Millie 167
 Mollie ... 166,167,168,169,171,172
 Mullie 169,170,171
 Nancy 317,326
 Peter 166,167,168,169,170,171,172
 Sallie 167,168,169,170,172
 Sullie 166,168,169
KNIGHT
 Ramsey 127

LAIRD
 Agnes J 227
LANE
 Hiram 254
LARNEY
 Almarine 22,23

Index

Bettie 73
Dave 22,23
Jacob 73
Nancy 22,23
LASLEY
  Lizzie 73
  Sam 73
  Wisey 73
LEONARD
  B V 11
LETT
  Dr William L 38
  Wm L 173
  Wm L, MD 38,173
LEWIS
  Delila 47,48,49
  Ella 47,48,49
  Jack 47,48,49
  Jimmy 177,178
  Thomas 177,178
LILLARD
  Thomas J 270
LINDSEY
  Cilla 73
  Freeland 73
  Phillip 73
LITTLEHEAD
  Nancy 201
LMB 2
LOLER
  Kizzie 22,23,24
LONG
  Jas A 245,247
  Wallace 143,144,147,149
  Wallace (Hicks) 143
  Yusie 143,144,146,147,149
LONGFELLOW
  L L 65,96,97,99
LOWE
  Sam 68,236
  Samuel 68,236
LUCAS
  John 27

  Martha 33
  S L 29
  Zoye 26
LUCUS
  Martha 31
LUCY 296
LYNCH
  Robert E 10,198
MCBETH
  John R 278,279
MCCLUSKEY
  W S 295,296
MCDERMOTT
  Charlie 85,86,87,88
  J 14,33,40,48,49,57,91,92,104,
    106,110,111,116,146,147,155,156,
    168,172,178,181,183,190,192,193,
    212,215,216,241,318
  Jesse 28,48,57,101,103,104,107,
    108,109,110,111,143,144,146,147,
    153,154,155,159,162,165,181,182,
    183,184,211,212,213,214,216,237,
    238,252,253,256,268,269,318
  Kizzie 85,88
  L H 85,86,87,88
  Lizzie 86,87
  Mary 85,86,87,88
MCFARLAND
  Sarah 205,206
MCINTOSH
  F A 15
  Mr 263
  Roley 264
  W J 300
MCKIM
  Minnie G 1,2
  Robert 1
  Robert A 1,2
  Willie Byno 1,2
MCNAC
  Annie 16
  Fred 16

Index

Lizzie 16
MALOT
  H G 9
MEAD
  L W 58,59
MEADOWS
  A 235
MELEHCHA 103
MELLOCHE 103,104
MERRICK
  Ed 160,166
  Edward 68,69,102,160,166, 237,283
  Lona..........25,27,32,66,69,74,101, 102,136,137,237
MICCO
  Katie 220,224,225
  Mary 136,137,140
MILLER
  J Y 40,116,212,230,298
  M J 53,54
  Minnie 175
MILLIE 283
MILLOCHE 101,102
MILLS
  B H 221,222,223,224,226,304
MITCHELL
  Lucinda 68,236
MONTARLEY 136
MOONEY
  Garland S 234
MOORE
  Ben 241
  Malissa C 58
  Wesley 299
MORTON
  J C 287
  Joseph C 287,288,289,290
  M M 112,139,140,142,150, 151,152
  Mattie 287
  Ohland 287
MOSER 317,325

MOSES 325,326
  Hannah 316
  Jennie 316
  Jesse 315,316,317,318,320,321, 322,323,324,326
  Jessie 325
  Maude 316
  Nancy 319,320,323,324
  Wiley 325
  Wylie ...315,316,317,318,319,322, 323,324,326
MOSS
  F L 7
MULLIE 283,284,285,286
  Sallie 286
MURRAY
  J L 273,274
MYERS
  J B 106,286
  James B 285,286
NASH
  Mary 133
NASLEY
  Mary 282
NAYLOR
  G R 229
NEEL
  S M 231
NELL
  J Z, MD 124
NELSON
  V S 228
NEWELL
  J O, MD 124
  J Q 126
  J Q, MD 126
NEWTON
  Eugene 134,135,136
  Ewell Durant 134
  Guy Jackson 135,136
  Sarah Elizabeth 134,135,136

Index

OKCHUN 102
OSAHWA 102
  Annie 103
OSBORN
  C M 169
OVEESTREET
  John W 115
OVERSTREET
  John W 116,117,118

P
  Alex 82
PARHOSE 136
PARRISH
  Zera E 271
  Zera Ellen 188
PATTERSON
  John B 44,45,291
PEACOCK
  J L 175
PEARSON
  J W 227,228
PELAH 302
PHILLIPS
  Jno H 112,151,152
  John 109
  John H 36,37,87,88,94,107,112,
  138,139,140,141,142,150,151,211
  M H 196
PIGEON
  Jennie 73
  Jim 73
  Nache 83
PLUMBLEE
  R S 198
  R S, MD 198
PORTER
  Chief 266
  James E 36
POSEY 27
  Alex 31,41,53,54,55,56,57,61,
  62,63,66,67,68,69,70,72,75,76,77,
  78,79,80,81,83,89,90,95,105,120,

144,154,170,171,207,235,237,238,
239,257,261,283,284,285,286,294,
305,308,310,311,312,319,320,321
  Andy 175
  Andy W 176,177
  Drennan C 170
  Lola Colesta 227
  Minnie 176,177
  Nellie A 227
  Nellie H 227
  Thomas Owen 176,177
  W A 228
  Willia A 227
POUNDS
  Nellie H 228
PROCTOR
  Dave 94,95
  Jaly 73
  Katie 94,95,220,224,225,226
  Leah 220,221,222,223,224
  Lean 220
  Lillie 94,95
  Mauda 95
  Nancy 73
  Sam 220,224,225,226
  Stella 220,221,222,223,224
  Sukey 73
  Wash 222,223,224,225
  Washington .221,223,224,225,226
  William 220
PURDY
  A H 272,273,275

RANKIN
  J Walter 134,135,136
REECE
  Fleta 215
  John H 234,235
  R C 215
REED
  Mr 256
REESE
  F S 214

Index

Mertie May 214
REGAN
  J T 60,64
RICHARD
  Annie 12,13,14,15
  Jasper 12,13,14,15
  Minnie 12,13,14,15
RICHARDS 214
  John D 138,140,141
RIDER
  Chas 60,61,64,312,313
RILEY
  Annie 281
  Maley 238,240,243
  Martha 281
  William 281
ROBERSON
  Lucy 292
ROBINSON
  Amos 41,42,43,46
  Amos R 45
  Amos, Jr 43,45,46
  James 41,42,45,46
  Lizzie 41,42,43,45,46
ROBISON
  Amos 39,44,46
  Amos R 38,39,40,41
  Amos, Jr 38
  Annie A 39
  Barney C 259,260,262
  Ben 39
  Christie 39,44,45,46
  Eddie 39
  Holmes 39
  James 38,39
  Josephus 39
  Leah 220,222,223
  Lean 220
  Lizzie 40,41
  Louisa 39,40,44
  Louisa Lizzie 46
  Louise 39
  Minnie 262

Richard Chisholm 39,40,41,46
ROGERS
  Melvina 196
SALLIE 285
SALT
  Anna 102
  Annie 103,104,105,106
  Edward . 101,102,103,104,105,106
  Melehcha 103
  Melicha 106
  Melloche 105
SANGEE 73
SANSON
  Thomas A 29
SAUL
  Annie 104,105
  Edward 103,104,105
  Melicha 103,104,105
SAYOCHEE 153,154
SCOTT
  L S 180
  Lambert 40
  Louina 109,111
  Lucy 44,45
  Lumber 40
  Nannie 67,236
  Sam 107,108
SEARCY
  Howard 195
SEF
  Lula T 116
SELF
  Dollie 19,20,21
  Edward N 20,21
  Ivory Bell 17,18
  James A 16,17,18
  John H 19,20,21
  M A 19
  Martha A 117,118
  Mattie 16,17,18
  Nellie E 16,17
  William K 19

338

Index

SELLER
  A V 200
SEWEL
  Ben 59,60,64
  Ellen 59,60
  Elliott 59,64
  Emma 59,60,64
  Sophia 59,60,64
SEWELL
  Ben 61,62,63
  Ellen 61,62
  Elliott 62,63
  Emma 61,62,63
  Sophia 62,63
SHACKLEFORE
  Wm R 123
SHELBY
  David 182,184,252,253,256, 268,269
SIMMER 144
  Andy 211,212,213,214,215, 216,217,218
  Charley 211,212,213,214, 215,217,218
  Kissie 215,216
  Kizzie 212,213,214,215,216, 217,218
SIMMONS
  Chippie 73
  Emma 83
  Louisa 12,15,178
  Walter 73
SIMMOR
  Charley 217
SIMON
  Emma 277,278,279
  Joe 277,278,279
  Levada 279
  Peyton 277,278
SIMPSON
  Agnes 5,7,8
  Estelle 207,208,209,219
  Mary Elizabeth 5,7,8

R L 6
Robert L 5,7,8
SIMS
  E W 124,253,254,255,267,268, 273,274
SKAGGS
  D C ... 31,41,54,55,56,61,62,63,69, 75,76,77,78,79,80,89,90,95,105,120 ,170,171,174,207,239,257,261,294 ,303,305,308,310,311,312,316,319 ,320,321
  Dremmam C 257
  Drennan C .. 31,41,54,56,61,62,63, 69,75,76,77,78,79,80,81,89,90,95, 105,119,120,204,206,207,239,248, 249,258,261,294,305,308,309,310, 311,312,319,320,321,322
SKAGGS, ... 75
SKEEN
  Amanda E 11
  H O 11
SKEETER
  Albert 253,254,255,267,268
  Poll 267,268
SKINNER 28
SLOAN
  Lillie 83
SMITH
  F L 265
  Frank J 214
  H C 232,233
  Jack 118
  Matilda 281
SNAKE ... 66,67,68,235,237,238,283
SNELSON
  A J 134,135,136
SOMA 107,108
SPANN
  Mary 189,195
SPARKS
  Neta E 231
STAMPER
  J B 86

Index

STARR
  Edward 168,169
  Lea 168
  Mollie 169,172
  Mullie 169
STODDARD
  Joseph 126,127,128
  Lousanna 127,128,129,130,155, 157
  Lousianna 154
  William 126,127,128,129,130, 145,147,148,156
STONE
  Ida B 228
  Varie 59
  W P 59
SUDDATH
  Bob 192,193
  Ida 189,192,193
  Levorn 189,191,192
  Phoebe 189,192,193,196
  Rosetta 189,190,193,196
  Willie 189
SUDDETH
  Phoebe 193
SUDDETHE
  Phoebe 192
SUDDTH
  Ida 197
  Levorn 197
SUDDUTH 190
  Bob 185,186,190,194,195,196
  Ida 190,191
  Levorn 190,191
  Levorne 184,185,186,187,188
  Phoebe 184,185,187,190,194, 195,196,197
  Rosetta 190,194,195,196
  William 185,188,190
  Willie 195
SULZBACHER
  Louis 29
SWAFFORD

  J H 238
SWINGLE
  Corda 24,25
  Hattie 24,25
  Willoughby 25
  Wiloughby 24
TAYLOR
  Lizzie 272,275
THLOCCO
  William 73
THLOPPA
  Sun 67,235
TIGER
  Ah-sey 266,267
  Cooper 297
  Dave 251,253,254,255
  David 251,252,255,256
  Eli 88,89,90,91,92
  George 53,54,137
  J E 200
  John 300
  Josie 252
  Jossie 253,254
  Mollie 252,256
  Mollie (Cowe) 252,255
  Mollie (Crow) 252,255
  Mollie Cowe 251,256
  Mollie Crow 253,254,255,256
  Robert 251,254,255,256
  Rose 88,89,90,91,92
  T W 3
  Thomas 88,89,90,92
  Tom 75,79,91,102,104
  Zoye 27,33
  Zoye Bullet 33
TISDELL
  Mr 263
TODD
  (Illegible) 161,164
TOLLESON
  W A 7
TON-TA 96

Index

TRENT
  Chaney 209,219

UPTEN
  Dan 109

USSERY
  J L 159
  Rebecka 161,164

VAN EMAN
  G S 121,122,124,125,126

WALKER
  Dr 185
  E H 264

WALLAS
  Chaney 278,279
  Cheney 278,279

WALTON
  Doctor 187
  Dr Willie W 187

WASHINGTON 185
  Claud 263,264,265
  Claude 264
  David 263,264,265
  M 7
  Millie 263,265
  Millie Ireland 264

WATSON
  Anna 205
  Annie 203,204,206
  Daniel 239,240,241,243,244
  Dave 203,206
  Johnnie 239,240
  Johnny 237,238,239,240,241, 242,243,244
  Katie 200
  Lela 204,205
  Louisa 68,236,237,238,239,240, 241,242,243,244
  McDaniel 239,242
  McDaniels 68,236,238
  Sally 204

Sandy 67,203,204,206,236
Sauta 205
Yanah 206

WATTIE 302

WATTS
  N V 208

WEBB
  J E 10

WEEKS
  Frank 180
  John W 180

WESLEY
  Victor 213

WEST
  Billy 67,235
  Emma ... 51,52,53,54,55,56,68,236
  Louisa 67,235
  Lumsey 52,53,54,55,56,68,236
  Robert 51,52,53,54
  Thomas 312
  Wiliam 51
  William 52,54,55,56

WHATLEY
  Agnes 6

WHITE
  J P 172,173
  Mary 172,173
  Romie Loundine 172,173

WILBANKS
  Dora 1

WILDCAT
  Losanna 66,68,69,70,71,72,236
  Peter 68,69,70,71,72
  Sandy 66,68,69,70,71,72,236

WILEY
  Andrew 207
  Andy 207,208,209
  Charlie 218,219
  Cora 207,208,209
  Haley 207,208,209
  Lizzie 207
  Susie 218,219

WILLIAMS

Index

Cinda 73
David 271
Davis 273,274,275,276,277
Nat 223,224,226
Rena 271,272,273,274,275,
276,277
Sam 271,272,273,274,275,
276,277
Sam B 275
Viola 271,272,276,277
WILLIAMSON
S S 235
WILSON
Horace 205,206
WINSTON
W W 118
WINTERS
Clara 244,247,248
Ed 244,245,247
Edward 246,248
Elijah 244,247,248
WISDON
John 250
WOFFORD
Shirly 4
WOLF
Lucy 202
WOLFE
Lucy 202
WOODARD
Edith 10
Herbert E 10
Nellie W 10
WORSHAM
D V 223,224,226
WRIGHT
Alva E 115
Ava E 115,116,117,118
Eva E 114
Lula F 115
Lula T 114,115,116,117,118
Walter C 114,116,117,118
Walter Clarence 115

Ynema B 114,115,116,117

YADEKE
John 294
Joseph 294
YAHOLA
Abraham 129,130
Billy 129,130,146
Fayeche 119
Winey 129,130,145,147,148
YAHOLAR
Chapley 221
YAMIE
Willie 315
YARBY
Hullie 26
YARGEE
John 266
YARHOLA
Winey 144
YELLOWHEAD
For-co-wee 252,256
Susie 254,255
YOUFKER 101
YOUNG
H L 145,147
YOUPKA 103

ZIMMERMANN
Frank 65,96,97,99

342

www.ingramcontent.com/pod-product-compliance
Lightning Source LLC
Chambersburg PA
CBHW020241030426
42336CB00010B/578